Economics of Information Technology and the Media

Linda Low

Department of Business Policy
National University of Singapore

World Scientific
Singapore • New Jersey • London • Hong Kong

SINGAPORE UNIVERSITY PRESS
NATIONAL UNIVERSITY OF SINGAPORE

Published by

Singapore University Press
Yusof Ishak House, National University of Singapore
31 Lower Kent Ridge Road, Singapore 119078

and

World Scientific Publishing Co. Pte. Ltd.
P O Box 128, Farrer Road, Singapore 912805
USA office: Suite 1B, 1060 Main Street, River Edge, NJ 07661
UK office: 57 Shelton Street, Covent Garden, London WC2H 9HE

British Library Cataloguing-in-Publication Data
A catalogue record for this book is available from the British Library.

ISBN 981-02-3843-6
ISBN 981-02-3844-4 (pbk)

Printed in Singapore.

To Wai Seng, Susan, Vincent and Peggy

Foreword

As we prepare to welcome the dawn of the new century, we feel increasingly overwhelmed by the development and application of new information and communications technology (ICT). The new media and new information technology (IT), in their ever-changing forms, are shaping every aspect of our lives from work to education to leisure to the management of interpersonal relations, from the office to the family to the school, and from politics to entertainment to culture to the economy. All indications suggest that we will see more new media and IT, in their hybrid and convergent forms, being developed and introduced as we enter the new millennium.

Sociologists tell us we are living in an information society, while economists stress the growth of the information sector of the economy. Communication researchers, on the other hand, focus on the changing process of communication, the new network of distributing and disseminating information and the social and political impact of the new ICT. What is missing is an analysis of information, information technology and the new media, as well as their content as economic goods. An analysis of the process of production, distribution and consumption of such goods requires a new perspective grounded in classic economics. Similarly, the laws of supply and demand can be applied, but only with some qualifications. Our understanding of modern communication would be incomplete without an informed analysis of the economic dimensions in this era of new ICT.

This book fills the gap. It applies an economics framework to an analysis of the nature and scope of information technology and the new media. It is a welcome addition to the scholarly literature in both economics and communication studies.

For the author, this book complements her earlier works on *Professionals at the Crossroads* (Times Academic Press, 1996), *Housing a Healthy, Educated Wealthy Nation through the CPF* (Times Academic Press, 1997) and *Political Economy of City-State: Government-made Singapore* (Oxford University Press, 1998). It introduces a new perspective for all students and researchers of new information technology and the media.

Eddie C. Y. Kuo
School of Communication Studies
Nanyang Technological University
Singapore

Preface

Information exploding through information technology and the media has become a central, rather than peripheral, resource in the knowledge-based production of goods and services involving suppliers, producers, information providers and information users. An economic framework using supply and demand to attain equilibrium to denote the efficient allocation of the factors of production and optimum welfare is appropriate in considering the economics of information technology and the media.

Information technology and the media is undergoing rapid change and development and defining the nature and scope of this area is not an easy task. Neither is it simple to analyse the field from an economics perspective since socio-political and legal dimensions are also involved. The impact of the information and communications technology (ICT) revolution is both shrinking and expanding the global economy and creating many paradoxes (Naisbitt, 1994), even as it breaks the tyranny of space and time or causes the death of distance (Caincross, 1997). This book tries to meet the challenge in four parts.

Part I addresses the economics of information. Chapter 1 introduces various concepts and definitions of information, information technology, knowledge and information economy and media. Chapters 2 and 3 cover relevant theories and principles in both macroeconomics and microeconomics.

Part II focuses on the players and markets in information technology and the media, namely, sellers and buyers (chapter 4) and the government (chapter 5). The impact on employment and labour (chapter 6), the role of technology (chapter 7) and the management of information, especially with multimedia (chapter 8) further highlight the relationships and interactions between players and markets.

Part III considers public policy in the national context (chapter 9) and the global sphere (chapter 10). Both national information infrastructure and global information infrastructure have spawned information and media networks in order to operate efficiently and effectively. Increasing and liberalising trade in telecommunications services allow more countries to enjoy the socio-political and economic benefits of a global economy connected in a fluid, seamless form. Finally, Part IV presents empirical evidence, applications and case studies from the Asia-Pacific region.

The book is motivated by a general lack of educational material on the economics of information technology and media. Yet, in many countries in the Asia-Pacific, mass communications and the media are growing in importance as subjects are taught at both the university and polytechnic levels within communications, management or engineering departments. The book can be used as a textbook, a source book or a structured synthesis for teaching, research or policy making on the subject. It will complement the extant literature on other technical aspects and project the contribution of economics and other social sciences on information technology and the media.

Linda Low

Contents

Part I

The Economics of Information

Chapter 1

Overview of Information Technology and the Media

Introduction

This chapter has three objectives. The first is to place the subject of this book, namely, information technology and the media, in the context of the revolutionary changes that are occurring, and to describe how information technology is a subset of overall science and technology development. The second objective is to draw out the boundaries of information technology and the media once the nature, scope and characteristics of information is understood and defined. A plethora of terminology has emerged surrounding information and knowledge in the literature. Some demarcation is attempted even as subtle distinctions are becoming blurred. The third objective is to discuss methodologies to measure information as a service sector, or even as a quarternary sector, over and above the traditional primary, secondary and tertiary sectors.

In unravelling these concepts and definitions, this chapter hopes to bring enlightenment and clarification to a number of terms and terminology. Until the nature, coverage and definitions of what is information technology and the media are clear and unambiguous, the analysis of issues, problems, challenges or prospects cannot even begin meaningfully. This chapter is a core chapter in this respect.

A Revolution in Information and Communications Technology

A convergence of trends in economics, globalisation, technology and industrial restructuring on one the hand, and socio-political transitions in the capitalist and socialist topography on the other, have occurred (Drucker, 1996, 1997;

Thurow, 1996). This mega shake-up was accompanied by an unprecedented economic boom and socio-cultural renaissance across the Asia-Pacific region (Naisbitt, 1995; Lassere et al., 1995). The East Asian economic miracle was made more stark by its relative eclipse of Anglo-Saxon dominance (McRae, 1994). Since 1997, fortunes have again changed as the Asian meltdown caught up with the hubris. With such frequent turns of volatility due to capitalism or technology, the age of uncertainty (Handy, 1994) is harder to predict.

The world is getting both bigger and smaller (Naisbitt, 1994) with new communications technology decimating the tyranny of time and space across a borderless world (Ohmae, 1990). The key force lies in the transition from Bell's (1973) post-industrial society to Drucker's (1993) post-capitalist society, which was envisioned as the third wave (or powershift) by Toffler (1980, 1990). A knowledge society featuring information technology (Campbell, 1991; Drucker 1996, 1997) or a digital economy (Tapscott, 1995), where individuals and enterprises create wealth by applying knowledge and networked human intelligence, has dawned.

An overview of new technologies

After steam power, coal, steel and oil, the fifth wave of technology is powered by microelectronics. Broadly understood, *technology* is the application of scientific knowledge, with information technology as an important subset that specifies ways of doing things in a reproducible manner (Castells, 1996: 29–30). More specifically, *information technology* comprises a converging set of technologies in microelectronics, computing (hardware and software), telecommunications, broadcasting, optoelectronics and even genetic engineering with its expanding set of developments and applications. The argument for including genetic engineering lies in its involvement in the decoding, manipulation and reprogramming of the information codes of living matter (Castells, 1996: 30). New technological trends that come with microelectronics include diminution, digitisation, computerisation, the globalisation of communication, instantisation, customisation, automation, robotisation and leisurisation (Makridas, 1990).

All technologies increase our ability to process matter and information. In particular, information technology increases the amount of information circulated and/or preserved. Apart from any technical or productivity aspects, the ability of information technology to enhance or erode the social structures that contextualise it implies that social relations are merely a reflection of the new technology (Couch, 1996).

The sequence of the information technology revolution

Technological changes and transformations occur so rapidly and in such quantum leaps that even the starting point of the development of electronics-based information technology is not an easy consensus. The telephone was invented by Bell in 1876, the radio by Marconi in 1898 and the first programmable computer and transistor only in the mid twentieth century. From the transistor (invented in 1947), which enabled the processing of electric impulses in a binary mode at a fast pace, further development of processing devices in semiconductors and chips has occurred. In 1971, Intel's breakthrough with a computer on a chip or microprocessor increased both the capability and portability of information processing power. The computer, as the mother of all technologies since World War II, was firmly and irrevocably established.

One timeline for the information technology industry describes a four-phase evolution (Moschella, 1997: ix; see Fig. 1.1):

(i)   a systems-centric system between 1964 and 1981,
(ii)   a personal computer-centric system between 1981 and 1994,
(iii)   a network-centric system between 1994 and 2005,
(iv)   a projected content-centric system between 2005 and 2015.

Corresponding to the four periods are four operating laws (Moschella, 1997: 15, 101, 264–65):

(i)   *Grosch's Law*. A computer pioneer, Robert Grosch, states that computer power increases as the square of the cost.
(ii)   *Moore's Law*. Intel's co-founder, Gordon Moore, states that the semiconductor's performance will double every two years for the foreseeable future.[1]
(iii)   *Metcalfe's Law*. Robert Metcalfe, inventor of the Ethernet and founder of 3Com, states that while the cost of a network expands linearly with increases in the network's size and semiconductor density, which doubles

---

[1] Moore forecasted that computing power will double every eighteen months to two years and that, by 2006, Intel's forecasts are that chips, together with smaller-sized computers, will be one thousand times as powerful and cost one-tenth as much as they did in 1996 (Cairncross, 1997: 9–10).

every 18–24 months, the value of a network increases exponentially. Thus, as networks expand, they become dramatically more cost-effective.

(iv) *The Law of Transformation*. It states that the extent of an industry's transformation will be equivalent to the square of the percentage of that industry's value-added, which is accounted for by pure information (bit), as opposed to atom-processing activity. This implies that the next technological wave will be grounded in the relationship between content and transformation.

	Systems-centric 1964–1981	PC-centric 1981–1994	Network-centric 1994–2005	Content-centric 2005–2015
Users	Business	Professional	Consumer	Individual
Technology	Transistor	Microprocessor	Communications bandwidth	Software
Law	Grosch	Moore	Metcalfe	Transformation
Network focus	Data centre	LANs	Public networks	Transparency
Supplier structure	Vertical integration	Horizontal integration	Converged horizontal	Embedded
Supplier leadership	US systems	US components	National carriers	Content providers

Fig. 1.1. A timeline for the information technology industry
(*Source*: Adapted from Moschella, 1997: ix)

The first wave featured a vertically oriented industry structure with the International Business Machine (IBM) as the overwhelming industry leader between 1964 and 1981 as it built, sold and serviced all of its key mainframe parts. Essentially, in a *vertically oriented industry*, speciality companies revolving around the central systems company (IBM, in this case) provide all the products and services. The vertical industry structure is a comfortable, if expensive, compromise for consumers. There is supplier and architectural stability, which simplifies user technology decision-making and facilitates long-term customer-supplier partnerships.

The first wave of vertical integration gave way to the second, highly disintegrated horizontal supplier structure. With a *horizontal supplier structure*, as seen in the personal computer market, every slice of the market is led by different sets of vendors. These vendors have an extraordinary level of supplier specialisation in keyboards, monitors, disk drives, floppy drives, compact disk-read-only-memory (CD-ROMs), dynamic random access memory (DRAMs), microprocessors, graphic chips, communications boards, sound cards, applications and delivery and service channels.

In fact, a unique trio of mutually self-reinforcing vendors—Intel, Novell and Microsoft—existed in a virtuous circle in the personal computer-centric system (Moschella, 1997: 34). Each occupied essentially neighbouring layers of the information technology value chain, which meant that what was good for one was almost always as good for the others. Faster Intel chips can run more powerful applications, which benefits Microsoft. Novell will also prosper as the need for more networking leads to stronger demands for faster chips and so on. A rare and powerful virtuous circle exists with each monopoly extracting very high profits, but their core interests are in such alignment that they may as well have been one company, or have been virtually vertically integrated as in the IBM example. Intel had nearly 90% of the microprocessor market, Novell enjoyed a near monopoly with some two-thirds of the personal computer local area network (PC LAN) operating system (OS) software market, and Microsoft had nearly 90% of the personal computer operating system market (Gates, 1995; Wallace, 1997).

Microsoft tried repeatedly, but unsuccessfully, to move into the local area network operating system (LAN OS) business in the 1980s, just as Novell tried to penetrate the DOS-compatible operating systems market with forays into the word processing and spreadsheet business. Apple's decision not to licence its Macintosh operating system gave Microsoft years to develop a comparable graphic user interface. The failed merger between Lotus and Novell in the early 1990s also gave Microsoft a clear way ahead. IBM eventually acquired Lotus and Novell acquired WordPerfect instead, losing its focus on its core networking business.

The three companies (Intel, Novell and Microsoft) enjoyed IBM-like power as the rest of the personal computer industry became increasingly commoditised (Moschella, 1997: 37). Other than the microprocessor, most of the hardware in a personal computer were commodity products, and nearly all of these components were produced by vendors other than the personal computer hardware vendor.

In the third wave of the network-centric power (1994–2005), the average cost of software will fall with virtually infinite supplier economies of scale. The marginal cost of an additional copy is next to nil, resulting in an asymptotic average cost curve (Moschella, 1997: 105). Metcalfe's Law shows that, as the cost of expanding a network tends to increase linearly as additional nodes are added, the value of the network can increase exponentially. Thus, the larger a network becomes, the greater its potential value. The more units of software sold, the cheaper each unit theoretically can become. The two forces become mutually reinforcing and this results in enormous value creation opportunities and the spawning of new economic activities. The same occurred in the telephone industry.

Convergence

Another phenomenon of new technologies is that of a global economy emerging as a product or convergence of capital, corporation, consumer and communications (the four C's), or the corresponding vectors of infrastructure, investment, individual choice and information technology (the four I's). With borderless economics, the four C's, or four I's, effectively spell the end of the nation-state and the rise of regional economies (Ohmae, 1995). The dysfunctional state becomes a symbol as these forces sweep across electronic highways.

In another interpretation, the evolution of markets in three vignettes starts with the circuit of capital first involved in the barter of commodities, that is, C-C (capital-commodity) (Perelman, 1991: 15–18). When money is used instead of barter trade, the vignette becomes commodity-money-commodity, or C-C-C, with the second C representing commodity used as money. By the time electronic money enters as another mode of payment, it creates its own interpretation in the more complex, modern economy where information becomes an important aspect in the C-C-C paradigm.

Many new communications technologies came with the advent of the Internet, which grew from a free and cheap academic application for data communications and transmission to commercial applications (see chapter 7). Companies are setting up intranets within single locations and extranets with branches and partners. *Intranets* represent a shift away from the internal company network using a local area network (LAN) to linking internal networks using both Internet technologies and Internet infrastructure within single locations. Its extension to branches and partners, including customers and suppliers, gives rise to *extranets*. The Internet offers a new platform as a fundamental technology for building new markets.

The Internet works on the simple philosophy that networks want to connect and once a universal way of getting networks to share data is broken through, a new paradigm in communications and exchange is unleashed (see chapter 7). Being in the public domain, nobody owns the Internet and nobody charges a fee for its use. The economics of cyberspace does not seem to exist as users surf and freeload for practically nothing after allowing for the monthly fees of Internet service providers and basic telecommunications charges.

There is no accurate way to count individual users of the Internet; the number of hosts or computer addresses is the next best proxy (*Far Eastern Economic Review*, 27 July 1995). Since 1991, the number has roughly doubled every year, but even host numbers can be misleading. A standard methodology assumes ten users for every host, translating to fifty million Internet users worldwide. But Asia has fewer users per host and fewer hosts per capita compared to Europe and North America, though this may be changing. The World Wide Web (WWW) offers an interactive brochure that serves as a table of contents to the Internet's vast resources and websites have multiplied tremendously.

As the Internet is mostly software driven, a concomitant growth in the software industry follows (see chapter 7). In turn, the booming computer industry (see chapter 4) is throwing a plethora of activities together, beginning with the merger of computers and telecommunications. The convergence of other industries includes office equipment and automation, electronics, recreation, entertainment, multimedia, education and many more. Industry lines are getting blurred, mixed and matched along the common thread of information technology.

As the power and reach of the communications infrastructure expands, the tools—namely, the computers—needed to harness that capability, shrink in size. Computers have become smaller, cheaper, lighter and more portable. Personal intelligent communicators, personal digital assistants (PDAs), personal communications devices (PCDs), or picocomputers, wireless communications and automatic interpreting telephony are already realities.

Alliances and raids as telephone companies invade each other's territories in partnership with cable companies are part of the new corporate terrain. Technology-driven strategic alliances produce strange bedfellows as traditional arch-rivals team up and cross-industry and cross-country alliances form as a result of deregulation, liberalisation and privatisation.

To dramatise the outcome of a seamless, global, digital network of networks, the parable of a theologian asking the most powerful supercomputer, "Is there a God?", was answered in the affirmative after it was connected with all other supercomputers, mainframes, minicomputers and personal computers in the world (Naisbitt, 1993: 98). Just as the space programme was about more than putting a man on the moon, the telecommunications revolution is about creating new technologies, expanding economic horizons, and accepting and meeting challenges. Digitisation will consummate the marriage among television, computers and telephones, and individual freedom will assume new meaning as this convergence takes place.

Digital technology allows broadcasters to send up as many as six separate sound tracks in different languages with the same video signal. Digital compression allows more channels to be packed into a smaller number of transponders. Signals can be received from new, powerful 25 cm dishes which cut costs to viewers and allow others, whose countries have banned the dish, to receive broadcasts as the dish is small enough to hide.

While the titans of media and communications wage war over the digital future, the Internet, a loose confederation of interconnected networks, which has been in existence for the last twenty-five years for scientists and academicians, has become more multimedia-oriented since mid-1993 (*The Economist*, 1 July 1995). A combination of software and a way of connecting documents that allows users to travel the network with pictures, sound and video became the rage of information, communications, education and fun. *Cyberspace* was spawned as a new medium based on broadcasting and publishing plus interactivity.

Industry value chain

The information technology industry *value chain* comprises vendor support and professional services, which account for about one-third of the total value added, followed by distribution channels, packaged software, peripherals, processors and semiconductors in fairly equal proportions (see Fig. 1.2). A distinction is made between software and content, where software refers

| Vendor support and professional services |
| Distribution channels |
| Packaged software |
| Peripherals |
| Processors and semiconductors |

Fig. 1.2. Value chain in the information technology industry

primarily to specific computer programmes, as in operating systems, tools, applications, interfaces, protocols and so on (see chapter 7). Software consists of a set of instructions while content revolves around some form of information as in text, images, sound, video or a combination thereof.

Figure 1.3 shows the value chain in the personal computer industry. Personal computer manufacturers are involved in the first four items in the hardware value chain: namely shape, colour, feature mix, service and price. Component manufacturers account for the rest of the value chain. As a result of the commoditised nature of the personal computer industry, the personal computer hardware vendor is responsible for only a small share of the value added in a personal computer. Even this portion generally consists of soft features such as shape, packaging, feature mix, service and others, including price (see Fig. 1.3).

	Shape, colour
Hardware Value Chain	Feature mix
	Service
	Price
	Monitors
	Keyboards
	Mice
Component Value Chain	CD-ROMs
	DRAMs
	Disk drives
	Microprocessors
	Other semiconductors

Fig. 1.3. Value chain in the personal computer industry

The inevitable result is that personal computer suppliers found it virtually impossible to differentiate their products as everyone uses the same component sources. Product competition shifted toward channel management, time-to-market, service, price, feature mix, and product and company branding, as best exemplified by Compaq Computer.

Over time, the four C's (computers, communications, consumer electronics and content) will become a converged information technology value chain

(Moschella, 1997: 114, 116–117). Digital technology has brought them together with multimedia, as manifested by the Internet, which is basically a merger of the computer and telephony industries. However, the overall horizontal information technology industry structure will remain; that is, five broad categories (hardware, software, transmission services, professional services and content businesses) of each of the four Cs will remain largely separate.

Nonetheless, components within each of these five categories will overlap, compete, merge and eventually become rationally structured to create a converged horizontal structure. The converged hardware market will link up end user devices and backbone network equipment. The integration of end user devices in personal computers, smart televisions, cable set top boxes, network computers, smart telephones, personal digital assistants (PDAs), video cassette recorders (VCRs), compact disc (CD) players and stereos is already happening to a greater degree than with network equipment.

Definitions and concepts

Some basic definitions and concepts are useful at this stage before looking further into the information and knowledge economy and society. The meaning of *information* is precisely and succinctly put as a reduction in uncertainty (Arrow, 1979: 306). A seminal definition of information is based on the concept of entropy (Shannon & Weaver, 1949). Total *entropy* represents complete randomness and lack of organisation; the greater the entropy, the higher the level of uncertainty. Thus, there is concordance with Arrow in that information is whatever reduces uncertainty. It also follows that information is only information if it represents something new, making a measure of information the "surprise value" of a message (Krippendorf, 1986).

Information is any experience or contact that adds new meaning or somehow changes events, lives or experiences. Information may be in the form of facts, opinions or algorithms, and may be transmitted and reproduced. While information is generally durable and permanent, as in a body of knowledge that has been built up, it can become obsolete if not updated, expanded and changed when necessary. It can be transmitted in many forms, as in audiovisual, sight, sound, touch, taste and smell which are not exclusive and can be mutually inclusive, as in a multimedia presentation of information. Information enables the user to know about something and to use that knowledge to relate, learn, think and decide as needed.

Information is the raw material of knowledge just as wood is the raw material for a table. Knowledge is a form of capital, and technology is an application of knowledge to work. *Knowledge* is cognitive information that has been generalised and abstracted from an understanding of the cause-and-effect relations of an event or phenomenon. *Cognitive information* is itself defined as logical and action-selective information that is a projection of the future or that is used for detecting and forecasting (Masuda, 1990: 160).[2]

The principal benefit of knowledge lies in the enhancement of the knowledge base and structure. An increment of information leads to a modification in the existing knowledge structure, which gives rise to a new knowledge structure as the old structure is modified with new knowledge (see Fig. 1.4).

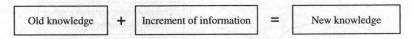

Old knowledge + Increment of information = New knowledge

Fig. 1.4. Change in knowledge structure

The omnipresence, variety and power of information can be structured such that the need for information varies with its position in an organisational hierarchy. But the value of information is inversely correlated with quantity; too much can lead to *information overload*, excessive information that is more useless than useful. To be of real value, information has to be processed (this is essentially information reduction) to unveil and highlight core information in a precise and direct manner.

Information is increasingly becoming a distinct fourth factor of production instead of being implicitly embedded or embodied in the traditional factors of land, labour and capital. In parallel, apart from the traditional primary, secondary and tertiary sectors, a fourth sector in information may be evolving. This *quarternary sector* would comprise a new classification of information-related industries distinct from tertiary service industries (see Fig. 1.5). As information becomes an important and distinct input to production, consumption and other aspects of daily life, the activities of generating, producing, processing, transmitting, disseminating, distributing, storing, archiving and retrieving information constitutes an *information industry*. While conceptually

---

[2] Cognitive information is distinct from *affective information*, which is based on sensitivity and the production of emotion as in all information that conveys sensory feelings (Masuda, 1990: 160).

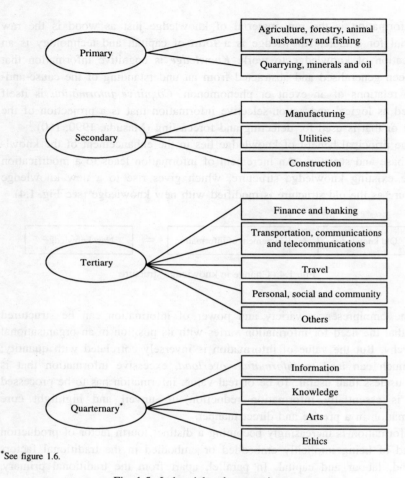

*See figure 1.6.

Fig. 1.5. Industrial and economic structure

distinct, the information industry is, in reality, pervasive and diffused across industries. The scope of the information industry is wide-ranging: from education to fun and recreation, or simply anything that involves information.

The impact of information in terms of economic, political, social, technological and cultural aspects are diverse, as the rest of the book will reveal. Information is power and various power roles may be discerned according to the organisation or hierarchy that controls the informational resources. Power relationships can exist at many levels including that of producer, authority, investor, client, auxiliary, creator, trade unionist, distributor, exhibitor, linking pin, facilitator, public advocate or members of the public in their various capacities.

Using a threefold definition, *information economics* is a framework of tools and concepts that enables: 1) a definition of value built on an expanded vision of benefit, 2) a definition of cost that includes explicit considerations of potential risk and 3) a decision-making process to make investment decisions in a manner consistent with business investment decisions (Parker & Benson, 1988: 5). Information economics looks at the supply side of production and investment in information infrastructure (dubbed infostructure) as well as the demand side, as in the consumption of information goods and services. The usual framework is in both microeconomics (consumer theory and firm theory) and macroeconomics (overall economy, public policies and the international arena).

Information seeking is the purposive acquisition of information from selected information carriers (Johnson, 1996: 9). Information seeking is beneficial as it is a moderator between perceived threats and the likelihood of taking action. It leads to an increased readiness to change. Ignorance and information are intertwined, though there can be some benefits to ignorance as well. Ignorance gives some comfort of denial, more anomie behaviour, lower information processing costs, lesser and lower conflicts, and less resistance to other's control and influence.

Knowledge economy

A distinction between information and knowledge follows, no matter how spurious it may be. The information economy, which will be elaborated upon shortly, is simply one that is knowledge-based. Both the knowledge economy and the information economy are associated with the digital economy as knowledge and information are conveyed in digital form. Following the revolution in information and communications technology, the emergence of the *knowledge economy* represents a shift from raw materials and capital equipment to information and knowledge as inputs for production.

In the information age, the resource that matters is intellectual rather than physical. The *raw material economy* premised on land (including all natural resources and climate) is uncoupled from the industrial economy, just as manufacturing is uncoupled from labour (Drucker, 1992). More precisely, the knowledge economy means a shift in the geographic centre from raw materials and capital equipment to information and knowledge, especially in education and research centres and man-made brain industries. The knowledge economy depicts the automation of labour-intensive manufacturing and service activities as well as growth in new service industries such as health care, distance learning, software production and multimedia entertainment.

The knowledge economy has altered traditional trade theories that explain why nations trade. The traditional factors of production and a relative abundance of factor endowment, based on geography under the Hecksher-Ohlin theorem as a basis of comparative advantage, seemed suited to agricultural products and some manufactured products. For new knowledge industries, such as in brain services, a theory of acquired or artificial competitive advantage (Porter, 1990) is more useful in explaining new activities associated with information technology. Competitive advantage can be simulated with policies to manipulate a conducive environment, whereas comparative advantage is based on the natural endowment of resources. With progressively shorter technology and product cycles, leapfrogging and more dynamic changes at a faster pace can occur with competitive advantage. This explains the role of information technology and information infrastructure in economic growth and development.

Information economy

The emergence of a knowledge economy is parallel to that of an information economy. To be clear, an *information economy* is one in which information is the core of a society's economic needs.

An information economy is dependent on knowledge and information, which are becoming increasingly science-based and applied to production (Carnoy et al., 1993: 5). At the global level, a new pattern of international divisions of labour will result as multinational corporations (MNCs) with information technology resources can wield immense power (chapter 10). This is precisely why the question of whither the nation-state in the new international economic order is posed (Ohmae, 1995; Carnoy et al., 1993). Moreover, the economic structure will change to involve the expansion of the public economy. The state has to strengthen its national information infrastructure (NII), or infostructure, as externalities are involved and set rules of conduct exist both domestically and internationally.

Because information technology is transmitted through digitised technology, the *digital economy* is one in which individuals and enterprises create wealth by applying knowledge, networked human intelligence and effort to manufacturing, agriculture and services. The meaning of a digital economy

(A) Information Industries

Private information industries	Investigators, forecasters, freelance writers and public opinion surveyors
Printing and publishing industries	Printing, plate making, bookbinding, publishing and photostat copying
News and advertising industries	Newspapers, news agencies, magazines, advertising and public relations
Information processing and service industries	Computer centres, data banks, software houses and time sharing services
Information machinery industries	Printing presses, computers, terminals, typewriters and duplicating machines

(B) Knowledge Industries

Privately operated knowledge industries	Lawyers and accountants
Research and development industries	Research institutes and engineering companies
Education industries	Schools and libraries

(C) Arts Industries

Private affective information industries	Novelists, composers, singers, painters, photographers, promoters and producers
Affective information service industries	Theatre troupes, orchestras, motion picture companies, television companies, movie theatres and recording companies
Affective information equipment industries	Equipment in photographic, musical, filming, recording and television companies

(D) Ethics Industries

Private ethics industries	Philosophers, religious leaders and prophets
Religious industries	Religious groups, churches, temples and shrines
Spiritual industries	Zen, meditation and yoga groups, spiritual training centres and volunteer service groups

Fig. 1.6. The quarternary of information-related industries
(*Source*: Adapted from Masuda (1990))

will probably become more entrenched as analogue transmission gradually gives way to digital technology and all forms of information (visual, audio, graphic, data and others) can be digitised.

An information industry, as distinguished from a knowledge industry, marks the attainment of an information-led type of industrial structure as the first stage of change in the economic structure (see Fig. 1.6). The *information industry* is responsible for the production, processing, storage and dissemination of information. It comprises the production of computer/office machinery, communications cables and equipment, information transmission, software, information processing services, information retrieval services, information storage and archival services.

The information industry is a generic one, including privately operated information industries (eg, investigators, forecasters), industries in printing and publishing (eg, printing, bookbinding), news advertising (eg, newspapers, magazines), information processing services (eg, computer centres, databanks) and information machinery (eg, printing press, computers). On the other hand, knowledge industries comprise privately operated knowledge industries (eg, lawyers, accountants), research and development industries (eg, research institutes, engineering companies), education industries (eg, schools, libraries) and knowledge equipment industries (eg, electronic calculators, computer-aided instruction equipment) (Masuda, 1990: 68). It is thus reasonable to distinguish information-related industries as quarternary industries distinct from tertiary or service industries in general.

Information society

Parallel to a knowledge-based information economy is the emergence of an information society. An *information society* is one that grows and develops around information and brings about a flourishing state of human creativity instead of mere affluent material consumption. More rigorously, the concept of an information society requires two premises (Masuda, 1990: 1). One involves the production of information values, not material values, as the driving force behind the formation and development of the information society. The other premise is that past developmental patterns of human society can be used as historical, analogical models for future societies.

An alternative definition of an *information society* is one in which the quality of life, prospects for social change and economic development depend increasingly on information and its exploitation (Martin, 1995: 3). One step beyond an information society with an ongoing information revolution is a *broadband society*, which is one where telecommunications has become the true catalyst for change. There is virtually unlimited access to information, and traditional universal telephone services will be replaced by universal multimedia information services. In fact, instead of an information society, many possible information societies may be spawned.

Information societies will result in economies in which information is the core of society's economic needs. Both the economy and society grow and develop around the core of production and use of information values. Information, as an economic product, will exceed goods, energy and services in importance (Masuda, 1990: 66). The information society will be a reality following four stages of computerisation (Masuda, 1990): big science-based computerisation (1945–1970), management-based computerisation (1955–1980), society-based computerisation (1970–1990) and individual-based computerisation (1975–2000).

Key features of an information society include the omnipresence of computers, synergistic production and shared utilisation in information resources, a participatory democracy and a voluntary community. A *participatory democracy* results when policy decisions are reached with the participation of people who are less satisfied with mere material wants and whose chief desire is self-realisation. The means to more information is available in an information society, but problems remain. Challenges include the creation of available, fair and accurate information, equal access to information, mechanisms for people to participate in matters concerning state sovereignty, and dealing with problems that cannot be solved by a simple majority since some minority rights have to be respected.

Simultaneously, people in a voluntary community are bonded by common goals and a shared philosophy; they voluntarily carry on life together under a common social solidarity. An application of this is the informational voluntary community, which is the technological base of computer-communications networks.

The goal of an information society is to satisfy human needs, which will have some new elements including self-determination. Societal productive power is the basis for the satisfaction of human needs and the production of information- and goal-oriented action. A vision of computer utopia, or computopia, is an ideal global society in which multi-centred, multi-layered communities of citizens, participating voluntarily in shared goals and ideas, flourish simultaneously throughout the world (Masuda, 1990).

Information societies are clearly underpinned by the telecommunications revolution, which changes economic production and consumption, spreads democracy and gives it urgency. The telecommunications industry, encompassing telephones, televisions, computers and consumer electronics, is struggling with four trends. The first trend is the blending of technologies in telephone/television/computer hybrids. The second trend is the swing towards strategic alliances. This, in turn, leads to the third trend: the creation of a seamless, global network in the form of a digital web of networks. Finally, there will be a growing phenomenon of personal computers for everyone as market forces push the diffusion of applications.

An information society based on knowledge creation and utilisation represents a transformation from an industrial society, which is a high mass consumption society, to a high welfare society and, finally, to a high mass knowledge creation society. In contrast, a post-Fordist, post-Taylorist economy represents, respectively, mass production in assembly lines and the application of scientific management. Some fundamental differences exist between post-capitalist industrial societies and knowledge societies in terms of organisation, behaviour and outcome (see Fig. 1.7).

Industrial Societies	Knowledge Societies
Hierarchy	Equality
Conformity	Individuality and creativity
Standardisation	Diversity
Centralisation	Decentralisation
Efficiency	Effectiveness
Exhaustion of natural resources and pollution	Resource-saving and symbiosis with nature
Consumption and material productive power	Technology assessment
Specialisation	Generalist, interdisciplinary and holistic
Individualism	Synergism
Maximisation of material wealth	Quality of life and conservation of material resources
Emphasis on quantitative content	Emphasis on quality of output
Security	Self-expression and self-actualisation

Fig. 1.7. Industrial societies and knowledge societies

The Nature and Scope of Information Technology and the Media

The core sectors in information technology lie in computers, telecommunications and semiconductors (Guysters, 1996: 4). They are the means, technology and mechanisms through which information is produced, processed, transmitted, archived and retrieved. Increasingly, the movement of information is not just among individuals, organisations, industries and other entities in disaggregated transactions or exchanges. Where information is public and more effectively processed and disseminated in an aggregate mode, the role of the *mass media*, as in newspapers and broadcasting (radio and television, as well as newer forms such as cable television) is apparent (see chapter 4).

Mass media and media systems imply interrelatedness and the existence of technological vehicles through which mass communication takes place. *Mass communication* is about the creation of messages, the use of technology, the involvement of large numbers of people, and the implications of it all. It is the industrialised production, reproduction and multiple distribution of messages using technological devices. Mass communication helps to shape people's understanding of the elements that make up society.

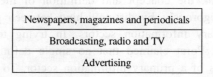

Fig. 1.8. The mass media industry

Figure 1.8 shows components of the mass media industry (compare with Fig. 1.2, which depicts the main players in the information technology industry—vendor support and professional services, distribution channels, packaged software, peripherals, processors and semiconductors). Newspapers, magazines, periodicals and other printed forms convey information on a mass basis. Broadcasting, as in radio, television, cable television, videos and such, is another mass media industry. Apart from conventional broadcasting, satellite broadcasting opens up a new window in mass communication. Advertising is considered a mass media industry, not only because it involves mass dissemination of information, but also because it is a vital form of revenue for other mass media players.

The Measurement of Information and Services

Conceptualising the information sector

Measurement necessarily comes after conceptualisation. A distinction is necessary between a sector and an industry. Traditionally, an economy has three sectors (see Fig. 1.5): the primary sector (ie, agriculture, forestry, husbandry, fishing, mining and all activities related to the land), the secondary sector (ie, construction, utilities and manufacturing) and the tertiary sector (ie, services). As noted, a quarternary sector may be the information sector. An *industry* is a collection of firms producing a similar category of goods or services. An information industry consists of all firms involved in generating, processing, disseminating or storing information. An electronics industry comprises all firms producing electronic goods. In other words, industries are clusters of firms that make up the sector.

Machlup (1962) was the first to conceptualise the *information sector*, leading to its measurement. His first listing identified five areas: education, research and development (R&D), communications media, information machinery and information services.

Porat (1977) took the concept and definition of the information sector further, and more rigorously, by distinguishing between primary information sectors and secondary information sectors. In trying to define a primary information market, Porat claimed that no single definition of information embraces all aspects of a primary information sector. To him, information is easier to define by example than by direct appellation. The end product of all information service markets is knowledge. Knowledge can be an end in itself, but it is usually applied in the acquisition of something. To qualify as an information service, knowledge does not have to be neither good nor true as distortions, inaccuracies and even lies also constitute information. Information is whatever enables a consumer to know something that was not known before.

In Porat's typology of primary information industries, which covers eight major parts, he showed the ways in which knowledge and information can be produced, processed, disseminated or transmitted. A *primary information market* is formed when firms, using a technology of organisation, produce and distribute information at an exchange price. The eight major parts of primary information industries, which in turn can cover hundreds of industries that, in some way, produce, process, disseminate or transmit knowledge or messages, are:

(i)   Knowledge production and inventive industries
    (a) R&D and inventive industries (private)
    (b) Private information services
(ii)   Information distribution and communications industries
    (a) Education
    (b) Public information services
    (c) Regulated communications media
    (d) Unregulated communications media
(iii)   Risk management
    (a) Insurance industries (components)
    (b) Finance industries (components)
    (c) Speculative brokers
(iv)   Search and co-ordination industries
    (a) Search and non-speculative brokerage industries
    (b) Advertising industries
    (c) Non-market co-ordinating industries
(v)   Information processing and transmission services
    (a) Non-electronic-based processing
    (b) Electronic-based processing
    (c) Telecommunications infrastructure
(vi)   Information goods industries
    (a) Non-electronic consumption or intermediate goods
    (b) Non-electronic investment goods
    (c) Electronic consumption or intermediate goods
    (d) Electronic investment goods
(vii) Selected government activities
    (a) Primary information services in federal government
    (b) Postal services
    (c) State and local education
(viii) Support facilities
    (a) Information structure construction and rental
    (b) Office furnishings

To be accounted in the primary information sector, the good or service must intrinsically convey information or be directly useful in producing, processing or distributing information. Inputs to information industries are excluded. While these inputs originate from industries that are closely associated with information industries, they do not sell information goods and services *per se*.

While the *primary information sector* produces information machines, or markets information services as a commodity, the *secondary information sector* comprises public and private bureaucracies that have planning, programming, scheduling and marketing activities. These activities are not directly counted in national accounts since information services and their values have to be imputed.

Input-output tables

There are peculiar difficulties involved in measuring intangible services, especially if they are transborder data flows (TBDF) or over-the-wire flows. Other difficulties involve the quality and productivity of services. Services are measured by the conventional system of national accounts (SNA) in terms of the total market value of all goods and services produced in a country, as in the gross national product (GNP), which is based on nationality, or the gross domestic product (GDP), which is based on geographic territory.[3]

The balance of payments records the export and import of services together with merchandise goods and other unrequited transfers in the current account, whereas capital flows are captured in the capital account. However, standard national output and income accounts are not conceptually organised to measure information industries. As information has become such a pervasive input in economic activities, the impact of the information sector is more clearly and effectively portrayed through input-output tables that show inter-industry linkages and transactions. Input-output tables enable multiplier analyses incorporating direct, indirect and induced effects. They show how changes in the final demand in one sector impinge on the others.

An understanding of input-output tables is germane at this stage (Jussawalla et al., 1988; Low, 1990; Low et al., 1994). Table 1.1 shows a simplified input-output table, also called a flow matrix, for four sectors in a hypothetical economy, namely, the primary sector, manufactured consumer goods, manufactured producer goods, and services. These four sectors form a matrix

---

[3] The total market value of all goods and services produced in an economy in a period (usually one year) by nationals inside and outside an economy is known as the gross national product (GNP), while the gross domestic product (GDP) is the total market value based on production within the economy irrespective of nationality. The difference between GNP and GDP is, thus, the net factor income from abroad. It is positive if there is more factor income accruing to nationals outside the country than factor income owing to non-nationals working in the economy.

Table 1.1. A hypothetical input-output table or flow matrix ($)

Row* / Column+	Primary	Mfr consumer	Mfr producer	Services	Total intermediate uses	Final uses	Total use
Primary sector	20	65	50	10	145	245	390
Mfr consumer goods	0	30	0	0	30	260	290
Mfr producer goods	50	60	70	15	195	50	245
Services	40	15	50	70	175	200	375
Total purchases	110	170	170	95	545		
Value-added	280	120	75	280		755	
Total output	390	290	245	375			1300

+ Column indicates use or destination of output.
* Row indicates source or where output is produced.

in Table 1.2, with the columns representing users, or output, and the rows representing producers, or inputs. Thus, a particular cell shows what a producer needs as inputs and what use or output has been made. Reading across the first row, the primary industry, as a producer, sourced $20 as inputs from itself, $65 and $50 each from both manufacturing industries and $10 from services. These total $145 in intermediate inputs. The column on final uses represents the final demand for private consumption, including government purchases and exports, which is $245. A total of $390 worth of production has thus occurred for the primary sector as required by these destinations, or users. The second row contains the same information for the manufactured consumer goods sector, and so on. The fifth row describes the total purchases of intermediate inputs from the domestic economy. In addition, other inputs that create value added, such as wages for labour services and profits for companies, are shown in the sixth row. Adding all the purchases in the first column yields the total output for the primary sector: $390. This figure matches the total as total use in the last column.

The main four-by-four transaction matrix, reporting flows across the four sectors or aggregations of industries, depicts the inter-industry linkages that form the basis of input-output tables. It shows how industries are related to one another in the whole economy. When the final demand in an industry increases, a chain reaction or effect, in terms of the greater output demanded by other industries because their outputs have become inputs in the user industry (the one whose final demand has grown), will take place. This, if the information industry can be singled out and identified within the overall services sector, is how its economic impact can be measured and evaluated. In reality, an input-output table can contain hundreds of industries; it is a matter of how practical it is to collect and itemise the statistics and data along these divisions.

Input-output tables are used to measure economic impact by converting the flow matrix in Table 1.1 into a matrix of coefficients as in Table 1.2. Each column in Table 1.1 is divided by its industry output total to yield the ratio of input to output for each industry. The result is known as an A-matrix, which represents a set of production functions for each industry (see Table 1.2). These fixed coefficient production functions are called Leontief production functions. The elements, or coefficients, designated as a_{ij} shows i for the input (row) and j for the output (column). Thus, a_{12}, or a value of 0.23 (65/290), is the output of the primary industry needed for each unit of manufactured consumer goods.

Table 1.2. Input-output coefficients

	X_1	X_2	X_3	X_4
Primary goods X_1	0.05	0.23	0.20	0.03
Consumer goods X_2	0.00	0.10	0.00	0.00
Producer goods X_3	0.13	0.21	0.29	0.04
Services X_4	0.10	0.05	0.20	0.18
Total purchases	0.28	0.59	0.69	0.25
Value-added	0.72	0.41	0.31	0.75
Total output	1.00	1.00	1.00	1.00

The assumption of a fixed coefficient has enormous implications, which also translate into a fundamental weakness of input-output analyses, namely, that technology has been held constant to derive these ratios. In turn, this basic assumption requires that the prices of inputs also do not change. If they do, factor substitution, cheaper inputs for more expensive inputs, would alter the coefficients or ratios just as technological changes would. The assumption is accommodated because, in reality, technology is quite constant. Hence, input-output tables are usually collated every five years, instead of annually, since technology does not change so fast or so drastically.

What is more important is that a Leontief matrix comprising the core four-by-four transaction matrix can be used to calculate the economic impact of one industry's growth on others. For a four-sector economy, the following equations may be written to show the total output for each of the four industries:

$$X_1 = a_{11} X_1 + a_{12} X_2 + a_{13} X_3 + a_{14} X_4 + F_1 \qquad (1.1)$$

$$X_2 = a_{21} X_1 + a_{22} X_2 + a_{23} X_3 + a_{24} X_4 + F_2 \qquad (1.2)$$

$$X_3 = a_{31} X_1 + a_{32} X_2 + a_{33} X_3 + a_{34} X_4 + F_3 \qquad (1.3)$$

$$X_4 = a_{41} X_1 + a_{42} X_2 + a_{43} X_3 + a_{44} X_4 + F_4 \qquad (1.4)$$

Suppose the economy is projected to grow at a certain rate, such that the final demand of all four sectors will be similarly projected (ie, final demand F_1 in the primary industry X_1, final demand F_2 in the industry X_2, and so on). It is a matter of solving the set of four linear simultaneous equations which have four knowns (the final demands of the four sectors) and four unknowns (the output of the four sectors). The use of computer packages to solve much larger systems for a real economy is not a problem. Neither is fine-tuning to allow for changes in the fixed coefficient if technological or input price changes become significant.

In addition, multipliers that measure the effect of changes (eg, output multipliers, employment multipliers and income multipliers) can be computed. An *output multiplier* for a primary industry reveals the total value of production in all sectors of the economy required to satisfy a dollar's worth of final demand in the primary industry. Usually, output multipliers have values greater than unity because of the indirect demand generated for intermediate inputs in all sectors. In other words, when the final demand in one industry grows, other industries do not expand output in direct inputs for that industry alone. They also produce more for other industries whose outputs have also expanded due to an indirect impact or chain effect that is created across the whole economy.

An *income multiplier* shows the total value added or income generated in that industry as a result of a dollar's worth of the final demand of that industry. By the same reasoning, an *employment multiplier* shows the number of jobs created due to an increase in the final demand of a particular industry.

Input-output tables and multiplier analyses are useful for planning purposes when target growth rates and certain industrial transformations are projected for the economy. More specifically, when an information industry is identified in an economy's input-output tables, the methodology of analysis involves computing the effect on the information industry as a result of changes in other non-information industries.

Chapter 2

Basic Economic Principles and Concepts

Introduction

The foundations of microeconomics, as applied to any economic activity, including information technology and the media, rest on the age-old concern of balancing scarce, limited resources with unlimited human wants. That, essentially, is the definition of *economics*: a discipline to match limited resources with efficiently produced commodities to satisfy unlimited human wants. *Microeconomics* looks at the economic problem from the perspective of individual units comprised of households or consumers (demand side) and firms or producers (supply side).

At the *macroeconomics* level, national aggregates such as employment, prices and overall growth are considered for the whole economy. In optimising resources, also known as *inputs* (or *factors of production*, which traditionally include land, labour and capital), to produce enough *output* (or commodities in goods and services) to satisfy human wants, economics may also be looked at in terms of three questions. Essentially, economics involves choices in terms of what goods and services to produce, how to produce them (ie, the method or production function) and for whom (implying the distribution of output).

Choice involves an *opportunity cost*, which is defined as the next best alternative foregone, such as when resources are allocated to produce more telecommunications services instead of highways. *Efficiency* implies that the maximum output is obtained from a combination of inputs; that is, no better means of allocating resources exists that can produce a higher level of welfare for most people in the society.

A *production possibility curve*, a locus of combinations of two products that can be produced given the availability of resources in an economy, is shown in Fig. 2.1. It illustrates the concept of opportunity cost and efficiency.

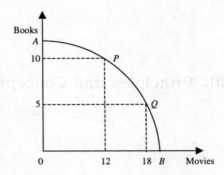

Fig. 2.1. A production possibility curve

Neither of the two extreme points on the production possibility curve are desirable since all resources would have to be devoted to books at A, or all to movies at B.

At P, the combination of ten units of books to twelve units of movies means that all resources have been efficiently deployed. This is not true for points inside the production possibility curve. A decision to move from P to Q implies choosing six more units movies at an opportunity cost of five units of books. Instead of a linear line joining AB (which has a constant slope and, hence, the same rate of substitution of the two goods or opportunity cost), a curve convex to the origin is more realistic. As more and more books are given up for more movies, the law of diminishing utility is operative.

The *law of diminishing utility* states that as books become more scarce, its *marginal utility* (the increment in total utility with every additional unit of books consumed) rises while the marginal utility of movies diminishes as more movies are consumed. Mathematically, the convex curve provides a steeper slope depicted at the tangent Q, which denotes a higher opportunity cost than at P. In consumer theory, an equilibrium in the consumption of books and movies will be attained when the marginal utility per dollar of books is equal to the marginal utility per dollar of movies. In other words, equilibrium occurs when each dollar spent on the two goods yields the same marginal utility. If the marginal utility per dollar of books is higher than that for movies, the consumer will continue to spend more on books until equilibrium is reached.

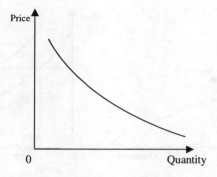

Fig. 2.2. A demand curve

The Laws of Demand and Supply

From these definitions of economics, two powerful laws in microeconomics are that of demand and supply. The consumer decides what to demand based on a number of determinants: the price of the commodity, prices of other commodities, income, tastes, time horizon, population size and structure, and even government policies, which affect consumption. Holding all other factors constant, or invoking the *ceteris paribus* assumption, a function or relationship correlating the quantity demanded, Q_d (a dependent variable), to the price of the commodity, P (an independent variable), a demand function is shown in Eq. (2.1) and a demand curve in Fig. 2.2.

$$Q_d = f(P) \tag{2.1}$$

The demand curve is downward sloping because the *law of demand* stipulates an inverse relationship between the price and the quantity demanded for all normal goods. The slope of the demand curve is negative because of the inverse correlation; that is, the price and the quantity demanded move in opposite directions.

The distinction between *movement* along a demand curve (due to price changes), and a *shift* in the demand curve (when any of the factors held *ceteris paribus* change), is shown in Fig. 2.3. In both instances, the movement and the shift have a similar effect (ie, a larger quantity of the commodity demanded) but different causes. In the former, the change is due to a fall in price, while, in the later, the increase in quantity demanded could, for example, be due to a rise in income while prices remained unchanged.

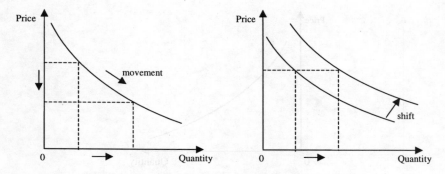

Fig. 2.3. Movements and shifts in a demand curve

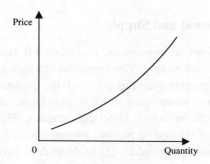

Fig. 2.4. A supply curve

The same analysis applies for firms using a supply function in Eq. (2.2) and Fig. 2.4. Factors affecting the production decision include the price of the commodity, prices of rival commodities, input prices, technology and government policy. Again, holding other factors constant, the *law of supply* stipulates a positive relationship between the quantity supplied, Q_s, and the price, P.

$$Q_s = f(P) \qquad (2.2)$$

Similarly, movements and shifts in a supply curve are illustrated in Fig. 2.5. In this example, the former is due to a rise in price and the latter is due to a change in any of the other factors held constant.

Market *equilibrium* is attained when the demand curve intersects the supply curve, that is, when demand equals supply and the market is cleared, such as at E in Fig. 2.6.

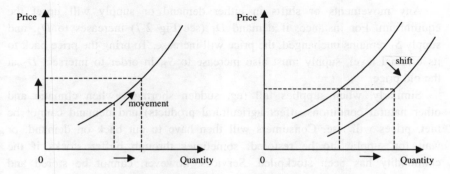

Fig. 2.5. Movements and shifts in a supply curve

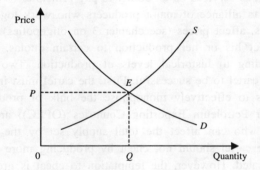

Fig. 2.6. Market equilibrium

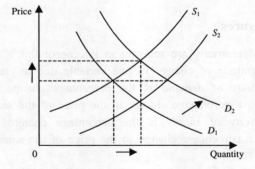

Fig. 2.7. Changes in demand and supply

Any movements or shifts in either demand or supply will upset the equilibrium. For instance, if demand D_1 (see Fig. 2.7) increases to D_2, and supply S_1 remains unchanged, the price will increase. To bring the price back to its original level, supply must also increase to S_2, in order to intersect D_2 at the old price.

Similarly, when supplies fall (eg, sudden shortages when climatic and other natural conditions affect agricultural products) and demand cannot be met, prices will rise. Consumers will then have to cut back on demand, or wait for supplies to be restored, sometimes through buffer stocks if the commodity has been stockpiled. Services, however, cannot be stored and excessive demand for services can cause overloads. To cope with this problem, telecommunications services offer lower rates for off-peak calls; this staggers demand and rations services on an ability-to-pay principle.

A *cartel* is an alliance of major producers who work together to control supply and, thus, affect prices (see chapter 3 on oligopolies). Each producer agrees to restrict his or her production to certain quotas, which may be allocated according to historical levels of production. Two conditions are important for a cartel to be successful. First, the cartel must include all major producers so as to effectively monopolise the bulk of production (eg, the Organisation for Petroleum Exporting Countries (OPEC)) and there are no new producers who can affect the total supply set by the cartel. Second, members of the cartel should not cheat by producing more than what they have been allocated. However, the temptation to cheat is great when prices are high as kept up by the cartel. Hence, the regular monitoring of output is crucial to maintain control over the total supply and higher prices.

Elasticity Measures

Four concepts of elasticity are relevant in microeconomics. Elasticity is the response or magnitude of change in one variable due to change in another. The *price elasticity of demand* is the percentage change in the quantity demanded due to a percentage change in the price of the same commodity.[1] The *price elasticity of supply* is the percentage change in the quantity supplied due to a percentage change in the price of the same commodity. A

---

[1] Algebraically, it can be shown that elasticity is the product of the reciprocal of the slope and the ratio of price to quantity. Thus, elasticity is not synonymous with slope, but the two are related.

notion of elastic demand or supply is when, for example, a 10% change in price brings about a larger than 10% change in demand or supply, respectively. Inelastic demand or supply exists when a 10% change in price brings about a smaller than 10% change in demand or supply, respectively. Unitary elasticity occurs when the changes in price and quantity are proportionate, (eg, exactly 10% respectively). Thus, if consumer demand is elastic with respect to the prices of telephone charges, for example, this implies that a slight reduction in prices will induce a fairly large change in demand.

Two factors affecting demand and supply elasticities are time and the availability of substitutes. When substitutes are available, such as in information services, the response of consumers to a change in price in one service will be elastic since consumers can switch to other services. The availability of substitutes is also a function of time. The longer the time allowed for habits and tastes to change, the more substitutes will be possible. A shorter time frame makes demand more inelastic.

Cross price elasticity shows the percentage change in the quantity demanded of one commodity as a result of a percentage change in the price of another. The two commodities are either *substitutes*, which compete with or rival each other, or *complements*, which are consumed together. The cross price elasticity of broadcast television and cable television, which are rivals, is positive in sign. The rationale is that if the price of broadcast television falls, more broadcast television and less cable television will be demanded. With both the numerator and denominator falling (in the same direction), the cross price elasticity is positive. If two commodities are complements, such as computers and printers, they move in opposite directions, yielding a negative cross price elasticity.

Finally, *income elasticity* measures the percentage change in the quantity demanded as a result of a percentage change in income. For example, if television sets are income elastic, a change in income will affect the purchase of such items. Necessities are more income inelastic: if a telephone is considered an essential commodity, its demand will not be greatly affected by changes in income.

Indifference Curves

Consumption preferences reflect the likes and dislikes of a consumer independent of income and the prices of goods. An *indifference curve* shows the combinations of two goods that the consumer is either indifferent to, or

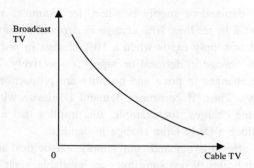

Fig. 2.8. An indifference curve

feels the same level of satisfaction about. This is shown in Fig. 2.8. It is a downward sloping curve, concave to the origin.

The slope at a particular point on an indifference curve measures the *marginal rate of substitution* (MRS), which is the rate at which one good is given up for another while remaining on the same indifferent curve. It is measured in absolute values. In general, if the slope is steep, the marginal rate of substitution is high. That is, more of the good measured on the vertical axis has to be given up in exchange for a small quantity of the good on the horizontal axis while remaining indifferent to the resulting combination of goods in overall satisfaction. If the slope is flat, the marginal rate of substitution is low. That is, a small amount of the good measured on the vertical axis has to be given up for a large amount of the good on the horizontal axis on the same indifference curve.

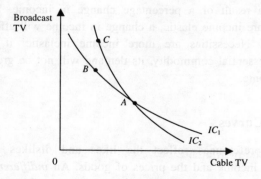

Fig. 2.9. Intersecting indifference curves

Indifference curves do not intersect each other. This is because, as a family of indifference curves, they represent a particular set of tastes. An outward, parallel shift of an indifference curve (away from the origin) indicates a higher level of utility or satisfaction. This is based on the assumption that tastes remain unchanged and larger baskets of goods are available. Intersecting indifference curves pose ambiguous results. In Fig. 2.9, since both A and B are on IC_1 the consumer is said to be indifferent to the combinations of broadcast television and satellite television represented by those points. Similarly, the consumer is said to be indifferent to both A and C on IC_2. However, C is preferred to A, as it is on a higher indifference curve, making indifference curves that intersect portray ambiguous results.

Budget Lines

A budget line shows the combination of two goods that a consumer can purchase with a given budget (see Fig. 2.10). Its slope measures the opportunity cost or trade-off between the two goods, which is the ratio of their prices. With prices remaining constant, the budget line moves outward or inward in parallel to depict an increase or decrease in income (or budget), respectively. Any change in the consumption combination is across the board: that is, income changes affect both goods proportionately since it has nothing to do with price.

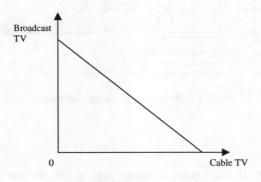

Fig. 2.10. A budget line

Combining the indifference curve and the budget line, Fig. 2.11 shows the optimum level of consumption whereby both utility and budget are maximised: the point of tangency, E.

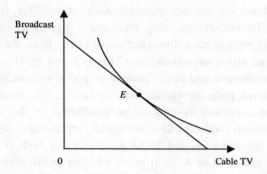

Fig. 2.11. Optimum consumption

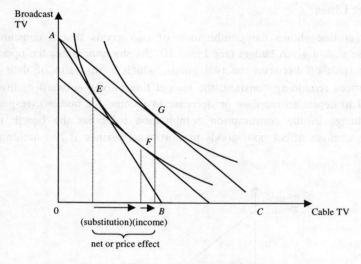

Fig. 2.12. Income and substitution effects

Price Effects

When the price of one good changes (eg, a fall in the price of cable television), its quantity demanded will rise while the quantity demanded of the other good (eg, broadcast television) will fall. This *price effect*, or net effect, in terms of the change in quantity demanded due to a change in price, can be broken down into an income effect and a substitution effect as shown in Fig. 2.12.

A drop in the price of cable television causes the budget line to shift outward from *AB* to *AC*, pivoting at *A*. The *substitution effect*, *EF*, is the increased demand for cable television due to its reduction in price. The price reduction is depicted by the tangency of a flatter hypothetical budget line that is parallel to the new budget line (new price ratios) *AC*, while remaining on the same indifference curve. The *income effect*, *FG*, is the increased demand for cable television due to its reduction in price. This is tantamount to an increase in the consumer's purchasing power, which enables him or her to attain a higher indifference curve. As cable television is a normal good, both its substitution and income effects pull in the same direction in terms of the larger quantities demanded due to its price reduction.

For an inferior good, the substitution effect is always negative; the price and the quantity demanded change in opposite directions. The income effect can also be negative; although the price reduction represents more purchasing power, consumers may still demand less of the good. For example, tastes may have changed such that the inferior good is no longer preferred. If the substitution effect is larger than the income effect, the good is only mildly inferior and more of it will still be bought on a net basis when prices fall. For a strongly inferior good, the net quantity demanded falls when the income effect outweighs the substitution effect.

Cost, Revenue and Profit

Profit is the excess of revenue over cost. Profit is increased by raising revenue or reducing costs. Profit after tax may be distinguished from gross profit, since tax is paid to the government. *Profit maximisation* (ie, to make the largest profit possible) is the conventional goal of a firm, although other goals such as sales maximisation (a strategy of high volume sales to generate profitability) may be pursued. Profit maximisation is synonymous with cost minimisation.

The economist's concept of profit is different from that of the accountant, as accounting profit is measured in actual dollars based on the firm's earnings and expenditures. Economists also consider the opportunity cost of allocating resources to produce a particular good in lieu of the next best alternative. As such, *normal or zero profit* (see chapter 3) is the minimum level of profit needed to encourage a firm to continue operations. *Excess or supernormal profit*, such as that enjoyed by monopolies, implies a sustained rate of return (before taxes on sales or invested capital) exceeding that of similar products or industries operating under similar conditions in terms of production, distribution and risks. In the long run, excess profits hold for approximately five to ten years. The decision to stay in the industry while earning normal profits, or to fix the rate of return for excess profits, depends on the market structure and can be rather arbitrary.

There is a need to distinguish between the concepts of average and marginal cost and revenue at the firm or industry levels. An *industry* is made up of all the firms that produce the same product (eg, the electronic industry). An individual *firm* can be privately owned (eg, a sole proprietorship incorporated but unlisted, or a private limited if listed on the stock market), or state-owned and formed to organise the factors of production in order to produce goods and services for the market.

A distinction must be made between the long run and the short run. The *short run* is defined as the period in which the plant size is fixed, no entry into the industry occurs and the output is functionally related to the amount of fixed input (eg, equipment, plant size) and variable input (eg, labour). In the *long run*, all factors of production (including technology) are variable, and firms can adjust their plant size as well as their production function in response to these changes.

At the firm level, *total costs* (TCs) are comprised of *fixed costs* (FCs), which are invariant to the level of output, and *variable costs* (VCs), such as raw materials, labour, rental of space. In the short run, as variable factors such as labour increase, the total output initially increases at an increasing rate, then eventually increases at a decreasing rate. This is known as the *law of diminishing returns*; as more and more of the variable input works with a constant amount of a fixed factor, total output cannot rise further until more of the fixed factor is made available.

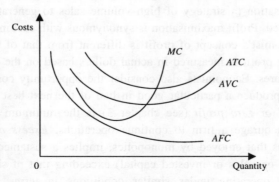

Fig. 2.13. Short-run cost curves

The a*verage total cost* (ATC) is the total cost divided by the total output (*Q*). It can be decomposed into *average variable costs* (AVCs) and *average fixed costs* (AFCs) as shown in Fig. 2.13. *Marginal cost* (MC) is the increment in total cost that results from producing one more unit of the product. Profit is maximised when the marginal cost is equal to the *marginal revenue* (MR), which is the additional revenue from producing one more unit of the product. In other words, a firm's profit maximising output is one in which the last unit produced adds as much cost as it brings in revenue. In symbolic terms:

$$\text{TC} = \text{VC} + \text{FC} \tag{2.3}$$

$$\text{ATC} = \text{AVC} + \text{AFC} = \text{TC}/Q \tag{2.4}$$

$$\text{AVC} = \text{VC}/Q \tag{2.5}$$

$$\text{AFC} = \text{FC}/Q \tag{2.6}$$

$$\text{MC} = \text{MR} \tag{2.7}$$

Scale and Economies

The *ATC*, *AVC* and *MC* curves are all U-shaped to reflect initially increasing returns to scale (ie, decreasing costs or economies of scale), then constant returns to scale (ie, constant costs) and, finally, decreasing returns to scale (ie, increasing costs or diseconomies of scale) associated with larger output. *Returns to scale* relate inputs to outputs, and *economies of scale* relate inputs to costs. Clearly, the amount of inputs used will affect costs. For instance, a 10% increase in inputs that gives rise to a more than 10% increase in output (or increasing returns to scale) is associated with decreasing costs or economies of scale since output is enlarged at an increasing rate, bringing down the overall per unit cost. The *AFC* curve is more hyperbolic since increased output brings down the fixed cost proportionately. The *MC* curve cuts the *ATC* and *AVC* curves at their minimum points.

The long-run average cost (*LRAC*) curve is also U-shaped and is derived from various short-run average cost (*SRAC*) curves as shown in Fig. 2.14.

Unlike in the short run, where at least one variable is fixed, in the long run, all inputs are variable, including the size of the plant. The firm can choose its profit maximising output level and its most efficient plant size. As output increases, the firm need not be confined to operating at the minimum point of $SRAC_1$. Even before that point is reached, the firm can build another plant and operate it at a lower-cost point using $SRAC_2$. With an infinite number of different-sized plants represented by the different *SRAC* curves, in

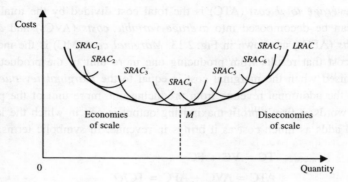

Fig. 2.14. Long-run average cost curves

the long run, there will be one unique minimum cost plant associated with each possible output level. Thus, the *LRAC* in Fig. 2.8 is an *envelope curve* of this infinite number of *SRAC* curves connected at the points of tangency. To the left of the minimum point *M* on the *LRAC*, economies of scale is enjoyed, and to the right, diseconomies of scale. In reality, *LRAC*s are L-shaped; that is, no firm will operate along the upward sloping portion of the *LRAC* making *M* the minimum efficient scale.

Economies of scale can be due to technical, pecuniary or financial reasons. Technical factors that lead to rising productivity include divisions of labour and the specialisation of tasks. On the other hand, diseconomies of scale may be due to managerial inefficiencies such as red tape and layers of bureaucracy associated with rules and regulations and the loss of effective, quick decision-making power.

Pecuniary economies of scale are commonly associated with the bulk purchase of inputs as suppliers reduce transaction and transport costs and pass the savings on to firms. In the media industry, larger buyers often receive discounts in advertising time and space. Also, because these products are often custom-made and specialised, the buyers can exert some oligopoly power (see chapter 3).

Economies of scale may be further split into *internal economies of scale*, which reflect the firm's efforts to reduce per unit costs, and *external economies of scale*, which are due to the industry's efforts. For instance, a concentration of firms from the same industry in one locale can be synergistic, especially when special services or utilities are required, such as the supply of water and electrical power or access for special transportation.

Economies of Scope

A distinction between economies of scale and economies of scope is important for multi-product firms. *Economies of scope* arise when a firm enjoys cost savings when it produces joint products or by-products as part of its normal production. The incremental costs involved in producing such by-products are lower than what it would cost another firm to produce them as a normal product. In other words, when a firm produces a bundle or range of related products, it enjoys overall cost savings due to technical reasons or to pecuniary economies of scale.

Economies of scope can enhance the overall barrier to entry into an industry, as additional efficiencies and cost savings provide synergies that a new entrant cannot have. Such synergies, leading to mergers and overlapping boundaries across industries, are not uncommon in information technology and in the media industry (as seen in chapter 1). Technology, research and development, purchasing, marketing, distribution, administration, treasury and financial functions are some areas where such synergies and cost savings apply.

Productivity

The *productivity* of a factor, as in labour productivity, is defined as the output per unit of labour input. Higher productivity can be achieved either by more output produced by the same labour input, or the same amount of output produced with less labour input.

Productivity is harder to measure in services because, unlike physical goods as in agricultural or manufactured goods, services have innate qualities and standards that are difficult to quantify. Some services, such as those in the government sector, are difficult to measure when they are not subject to the usual market criteria of profitability such that neither output nor input need be constrained by conventional standards of efficiency and effectiveness. In general, productivity levels tend to be lower in the service sector than in manufacturing.

Productivity is easiest to measure at the national level: it is the total *gross domestic product* (GDP), or the *gross national product* (GNP), divided by the total labour force. Both GDP and GNP are equivalent to the market value of all goods and services produced (see footnote 3 in chapter 1 for GED and GNP). The distinction is that GDP measures total output based on a territorial or geographic concept that uses all factors of land, labour and capital available to produce the output regardless of nationality. In contrast, GNP measures total output based on a nationality concept that excludes factor income owing to non-nationals in the economy but includes factor income accrued to nationals from abroad. If the factor income owing to non-nationals is greater than the factor income owing to nationals, the net factor income is positive, making GNP greater than GDP.

Productivity measured at the industrial level (eg, the broadcast industry) is the total output of the industry divided by the total number of workers in that industry. Productivity at the company or firm level is the firm's output divided by the total number of workers in that firm. Since modern industrial production emphasises team or collective efforts, individual productivity is difficult to measure, and can only be based on the qualitative assessment of the individual's supervisor or manager. In certain situations, such as promoting sales, individual effort can be directly attributed and rewarded on commission.

Public Goods and Externalities

The distinction between a public good and a private good lies in two consumption characteristics: non-exclusion and non-rivalry for public goods. *Non-exclusion* in consumption means the market fails, as the pricing mechanism cannot be used to exclude people who do not pay from enjoying a public good. The second characteristic of a public good is that it is indivisible, jointly consumed and *non-rivalrous* in that someone watching broadcast television does not leave less of it available for the next person. Because of these two features, *market failure* occurs in the sense that the price system, as the "invisible hand" that matches demand and supply, cannot operate. As such, public goods have to be produced or provided by the state, using consolidated tax revenue, rather than by pricing according to the quantity demanded. In this case, the quantity of public goods produced is a collective decision made by the government.

An issue of *freeridership* occurs with public goods since not everyone pays tax in a progressive tax system based on one's ability to pay. The tax structure fulfils the function of income distribution and equity, and lower income groups are subsidised by higher income groups. Freeridership is another reason why the market fails and the government has to take care of public goods—either directly by producing them, or indirectly by financing their production in the private sector.

Some private goods may have an *externality*, or third party effect, in that their consumption benefits not only the consumers, but also the rest of society. Further, if these goods and services are of a meritocratic nature, they are *merit goods* whose consumption is usually made compulsory to ensure that their benefits are gained. Examples of goods that have externality or meritocratic features are education, health, housing and transportation.

Chapter 3

Market Structure and Competition

Introduction

This chapter presents various types of market structures and competition ranging from perfect competition at one extreme to monopoly at the other, with monopolistic competition and oligopoly in between. Public policy interventions to stimulate competition will be considered at the end of this chapter, leaving the substantive role of government and its regulatory functions to be discussed in chapter 5. Given the global market structure, this chapter concludes with the competitive landscape in information technology across industries and countries.

Market Structure

Market structure depicts how firms are organised according to their degree of market power, which ranges from perfect competition (the lowest degree) to a monopoly (the highest degree). The factors affecting market power include the number of buyers and sellers, the nature of the product (ie, homogenous or heterogeneous), entry barriers and availability of information.

The number of firms is critical to market power and its distribution. Some idea of the *concentration ratio* reflecting aggregate market shares (in terms of sales, value added or assets) of the largest four, eight or even twenty firms is useful. There are no hard and fast rules but, generally, a high concentration ratio, such as attributable to a tightly knitted oligopoly, would have the four largest firms holding more than 50% market share, or the eight largest firms holding more than 75% market share. Milder oligopolies have moderate concentration ratios of between 33% and 50% for the four largest firms and between 50% and 75% for the eight largest firms. For monopolistically competitive firms, the four largest firms have less than 33% market share, and the eight largest firms have less than 50%.

Just as sellers wield market power, buyer concentration is also possible. The counterpart of a monopoly is a *monopsonist:* a single buyer in the market. Buyer concentration can be measured using concentration ratios applied to aggregate market shares purchased by the four largest buyers. The concept of buyer concentration in the media is relevant, as products (eg, newspapers, television and radio programmes) tend to be highly specialised or tailor-made for a particular medium such as broadcast television or cable movies.

A broadcast firm, or a small group of broadcast firms, can exercise monopsony power as buyers. The elasticity of the overall supply of inputs impacts programme production and other matters relating to inputs. The exercise of monopsony power has to be distinguished from the exercise of bargaining power. If the supply is very elastic, broadcast firms cannot exercise monopsony power, but they may still exercise bargaining power. Such *bargaining power* affects how firms divide rents for popular programmes, but is unlikely to harm efficiency. On the other hand, the exercise of monopsony power is likely to harm efficiency since it restricts the supply to market and increases prices to the eventual consumer.

Regardless of the type of market structure, all firms maximise profits according to the *MR = MC* rule (see chapter 2). However, pricing and profit arising from various market structures affect consumer welfare and resource allocation differently. It is thus germane to discuss the concept of consumer surplus and deadweight loss before the four types of market structures are presented.

Consumer surplus and deadweight loss

Consumer surplus is the difference in price between what a consumer is willing to pay and what he or she actually pays. Given a downward sloping demand curve, the triangle represented by the area under the demand curve and above the price line measures the size of the consumer surplus (triangle *abc* in Fig. 3.1). A parallel concept is that of *producer surplus*, which is the difference in price between what a producer is willing to produce something for, and what he or she actually gets. The size of the producer surplus is represented by the area above the supply curve and below the price line (triangle *bcd* in Fig. 3.1).

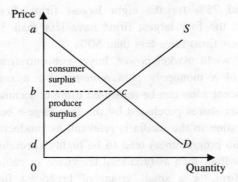

Fig. 3.1. Consumer and producer surplus

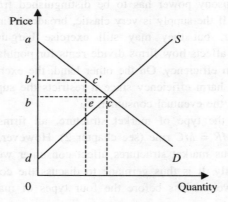

Fig. 3.2. Consumer surplus and deadweight loss

When prices are raised, consumer surpluses are reduced (triangle *ab'c'* in Fig. 3.2); the opposite occurs when prices are lowered. Producers may gain from a loss in consumer surplus, but only to the extent of rectangle *bec'b'*.

Since the quantity demanded falls after prices increase, triangle *cec'* in Fig. 3.2 represents the *deadweight loss* in welfare suffered by the consumer consuming less, since less resources were allocated to produce the output level before the price increased. This is considered a misallocation of resources if the price increase is caused by the firm or producer holding market power.

Alternatively, the price increase may be due to a tax, in which case rectangle *bec'b'* goes to the government as tax revenue. There may be some sharing of the tax burden between buyers and sellers depending on the elasticity of the demand or supply. When demand is inelastic, the consumer's burden is greater; when supply is inelastic, the producer bears the tax burden. But the deadweight welfare loss is still sustained. Less resources are allocated to this industry as demand falls and output falls and a misallocation is deemed since market efficiency, guided by the free forces of demand and supply, is now distorted by the tax. The rationale for the tax may be based on non-economic arguments, such as deterring consumption of harmful or undesirable products (eg, cigarettes), but resource allocation is judged based on economic efficiency.

Perfect Competition

A perfectly competitive market has a large number of buyers and sellers producing a homogenous product. The presence of identical products and many sellers causes firms to be *price-takers*, where the price is set by the industry rather than the firm. Information is assumed to be freely and easily available, which also intensifies competition.

Figure 3.3 shows a perfectly competitive industry and firm in the short run. The industry, comprising a large number of firms, has the usual downward sloping demand curve and upward sloping supply curve that intersect to

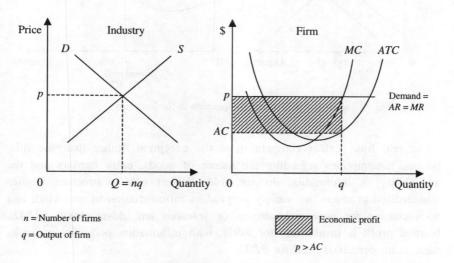

n = Number of firms
q = Output of firm

Economic profit

$p > AC$

Fig. 3.3. Perfect competition in the short run

determine the equilibrium price and quantity. As price-takers, individual firms cannot influence the price, and hence face a perfectly horizontal, or elastic, demand curve. Since firms produce identical products, one firm's output is perfectly substitutable with that of other firms. The demand curve, or price line, is also the perfectly competitive firm's *AR* and *MR*. At the firm's profit maximising output level, where *MR* = *MC*, the shaded region represents *economic profit* since the price is higher than the average cost.

In the short run, when there is economic profit and entry is possible, more firms will be attracted to join the industry, which will raise supplies and push down the price. As shown in Fig. 3.4, this process will continue until the *LRAC* of the firm is tangential to the price, and *normal profit* is earned (since the price equals the average cost). When there is no incentive for entry or exit, the industry is in a long-run equilibrium, and the profit maximising output is where *MR* = *MC*.

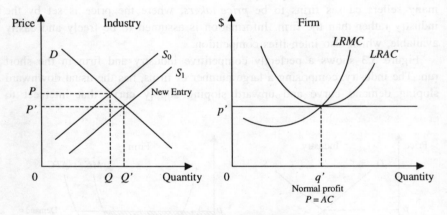

Fig. 3.4. Perfect competition in the long run

In real life, perfect competition is the exception, rather than the rule, because assumptions regarding the nature of goods, entry barriers and the availability of information do not hold. Perfect market structure implies standardised products, no variety or product differentiation of any kind, and no incentive for new technologies or research and development (R&D). Normal profit is insufficient for R&D; with information perfectly available, there is no perceived need for R&D.

Monopolistic Competition

There will still be a large number of buyers and sellers in monopolistic competition, but not as many as in perfect competition such that they have no market power. Instead of a homogenous product, *product differentiation*, through brands, service, location and, most of all, advertising, encourages buyers to made purchasing decisions based on perceived differences in quality and price. Brand loyalty and market power will increase, the more the firms succeed in niche markets.

Advertising can be informative, but more manipulative advertising tries to make the demand curve steeper, or more inelastic, rather than completely horizontal. With some competition from substitutes, the demand curve for monopolistic competitive firms is downward sloping since these firms are no longer price-takers and they enjoy some customer loyalty. However, the demand curve will be relatively elastic, though not as inelastic as oligopolies and monopolies, which have higher market power.

A simple relationship between demand (ie, *AR*) and *MR* curves exists: namely, once the demand curve is determined, the *MR* curve lies mid-way between the demand curve and the vertical axis. In other words, the *MR* curve bisects the horizontal distance between any point on the linear demand curve and the vertical axis.

Mathematically, the total revenue for any output measured as the area under the *AR* or demand curve (the product of price and quantity, or *OQCP*), must equal the area under the *MR* curve (*AOQD*). This implies two other equalities, namely, *PB* = *BC* and *AP* = *CD* in Fig. 3.5.

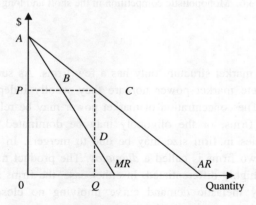

Fig. 3.5. The relationship between *AR* and *MR*

Figure 3.6 shows the short- and long-run equilibrium points of monopolistic competitive firms. Excessive profit, which attracts new firms, is possible in the short run at the profit maximising output where $MR = MC$. Equilibrium is reached when $MR = LRMC$ and $P = LRAC$, squeezing out excess profit. In monopolistic competition, some resource misallocation occurs when the price exceeds marginal cost and becomes higher than the price under perfect competition. Persuasive advertising and product differentiation do not give rise to real economic utility. While product differentiation generates some variety, the *excessive capacity*, as in higher costs associated with accentuating differentiation through advertising, is deemed less economically efficient than perfect competition. Economic efficiency occurs when there is no misallocation of the resources required for production.

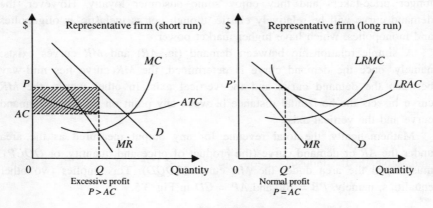

Fig. 3.6. Monopolistic competition in the short and long run

Oligopoly

An oligopolistic market structure only has a few firms. As such, the firms do not have complete market power nor are they wholly independent of each other's actions. The concentration of market power may be relatively balanced between a few firms, or the oligopoly may be dominated by one or two leaders. Disparities in firm size may be due to mergers. In the extreme, an oligopoly with two firms is called a *duopoloy*. The product may be relatively homogenous or highly differentiated. In either case, the firms and the industry face a relatively inelastic demand curve implying no close substitutes as product differentiation is practised.

Market power is higher in oligopolies than in monopolistic competition due to higher entry barriers in the form of economies of scale and economies of scope or absolute cost advantages. However, because there is a high concentration ratio reflected in the dominantly large market shares held by the top four or five firms, a *mutual interdependence* is perceived by rival firms. The actions of one rival cannot be ignored by another, giving rise to a number of oligopolistic models.

In cases where rivals cannot totally ignore the actions of another, when one firm reduces its price and initiates an advertising campaign, others do the same. A *price war* and advertising blitz result until all excess profit is squeezed out and the resulting market shares are similar to what they were initially. This oligopolistic model is more akin to monopolistic competition.

Another possibility is the *kinked demand* model of an oligopoly where rival firms closely monitor each others' reactions, mistrusting each others' motives and believing rivals are out to inflict their worst damage. A kinked demand curve (solid line d_1d_2), shown in Fig. 3.7, is a combination of an elastic (d_1) and an inelastic (d_2) portion of the demand curve, which represent, respectively, price increases that will not be matched by rivals and price decreases that will be matched by rivals. The *MR* curve is discontinuous, reflecting the differing slopes of the elastic and inelastic portions of the demand curve.

Profit maximisation occurs at $MC = MR$, and the price is relatively rigid and stable for the industry as long as MC cuts MR along its vertical portion,

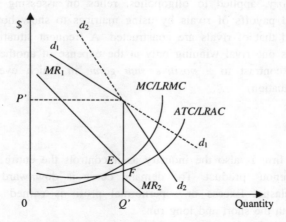

Fig. 3.7. The kinked demand curve of an oligopoly in the short and long run

EF. The kinked demand curve model of an oligopoly is typical of new industries and ones in which companies have entered through acquiring others; such firms are often unfamiliar with the industry and mistrustful of others.

Yet another model of an oligopoly is a hybrid of the above two models. Firms learn from past actions and are willing to trust each other to the extent of recognising their mutual right to exist. Under this model, firms recognise the self-defeating futility of price and advertising wars. They believe that it is wiser to cooperate to maintain high product prices, low input prices and reasonable advertising expenditures. Through cooperation, each firm's profit can be higher than if it acted independently and engaged in rivalrous behaviour, but agreement or collusion is tacit rather than explicit.

In the extreme, a cartel or an explicit agreement to collude occurs. Collusion means jointly controlling supply in order to command a high price and maximum profit for all. A cartel involves the oligopolists getting together to fix the total supply to be shared through quotas, which may be based on historical output or negotiated through bargaining. Two conditions are required for a successful cartel. First, the cartel must include all the major producers and command the dominant if not the total supply. New producers are attracted by high prices but the increase in supply will eventually lead to lower prices. Second, existing members do not cheat by producing more than their allocated quotas. Like new producers, existing members may be tempted by the high price to supply more, which would defeat the purpose of the cartel.

Game theory, applied to oligopolies, relies on assessing the expected behaviour and payoffs of rivals by using matrices to show how one's own behaviour and that of rivals are constructed. A frequent situation of a *zero sum game* has one rival winning only at the expense of another (a win-lose situation) in contrast to a *positive sum game* in which everybody wins (a win-win situation).

Monopoly

A monopoly firm is also the industry as it controls the entire market share for a homogenous product. The demand curve is downward sloping and relatively inelastic. Excess or supernormal profit is earned as shown in Fig. 3.8 in both the short and long run.

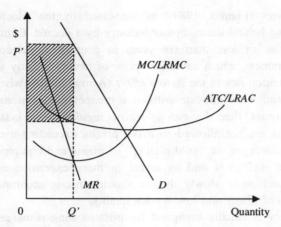

Fig. 3.8. Monopoly in the short and long run

Entry barriers to a monopoly are varied and include: features of a natural monopoly; statutory or legal provisions; and ownership of patents, specific factors or inputs. A *natural monopoly* is one in which economies of scale and economies of scope enable one firm to serve the market more efficiently than several firms. The *LRAC* is downward sloping, implying that lower per unit costs can only be attained with larger output levels. Breaking up a natural monopoly raises costs and increases inefficiency as smaller outputs are shared among a few firms without any benefits of scale.

The telecommunications industry is a natural monopoly if there are *technical economies of scale* in transmission associated with the economies of scale in telecommunications switching equipment. A *system economies of scale* exists when, for example, the value of a telegraphy or telephone network increases dramatically with an increase in the number of users (Duysters, 1996: 84). *Economies of scope*, such as the less costly production of two or more products simultaneously (rather than producing them separately), are clearly demonstrated in the production of the public telephone and telegraph (PTT).

In defence of artificial monopolies (eg, AT&T) due to regulatory and patent practices, the supernormal profits earned through such monopolies make R&D and innovative activity possible. In 1994, the ten largest telecommunications giants made more profit than the twenty-five largest commercial banks (*The Economist*, 30 September 1995). However, regulated industries are characterised by slower technological innovations compared to unregulated ones (Flamm, 1989), as witnessed by the telecommunications industry lagging behind the computer industry by a decade. Computer products have life cycles of less than six years in contrast to telecommunications switching equipment, which have life cycles of twenty to forty years.

One explanation lies in the *Arrow effect* (Arrow, 1962b) where monopolies have less incentive to innovate without a competitive environment. Another explanation argues that the *rate-of-return regulation*, a system in which regulated firms are not allowed to make profits exceeding a certain rate of fair return, encourages the "gold-plating" of plants and equipment. Firms are induced to be inefficient and to invest in more expensive equipment that depreciates much more slowly than it should; this is accompanied by high tariffs, long-lived plants and low service quality.

A monopoly is usually maligned for misallocating resources, imposing a deadweight loss and earning excessive profits as the price exceeds the *LRMC*. Absolute control of a market by one firm is an uncomfortable concept in a market economy with no external checks and balances on its behaviour. In the extreme case, a monopoly can dictate its own self-interests upon the economy and society.

However, a monopoly also has redeeming features: namely, its ability to use excess profits for technological upgrading in R&D. It may be a myth that, since it is the sole producer, a monopoly does not need to ensure that its absolute market power is maintained. Unless it is legislated as a state monopoly with an "iron rice bowl" constitution, a monopoly cannot last forever if it continues to be inefficient and becomes a drain on the state for subsidies.

Apart from market and ideological reforms, which are breaking up inefficient monopolistic state-owned enterprises in many command economies, there is actually a strong incentive for a firm to defend its monopoly power. Supernormal profits provide that incentive, but also attract others to enter. As such, even as the sole producer of a homogenous product, it pays for a monopolist to invest in R&D in order to maintain its market share.

Hence, all forms of monopolistic power, notably, monopolies and oligopolies, can be credited for their expenditure on R&D, which ensures that technology on the whole improves. Perfect competition has neither the profits nor the incentives (given free entry and the availability of information) to bother with R&D and technological improvements. The other party most likely to drive technology, R&D and scientific creation and innovation is the state and the overall public sector. But the public sector cannot be wholly relied upon for R&D since private sector initiatives, dictated or guided by the market, have to be more efficient. State funding is, however, always welcome and necessary in some cases.

Regulating a monopoly

Even in a natural monopoly where the justification for its existence is high in terms of public interest, necessity and convenience, some *regulation* (eg, placing maximum limits on its prices and profits) is desirable. Regulated monopolies are common in utilities such as telecommunications. Usually, a *cost-plus* principle is used to allow certain prices or tariffs to be charged, which helps a monopolistic firm earn sufficient revenue to cover its overhead or outlay in infrastructure costs, plus a fair rate of return on its investment. The concept of normal profit is used (see chapter 2). The level of normal profit is the approximate outcome of a cost-plus basis of pricing.

The cost concept employed is the average cost, or it uses *average cost pricing* to determine the cost-plus regulation. Figure 3.9 shows the regulation of a natural monopoly. The *LRAC* of a natural monopoly is L-shaped and downward sloping to reflect lower costs as output increases. The *LRMC* is relatively elastic and almost horizontal such as in perfect competition. This is

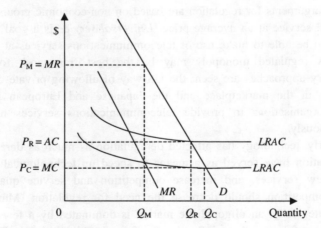

P_C, Q_C for perfect competition
P_R, Q_R for a regulated monopoly
P_M, Q_M for an unregulated monopoly

Fig. 3.9. Regulating a natural monopoly

because the objective of regulation is to try to get a naturally monopolistic firm to operate as efficiently as a perfectly competitive one. With profit maximising at $MR = MC$, an unregulated naturally monopolistic firm will charge the price revealed by the demand curve at $P_M = MR$. A perfectly competitive firm produces much larger output (where MR, as in its demand curve (demand $= AR = MR =$ the price in perfect competition), cuts the $LRMC$) and prices the output at $P_C = MC$. Clearly, in perfect competition, both output and price are, respectively, larger and lower compared to a natural monopoly.

Regulations based on average cost pricing will put a natural monopoly at an output where the demand curve intersects the $LRAC$ and $P_R = AC$. The regulated price and output is closer to the perfectly competitive ideal but, of course, never equal such perfect outcomes. As long as the $LRMC$ lies below the $LRAC$, forcing a natural monopoly to any price equal to the MC would cause the firm to incur an economic loss. Thus, the practical solution is a regulated environment that lies between an unregulated monopoly and a perfectly competitive market. The natural monopoly is guaranteed its total cost, covering all outlays and expenditures, plus a fair rate of return. The regulatory body verifies that the total revenue (the product of the quantity and the price) does not exceed the total cost and let the natural monopoly decide its rates or tariffs.

The arguments for regulation are based on non-economic grounds, including universal service at an average price. *Universal service* is a goal to enable all people to be able to make use of telecommunications services at a reasonable price. A regulated monopoly may be the best framework for this. Two regulatory approaches are seen: the US way of allowing private companies to compete in the marketplace and the Japanese and European provision of public organisations to provide telecommunications services more or less autonomously.

Clearly, technology has affected deregulation as much as deregulation and liberalisation have served as a means to speed up technological innovations, boost new services, and increase competition and service quality. Ideally, more competition should decrease the need for regulation (Mansell, 1993). But, strategically, an oligopolistic market is dominated by a few large global firms powerful enough to influence the future public network. The customer premises equipment and services markets resemble the idealistic model, while the switching and transmission markets fall under the strategic model. There are still enormous upfront costs in switching equipment, satellite systems and fibre optics. Economies of scale and shrinking product life cycles give oligopolistic firms the edge in capturing market shares.

The other redeeming feature of a monopoly lies in its ability to price discriminate. This allows some classes of consumers to be brought into the market to consume goods that would otherwise have been prohibitive given a single price. Price discriminating monopolies can take fuller advantage of economies of scale and economies of scope and enlarge possibilities in both output and variety.

Price discrimination

A regulated monopoly, operating at a price and output in between that of an unregulated monopoly and a perfectly competitive market, would lower the inefficiency associated with deadweight loss. Allowing for *price discrimination*, the ability of producers to charge different categories of consumers different prices for similar goods instead of a single monopoly price, also helps. Price discrimination so defined is not synonymous with *price differentiation*, where different prices are charged based on perceived differences in goods. Price discrimination enables a monopolist to earn higher profits than under a single price regime.

Price discrimination requires two main conditions to work successfully. First, consumers are physically separable based on different elasticities of demand; the physical separation may even be across countries. Second, no resale or arbitrage takes place among various classes of consumers. The principle of price discrimination works on consumers faced with a more inelastic demand curve who are willing to pay more for the same good. Consumer surpluses confiscated from this category of consumers into producer surpluses enable the monopolist to charge lower prices to, or even incur a loss for, other consumers who have more elastic demand. Such price discrimination, or cross-subsidising across countries to penetrate new markets, is deemed as *dumping*.

Figure 3.10 shows price discrimination practised among various groups of consumers. The first class, C_1, has the most inelastic demand paying, P_1, followed by the second class, C_2, paying, P_2, and so on. Even if a loss is incurred—for example, if the monopolist charges the fifth category of consumers a price of P_5—the monopoly still makes more profit than it would have by charging a single price, P_3, under maximising profit at $MR = MC$. Total consumer surplus, represented by the rectangles under P_1, P_2 and P_3 exceed that of just P_3 if a single price were charged.

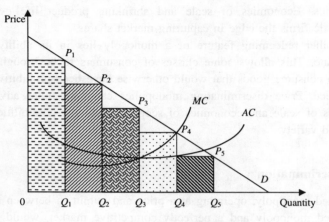

Fig. 3.10. Price discrimination

In telecommunications, price discrimination is practised in peak and off-peak pricing to smoothen demand and loads and to promote a more even distribution of resources and capacity utilisation of equipment and resources. As product lines and customer bases multiply and grow, the conditions for price discrimination become more favourable.

Natural monopolies in telecommunications

The end of telecommunications as a natural monopoly is as much pushed by technology as by deregulation policies that encourage networks. New entrants come from three directions: through networks of their own, by leasing infrastructure from others and by using new infrastructure such as cable television and wireless spectrums. The effect is the same: the increase in supply drives prices down and increases the range of services.

Large businesses with their own internal networks of personal computers and telephones would work more on private networks. There are about 700,000 private networks in the US, compared to only 14,000 in the European Union (*The Economist*, 30 September 1995). Once private networks are constructed, companies can lease out excess capacity to others and thus enter into competition with traditional providers so long as legislation permits them to do so.

Large wholesale markets also sell excess capacity to specialist companies and, as restrictions are further loosened, other resellers enter the market too.

With the freedom to price and compete, they may undercut the dominant market players and create niche markets for themselves.

High monopoly profits always attract entrants, such as in the proliferation of *call-back services*, which allow callers to pay lower rates using calling cards and the call-back market (see chapter 4). Essentially, a caller in a high-cost country such as Singapore first telephones a low-cost country such as the US. Without answering the telephone, a computer identifies the caller and calls him or her back to connect the subscriber to the desired country. This way, the Singapore caller enjoys US rates when making calls to other countries since tariff rates are no longer a function of distance, but are more artificially created through pricing policies. High rates are also due to a complex settlements system for splitting the proceeds of international calls among oligopolies. But competition has led to a reduction in the rates of international calls. Using profits from international calls to subsidise domestic rates—as well as other forms of price discrimination—will have to change.

Public Policy and Competition

Competition policy is any public policy meant to remedy the anti-competitive inclinations of economic agents—be they producers or consumers—in order to foster efficiency, effectiveness and entrepreneurship, and to combat collusion and the abuse of market power (Welfens & Yarrows, 1997: 429). Anti-trust institutions that enforce competition policies include those at the national level such as the UK Monopolies and Mergers Commission, the regional level such as the European Commission, and the international level such as the World Trade Organisation (WTO). A regulatory framework is constituted within which these institutions operate and supervise.

Regulation provides a set of laws, rules and regulations to ensure a level playing field for all participants. It does not necessarily conflict with the "invisible hand" or price mechanism under the free forces of supply and demand since regulation can be a tool of market economies. Universal regulation is as safeguarding competition and public interests, especially where self-regulation is not perfect in imperfect markets; that is, economic agents are not concerned with the common good as such.

Imperfect as it is, regulation is one alternative since market forces alone cannot prevent the exercise of market power. But others may disagree and argue for deregulation of telephony because the traditional *raison d'être* for regulation has been undermined by technology, and the elimination of rate distortions would enhance static welfare gains (Alexander, 1997). Another alternative is regulation by constraining the price to the measured cost of service, but this may fail to give suppliers adequate incentives to minimise costs. Limiting the price or price increases without measuring costs, such as a price cap, also may not give suppliers the incentive to choose desirable improvements in programming quantity or quality. Suppliers generally fail to provide an optimal level of service quality.

An alternative to regulation is to reinforce competitive forces by modifying policies that directly or indirectly limit new entries or the competitiveness of existing rivals. This requires evaluating the effect of allowing additional entries on competition and efficiency, and balancing competition objectives against other objectives. But the increasing role of market forces in determining supply is leading to a fundamental conclusion that competition policy should ensure efficiency to satisfy the demands of consumers.

The end product of all information service markets is knowledge. An *information market* simply enables a consumer to know something that was not known before. The forms in which information can be marketed include exchanging a symbolic experience, learning or relearning something, changing a perception of cognition, reducing uncertainty, expanding one's range of options, exercising rational choice, evaluating decisions, controlling a process, and communicating an idea, fact or opinion.

In information technology, telecommunications and broadcast services, competition policy tries to prevent firms from reaching agreements to consummate mergers in oligopolies with enhanced market power. Similarly, horizontal agreements among competing firms to reduce competition via collusion have to be scrutinised. The objective is not to preserve the viability of individual competitors, but to preserve the process of competition and the efficient functioning of markets.

Market power and entry are based on economic factors and the influence of public policy. If entry is unlikely to be sufficient to prevent the exercise of market power, the question is whether existing suppliers in the market have the ability and incentive to prevent the exercise of market power.

Public policies affect the entry of new competitors either directly, by controlling entries, or indirectly, by affecting the entrant's prospects for profits. Policies may also affect competition among existing suppliers. How public broadcasters react to attempts by other firms to exercise market power depends on their mandates and structure. The competitive responses of private firms are affected by broadcast policies that change their ability or incentive to expand supply or undercut the prices of a rival who tries to exercise market power.

Competition policy can help shape media policies and regulations by evaluating their effect on the competitive process. The goals of competition and regulation extend into non-economic objectives with possible conflicts on competition or economic objectives. Socio-cultural and political values, pluralism, the freedom of expression and other fundamental attributes of a democratic society are involved. The promotion of efficient markets would not take over the primacy of these goals, but competition issues have to be considered alongside public policies in decisions affecting the provision of telecommunications, broadcast and other services. A balance among the various objectives has to be made.

In broadcast services, for instance, allowing market forces to play a role in determining supply is to take advantage of opportunities that new distribution technologies offer. They can break through limitations of spectrum allocated to traditional broadcasting and satisfy the consumer's demand for an increased supply of broadcast services. New means of delivering broadcast programmes do not require over-the-air terrestrial transmitters or the use of a broadcast spectrum with delivery by cable, direct broadcast satellites (DBSs) and microwave multichannel distribution systems (MMDS). With lower costs due to technology, suppliers can now tap demand through subscription fees. Similarly, call-back services in telecommunications have started along that line of demand and supply economics.

Historically, broadcasting was reserved for public service broadcasters, or controlled and regulated by government policies. With new technology, media services are increasingly supplied by private firms, giving rise to two types of competition issues. First, competition policy must ensure that markets function as efficiently as possible. Growing private firms, mergers, contractual and other relationships shape the structure of markets. Second, competition issues are also created by government rules and regulations.

In general, competition policy issues involve four broad areas (OECD, 1993). First, they entail a basic analysis of the ability of firms to exercise market power as sellers, or monopsony power as buyers. Second, they involve an analysis of how the competitive process is effected by vertical contract relationships, vertical integration between programme producers and programme services or networks, and vertical integration between programme services and video distributors. Third, the issues call for an analysis of how concentrations in media ownership affect competition. Finally, an analysis of the ability of market forces or regulatory options to control the exercise of market power by multichannel distributors, especially by a single supplier of cable service, is necessary.

Areas where public policies remain relevant in broadcasting include licensing requirements; controls on subscription fees for cable and other new distribution systems; regulations on the permissible quantity and type of advertising; regulations on the permissible concentration of broadcast properties or of broadcast or other media; requirements concerning minimum amounts of particular types of programming, programmes produced by independent producers or programmes produced within the home country.

Who's Who in Competition

Information technology

The US dominated the information technology industry until the mid-1980s when Japanese companies took over as the personal computer turned computer hardware into a consumer electronics commodity. South Korea and Taiwan also entered the computer market on the hardware side. As semiconductor memory became the core chip design and manufacturing competency, Japanese dominance of the DRAM market became a precursor to its dominance in the semiconductor industry.

Japan's domestic information technology industry soared with its overall economy compared to US sluggishness in the late 1980s and the break-up of AT&T and deepening problems at IBM. Cross subsidisation and predatory pricing by huge diversified Japanese keiretsus, immense sums spent on R&D and Japan's trade barriers crushed US rivals in a sector-by-sector strategy (Moschella, 1997: 43).

Hardware

Competition in global hardware is between the US, Japan, South Korea and Taiwan. Europe has lost much of its vitality even as it remains a source of information technology production. Europe accounts for one-third of consumption in the global information technology market but is a minor in global supplier leadership. It appears generally stuck in the middle as personal computer-centric markets pass by Europe.

Within the hardware sector, competition revolves around two main dimensions: strength in technology and overall time-to-market (Moschella, 1997: 54). Particular country competencies show US vendors in fast-moving, high technology sectors while Japanese strengths are in slower moving but still high technology markets such as mainframes, high-end disk drives, flat panel displays, DRAMs and others. Both Japan and the US are undoubtedly leaders in hardware technology; Europe follows.

Lower down the technology curve, Korean and Taiwanese firms have carved out significant and generally different positions. Taiwanese firms are fully integrated in the global information technology production value chain, dominating many low cost personal computer commodities such as keyboards, mice and motherboards (except between 1995–1996 when Intel posed the competition in motherboards).

In the 1980s, Korean firms started to challenge US and Taiwanese firms but have succeeded only in the low-end floppy disk and monitor markets. Re-emerging with a powerful overall strategy in the early 1990s, Korean firms, including Hyundai, Samsung, LG Electronics and Daewoo, changed their target to Japan and pursued high technology commodity products, grabbing a large share of worldwide DRAM market and becoming active in flat panel displays.

Singapore has become the world's largest producer of disk drives and produces high volumes of printers, computer subassemblies and, increasingly, semiconductors. Its Creative Technologies is a major player in the sound and video card markets and Singapore is emerging as an important regional centre for US information technology firms, replacing Hong Kong. Hewlett-Packard, Compaq, Intel, Digital and Seagate have regional headquarters in Singapore. Malaysia, China, Thailand and Indonesia play similar offshore manufacturing roles.

Japanese hardware vendors need to be more competitive in the face of rapidly rising Korean competencies, which augur well for long-term capital-intensive markets. Taiwanese vendors face competition, in terms of time to market, from Singapore, Malaysia, China, Thailand and Indonesia; some of these countries are also moving up the technology curve. The strategic question for these Asian newcomers is, can they follow the Korean route, which adopted the Japanese strategy of targeting high technology commodity products? They are unlikely to pursue the US model of developing strengths in technology and time to market simultaneously.

Software

Software pricing seems to defy conventional microeconomics (see chapter 4). The puzzle of software pricing is that entry costs into the software industry are low, and it is almost impossible to co-ordinate the market. Also, potential buyers cannot fully understand the strengths and weaknesses of software programmes until they have used them for a certain period. The search for an appropriate programme may be more costly in time and effort than any possible savings from purchasing a cheaper product. As software firms attempt to gain market presence through intensive marketing and promotion, which are more effective in generating profits than perfecting the product, the process of computer technology is lost in the process.

Software and services account for half of the global information technology market, and the competitive landscape is different from the rest of the market. In both software and services, the two competitive drivers are skills and organisational reach; the US dominates this area, followed by Europe (Moschella, 1997: 58). Human skills (principally in design, consulting, implementation and project management) and organisational reach or ability to project these skills globally are crucial.

Countries like India, Russia and Hungary have high competitive skills but extremely limited market reach. Asian nations essentially have neither. Asia's weakness is not due to an inherent lack of software proficiency, but to the global emphasis on English language products as the starting point for new applications and tools. Asian firms also have to pay more attention to the relative lack of intellectual property protection. European firms are again caught in the middle with a generally good skills base but with market access confined to domestic and former colonial markets. Unlike the hardware market, US firms, with some co-operative efforts with India and other countries, may preserve their competitive edge since there is no looming threat from Asia in software. Both South Korea and Taiwan are at the lowest end of the software and service markets by the criteria of skills and organisational reach, while Japan is about mid-way between Europe and other Asian countries.

Services

Information services are in information technology consulting, project design, custom programming, training and support, systems integration, maintenance, operations and outsourcing. Although skills bases are comparable in a number of countries, global market reach varies considerably and no nation, including the US, has a truly global information service industry. American systems vendors such as IBM and Digital come closest in terms of global reach but they have competencies only in their own product offerings.

The task of building a fully capable unit in significant country markets remains daunting unless partnerships and occasional acquisitions are accommodated. Only the US can do this. Europe is barely keeping up with viable pan-Europe capabilities let alone going global, and no Asian firm has made a serious attempt outside its home country in information services.

The whole information industry structure is still multi-layered, with fewer layers in hardware and software, and services staying largely separate. Less layers, however, do not mean consolidation of the overall industry. The converse is true: that is, less layers mean steadily fragmenting supplier market shares.

Some division is implicit with Compaq staying out of services, Intel out of software and Microsoft out of hardware. Intel is moving upstream in the hardware market and its cosy relationship with Microsoft will wane without being totally indifferent. Microsoft and Novell are increasingly locked in direct competition. The rare triumvirate of mutually reinforcing monopolies is likely to break with strategic distancing.

Within these broad categories, changing technology is offering the possibility of a more homogenous technology base for hardware and software platforms. The effect on the personal computer business and the business environment will be profound, especially with the growth of new areas including the Internet and the World Wide Web.

The services industry is relatively more stable for a number of reasons, including being more fragmented due to a lack of dominant leadership. Technological innovations in the services industry (eg, breakthroughs in business models, management practices and human resource management) are less tangible than innovations in the hardware and software industries. The services industry offers a completely different type of investment opportunity. With multi-year services contract arrangements, the business is more predictable and stable.

Part II

Players and Markets in
Information Technology and the Media

Chapter 4

Information Technology and Media Markets

Introduction

This and the next three chapters focus on the players in the information technology and media markets. This chapter considers the hardware and software vendors in the telecommunications, computer, semiconductor and media industries. The later includes radio, television, cable television, newspapers, magazines, periodicals and advertising. The individual treatment of these markets is being stirred and shaken with technological convergence, networks and multimedia (see chapter 7). Chapter 5 is devoted to the government as both a player and a regulator in the information technology and media industries. The impact of information technology on employment is discussed in chapter 6 while chapter 7 looks at technology and the market.

Terminology and Etymology of the Mass Media

The word *mass* (as in a multitude) in economics suggests mass production of a commodity, together with connotations that the commodity is cheap and short-lived. The word *media* (as a plural of the word *medium*) conveys an intermediate position or agent as a linking instrument that is part of the communications process. Seven broad forms of mass media may be identified in terms of the largest audience and impact: they comprise newspapers, magazines (Daly, 1997), broadcasting as in radio and television (including cable and satellite broadcasting), books (Greco, 1997), sound recordings, film and advertising.[1] Other forms of mass media include posters, buttons,

---

[1] It is estimated that, in 1996, television broadcasting enjoyed the highest rate of operating margins (about 18%), followed by radio broadcasting (17%) and newspaper

billboards, direct mail, comic books, matchbooks and others. Recording (Hull, 1998) and motion pictures (Litman, 1998) have taken over some of the audience from live theatrical exhibitions. Similarly, cable television (Parsons & Frieden, 1998) competes with broadcast television (Walker & Ferguson, 1998). The blurring and convergence of lines are due as much to economics and technology as to electronic publishing (Paulick, 1997; Grycz, 1998).

Media experiences are synonymous with human experiences, encompassing many aspects of social science. Whereas people and individuals are different according to their culture, age, education and technical abilities, they experience and respond to media similarly. As with all social and natural responses, the reaction is automatic—without any conscious or strategic thinking—as long as the media is kept simple and comfortable.

The media equation is about how people treat computers, television and new media, and it is equal to real life (Reeves & Nass, 1996: 251–6). The media equation is automatic with minimal cues. What seems true is more important than what is true. People respond to what is present and people like simplicity. These findings on the media equation—the need to keep things simple and short—allow improvements in media design to evaluate media and provide new methods for research and the study of issues, such as whether the media is a tool to serve people's needs, and whether people become guilty of anthropomorphism (the mistaken belief that inanimate objects are human).

Different media may have different sets of audiences. An *audience* is broadly defined as a set of people who use mass media for information. It can move from people to the public in general; it can also evolve into a more unorganised and amorphous body. The mass media audience is more mass-based than, for instance, an arts audience that only goes for theatres and concerts.

Measurements of audience size and behaviour (eg, who reads the publication? who sits in front of the television? what is their attention span?) helps various industries gauge the effectiveness, popularity, etc. of their work. An immediate implication of such data is the attractiveness of a particular form of mass media to the advertising on which it depends for revenue. However, care must be cautioned on such measurements as statistics and the use of percentages can be abused, self-serving and adapted to certain aims.

---

publishing (over 15%) (*The Economist*, 28 March 1998). Pay television and recorded music had operating margins over 10%. Margins for films, magazine publishing and book publishing were around 10%.

The role of the mass media

The use of mass media is basically to inform, entertain, convince or a trilogy of information/entertainment/influence based on a market model that operates on demand and supply principles. Beyond the market model, mass media is also used for socialisation. The symbolic function is obvious and can be decisive in dictating or directing pivots of social behaviour. On the other hand, mass media can enable debate and consultation to assimilate into the lineaments of national identity. It can stimulate collective action in communities and engender co-operation and participation. Public opinion thus evoked and embellished can also pre-establish divisions.

For most people, daily encounters with the mass media are a social rite. Buying a newspaper, putting on the news or accessing the Internet for current affairs and information can be ritualistic. Such rituals have a social function since repetition–compulsion is an impulse to repeat the same gestures or recreate the same situation with an innate tendency to revert to earlier conditions. Since routine is a response to the challenges of life, rites are created as a defence against the pressures of the environment. Responsible and accountable mass media recognise their potent influence in moulding thinking, opinion and behaviour in socially and morally right directions. This role in education is more edifying than to cause defiance toward unobtainable goals, to create mischief or to attain pure pecuniary gains such as with tabloid sensationalism and the paparazzi.

On the other hand, communication may just be a form of social exchange, with no real information sought. Noise fills up letters, conversations, encounters and exchanges. A functional approach to satisfy this kind of audience is to provide perspective, generate useful concepts and generally promote an awareness of diversity rather than dysfunctionally portraying negative, harmful views. The mass media also provide surveillance by giving warnings on threats from weather, volcanic eruptions or inflation. They supply instrumental surveillance through coverage of parliamentary sessions or public hearings. News is important to verify, create credibility, confer status for endorsement, interpret as well as lead public opinion.

Whatever the specificity or role of mass media, the idea is to create links, transmit values and socialise individuals such that they adopt behaviour and values as a group. Competition for attention, audience and the technology that enables capability and capacity to be generated together with cost and price effects does, however, create many possibilities and modes. Some postulate the end of mass media with segmentation, fractionalisation and cannibalisation.

The Telecommunications Industry

Origins

The birth of modern telecommunications came in England in 1837 with the invention of an electric telegraphic instrument by Cooke and Wheatstone, followed a few months later by Samuel Morse's dot-and-flash-based codes over copper wire cables (Duysters, 1996: 65). The telegraph was an expensive service used only by time-sensitive industries like stock markets, newspapers and the military. In the US, such services were virtually monopolised by the Western Union Telegraph Company, which owned the Morse code patent and exclusive railroad contracts that enabled it to construct the largest telegraph network by far. By the mid-1850s, extensive telegraph systems covered the US and Europe, remaining uncontested until the invention of the telephone by Alexander Graham Bell in 1875.

The telephone, a new technological paradigm using analogue voice communications, coexisted with the telegraph as a complementary product that covered short distances and supplemented the long-distance telegraph. Bell's patent was filed a few hours before a similar invention and patent by Elisha Gray that came under Western Union, starting a strong rivalry between it and the Bell Company. An agreement made in 1879 gave Bell a virtual monopoly over the telephone and gave Western Union assurances of no competition in the telegraph market; this agreement established the American Bell Company and the American Union Telegraph respectively. The apparent myopia of Western Union at the time was because the telephone was barely functional up to twenty miles under the best possible conditions.

Both the telegraph and telephone technologies had similar difficulties in using copper wires to transmit signals manually. Research was directed at lowering the resistance of the transmission wires and improving the distance to be connected. Shielded by its patent and monopoly, American Bell reaped economies of scale. But it neglected rural areas in the US and many independent companies overcame the high entry barriers within fifteen years after Bell's patents expired. However, Bell still dominated long-distance services and, by refusing interconnection, kept local systems relatively isolated. After failing to compete by following the low-price strategy and filing patent suits against major competitors, the company turned to acquiring weaker competitors instead.

Diversifying away from Massachusetts, American Bell relocated its stocks to the New York-based American Telephone & Telegraphy Company (AT&T)

in 1899. AT&T was criticised of monopolising the industry and, to avoid nationalisation, it accepted regulation instead. By agreeing to strict government regulation, AT&T retained its virtual monopoly of the US telecommunications industry.

In 1907, the invention of the vacuum tube enabled signals to be amplified through thinner wires and vacuum-tube repeaters. This doubled transmitting distances. The combination of vacuum-tube repeaters and frequency division multiplexing paved the way for more low-cost long-distance telephony, a distinct triumph over the long-distance telegraph. But AT&T's next challenge came from Guglielmo Marconi's invention of radio transmission, which led to wireless voice applications and, with the start of World War II, lucrative military contracts. Radio communications over the air broke AT&T's hold over the wired network.

The growing complexity of technology and economics posed regulatory problems, resulting in the US Congress's 1934 enactment of the Federal Communications Commission (FCC) to regulate interstate long-distance telecommunications and broadcasting. Meanwhile, research focused on electro-mechanical switches to replace manual switching. The transistor invented at Bell Laboratories in 1949 replaced the vacuum tube and initiated the digitisation process. By the 1960s, the age-old switchboard problem was finally solved by smaller, faster, semi-electronic exchanges in high capacities. Computers and switching equipment were driven electronically, and the convergence of information technologies in the telecommunications, computer and electronic industries provided economies of scope (see chapter 7). With the increased capacity and flexibility of switching equipment, the next challenge was transmission speed and capacity.

Reliability, speed, size and power consumption were further improved with the invention of the integrated circuit, which led to a fully electronic telecommunications network. The pulse code modulation system invented in the 1930 became economically feasible with more sophisticated solid state electronics to translate analogue signals into digital form. Another impetus to the digitisation of the telecommunications network came from stored programme control in electronic exchanges.

Meanwhile, high-capacity coaxial cables replaced copper wires. The invention of the microprocessor in the 1970s and other developments in computer and semiconductor technology (see chapter 7) speeded up digitisation. Satellite transmission and fibre optic cables have further enabled signals to be transmitted, switched and received in digital form. Satellite systems avoid the upfront costs of wired networks, which intensify competition as much as they improve on distance and point-to-multi-point transmission, but they do face competition from fibre optic cables, which became cost effective in the 1980s.

Fibre optic cables are characterised by large bandwidth coupled with reliable data transmission at very high speeds. *Broadband* describes the bandwidth needed to carry one or more full motion, television-quality, video signals (Miller, 1996). Fibre optic cables are used extensively in local and wide area networks (LANs and WANs) and in integrated services digital networks (ISDNs). ISDNs became commercially available after 1988 and use a multi-purpose fibre optics cable network as the backbone.

Developments in transmission speed and cost effectiveness were accompanied by progress in digital time-division switching equipment in the 1970s. Hybrid intelligent networks, new interactive services and value-added services (eg, electronic mail, electronic banking and data storage, retrieval and processing) allow users in distant locations to share processing capacity and information sources. Increasingly, the boundary between the regulated telecommunications industry and the unregulated computer industry is blurring and converging. The distinction between voice and data communications is becoming artificial. Microwave transmission further enabled private systems, such as Microwave Communications Inc (MCI), to bypass AT&T's network.

As capabilities rise and distance matters no more, demand will be further boosted by falling telecommunications charges. Profitability in the international telephone business is currently propped up by agreements between governments and big national telephone companies. A national monopoly carries a call to the border and allows another monopoly to take over until the message is delivered; costs, through *accounting rates*, are appropriately shared. This regime is breaking down due to monopoly power being scrapped and to the elimination of the settlement payments system.

International simple resale (ISR) allows carriers to lease or buy international transmission capacity in bulk, plug it into the public network at each end and resell it one call at a time (*The Economist*, 13 September 1997). Besides avoiding settlement payments, customers can enjoy a big price advantage with international calls billed at close to domestic long-distance rates. A stretch of international route at bargain prices will attract calls from a direct route to a more indirect path since some countries do not yet allow international simple resale.

As telephone companies acquire more freedom to channel calls along low-cost routes, some incentives to misbehave through the accounting-rate system appear. If a carrier picks up more calls to deliver to another country than it receives, it must make a settlement. On the other hand, if it receives more calls than it sends, the carrier receives a settlement, making it attractive to manipulate permutations of public networks and private lines to ensure that more calls are received than are sent over public networks.

Two ways of smuggling calls are possible. The first, called refile, is when a carrier in a country with high accounting rates and sending rates calls another carrier that also has high accounting rates by first sending the call over the public network to a country with low accounting rates. The latter sends the call to the desired destination, charging the first country a cheaper accounting rate than if the first country had sent the call directly. Telephone companies loathe this practice since it is tantamount to smuggling calls.

Another technique for exploiting the accounting-rate structure, the *call-back*, employs the same principle as refile, but does not use public networks (see chapter 3). The caller dials a local number that puts the call through to a switch in a country like the US where call charges are low. This American switch reads the caller's number without answering, rings the original caller back, simultaneously ringing the party being called and connects the two together. Call-back services are viable wherever the price of a direct call made on the public network is higher than the price of the two legs from the computer switch, forming a telephone arbitrage.

The call-back is one of many ways in which a call that originates in a country is effectively turned around and becomes, in effect, a call into the country. In 1995, an estimate by the International Telecommunications Union (ITU) put such services as accounting for 22% of the traffic from Asia to the US (*The Economist*, 13 September 1997). With settlements following the direction of the calls, the outcome is to replace calls that require a payment from Asia with calls that involve a payment from the US to Asia.

New entrants are attracted by the relative ease of establishing a service and earning profits. Companies provide least-cost routing with software installed on the customer's premises. Calls can then be routed to undercut the notoriously high costs of national monopolies. Clearly, call-back services have a role as long as price differentials exist. Once international tariffs fall with such competition, call-back services will have served their function.

Other ways in which the accounting-rate system is attacked have come from the US, which has relatively low international charges. Many more international calls appear to originate in the US than terminate there due to the proliferation of the routing described above. To stop this, the US plans to impose price caps from 1999 on American carriers for calls terminated overseas. American carriers presently pay more in settlements than they receive, implying a subsidy to foreign telephone companies by American consumers. Developing countries are displeased since they cannot recoup their investment in telephone networks by enjoying high international tariffs.

Competition is a clear trend. The accounting-rate system will probably not survive on busy routes, and will be replaced by a system of call-termination charges. The carrier that delivers the call to its destination will charge the carrier fee no matter where the customer resides.

Not only did AT&T face intense competition in the customer premises equipment market, but low-priced products from Japan, Taiwan and South Korea confronted both American and European telecommunications manufacturers (see chapter 3). Office equipment suppliers encroached on the customer premises equipment market to reap economies of scope from the same technology base. The convergence and integration of these markets occurred in spite of domination by telecommunications giants like AT&T, Alcatel, Siemens, Ericsson and NEC.

The break-up of AT&T, the world's largest corporation, in 1994 into AT&T Communications, AT&T Technologies and AT&T International was paralleled by deregulation elsewhere. In Japan, Nippon Telegraph and Telephone Corporation (NTT), created in 1952, is a public organisation for domestic telecommunications and Denshin Denwa Company Ltd (KDD) is a private monopoly for international telecommunications services. Further deregulation occurred in 1985 as NTT faced competition in all its core markets. In Europe, state-owned postal, telegraph and telephone (PTTs) administrations faced similar, if somewhat more gradual, pressure to liberalise, starting with British Telecom (BT) in 1981 until its final privatisation in 1984.

International and intergovernmental organisations involved in the telecommunications industry that help in networking, standardising quality protocols and architecture, regulation and other issues include: the International Telecommunications Union (ITU), the International Telecommunications Satellite Organisation (INTELAT), non-governmental bodies (NGOs) such as private communications carriers (eg, RCA Global Communications, ITT World Communications, Western Union International, SWIFT for interbank transfer systems, SITA for airline networks in Europe), data processing service bureaus, multinational corporations (MNCs) and other transnational associations.

The Computer Industry

Origins

The modern computer industry started in 1907 with the vacuum tube as the signal-amplifying device that kicked off the electronics revolution. World War II provided prospects for computer applications for military use but commercial exploration did not occur till 1945 when a general-purpose electronic computer came out of University of Pennsylvania based on a paradigm of digital electronics (Flamm, 1988). With John von Neumann's architecture or concept of a *computer* as containing a central processor, memory devices, input-output devices and using sequential programming, the UNIVACI (Universal Automatic Computer) was built. It became the basic design in computer technology. As commercial prospects improved and technological uncertainty diminished, a number of large industrial firms, including IBM, entered the computer industry. The industry is technology-driven with each successful innovation creating its own demand. Research focused on innovation rather than production efficiency.

In the mainframe market, product differentiation associated with big firm reputations gave large companies such as IBM a foothold over smaller firms, which ended up being acquired. After a hesitant beginning in the late 1940s, IBM's large scientific computer, followed by a small-scale computer, established its leadership in the industry (see chapter 1). As "Snow White", IBM accounted for 74% of the computer market and, together with the seven "dwarfs", the combined share (or concentration ratio in the US) of the eight companies was 98% in the late 1950s (Duysters, 1996: 41).

The invention of the integrated circuit in 1959, together with progress in miniaturisation, reliability and performance, made possible the integration of a number of components on a single chip. The technological trajectory of the computer industry was further propelled by the entry of mini-computers and the lowering of software costs in compatible central processing units, standard programming systems and interface standards for peripherals. The microprocessor built by Intel in 1971 literally built an entire computer on a single chip. The shift from a technology-driven to a demand-led industry followed in the 1970s implying that firms have to be competitive in costs in price sensitive markets.

The mainframe computer market also reached a concentrated mature stage, coexisting with supercomputers and minicomputers. All in all, industry leadership has ranged from IBM in sales and marketing to brilliant engineers at minicomputer vendors such as Digital, Data General, and Wang to hardware and personal computer executives who are relatively young, open to technology and closer to the marketplace than their counterparts in the bureaucratic mainframe industry. The 1980s saw more personal computer networked usage than stand-alone personal computer usage. Network-centric applications such as electronic mail, information access for education and training, electronic commerce, audio-on-demand and video-on-demand are already evident, as discussed in chapter 1.

Similarly, a converged professional services market between professional services (as in consulting, programming and systems integration) and communications services (as in analogue and digital transmission) has emerged (Duysters, 1996: 121). There is also a growing body of converged content and applications market in television, music, newspapers, magazines, sports and all forms of entertainment using multimedia technologies.

Computer hardware

The *electronics industry* as a whole can be defined as a cluster of closely linked industries within the electronics technology chain (see chapter 7). An industry is defined as a collection of companies that produce the same kind of goods and compete in the same market. It can vary in its spectrum of products as well as in its competitive scope, which can range from domestic to multi-domestic to global. The definition of the electronics industry is straightforward and unequivocal: it is the assemblage of enterprises engaged in the manufacture of electronic devices (Todd, 1990: 3). At a deeper level, electronics has always been bracketed by electrical engineering and keeping the two separate is no mean feat. Technological trends and the structure of the electronics industry following these developments will be discussed in greater detail in chapter 7.

The emerging global economic order—in which the electronics industry is a key player—is one of greater interdependence. This was brought about as much by the end of the cold war as by the sheer costs and impossibilities of independent R&D and other infrastructural support that have externalities extending beyond national borders. Issues include those of global competitiveness, global infrastructure and infostructure (electronic highways and such), intellectual property rights and protection. Moreover, the political economy of international trade, more than simple international divisions of labour and the proliferation of revolutionary technologies, have telescoped and accelerated technology cycles at unprecedented rates. The freedom of exchange in trade and ideas, the freedom of access and the freedom of enterprise are as much expressions of democracy as of economic freedom.

Dilemmas confronting industries and firms include short product and technology cycles, forcing as much competition as collaboration in R&D to lower costs. Oligopolistic firms in the electronics industry have made strategic alliances to avoid extreme cannibalisation since they see value in some cartelisation to the extent legally and structurally permissible. With contestable markets, strategic yet still oligopolistic alliances among hegemons at the industry and national levels may forever frustrate the ambitions of developing countries. Their dependence on foreign technology will remain almost indefinitely and their only bargaining point lies in the potential of their large population bases and growing affluence. If these can be wielded wisely and rationally, without compromising international competitiveness as the ultimate source of growth and prosperity, as well as insulation against external challenges, developing nations would be better partners to advanced industrial nations.

The economics of computer software

Computer software refers primarily to specific computer programmes such as operating systems, tools, applications, interfaces, protocols and so on. Software is not the same as content: software consists of a set of instructions while *content* revolves around some form of information such as text, images, sound, video or a combination thereof.

In software, there are two aspects of convergence (Moschella, 1997: 118). As noted, software and content are distinguished and the two markets have fundamentally different market characteristics. Software markets are more horizontal and monopolised. Content markets are quite fragmented and highly driven by individual consumer tastes. However, on the Web and in a converged industry, the distinction breaks down in interactive applications where programme instructions and content are interwoven. Competition will change.

Programming and systems development spawned terms such as *structured programming* and *software engineering* to describe and prescribe systems development to achieve greater direct management control over development projects. A waterfall model of the life cycle of a development project is shown in Fig. 4.1.

Initial objectives
Requirement specifications
Systems specifications
Systems design (in the form of modules)
Programme/module coding and debugging
Implementation
Operation
Maintenance/enhancement

Fig. 4.1. The waterfall method in the life cycle of project development
(*Source*: Adapted from Dutton (1996: 164))

The waterfall method creates flexibility and ensures that new automation projects work with others as much as it allows the system to be updated and improved through maintenance. Computer-aided software engineering (CASE) automates part of the process of programming.

Software production defies economics: once written, it costs nothing to manufacture and market it. Once market share is gained, it is easier to sell follow-on products at higher prices, hence competitive upgrades by Microsoft. Software economics also stretches the *law of diminishing returns* since owners of competing software can buy Microsoft's version at a huge discount and each copy costs Microsoft only a fraction of discounted price. But each sale generates revenue the firm would not have had otherwise and produces new customers who might be persuaded to buy the next upgrade at the full price.

The implications of stretching the law of diminishing returns are, as with all high technology products, similar to those for pharmaceuticals. First, software products have development costs but low production costs. Second, networks of users want compatible software and, third, customers tend to "groove in" once a programme is selected. Learning the software takes time and information saved in proprietary file formats makes switching painful. This supports an economic model of increasing returns, resulting in a tendency for market leaders to get even further ahead. Market leaders have the same costs of development as other firms, but the leader makes more money, can invest more in developing new products and maintain the lead, creating a winner-takes-all outcome.

Thus, *increasing returns to scale*, such as in a proportionately higher increase in output to a given increase in input that will also reap decreasing costs or economies of scale, will rule. Whereas returns to scale relate output to input, cost economies or economies of scale relate output to costs (see chapter 2). The two are clearly interrelated: increasing returns to scale bring about decreasing costs since more output proportionately lowers the cost per unit of production. In turn, the industry reaps increasing returns as profits.

Examples of increasing returns to scale are found in the financial sector. For example, on-line banking means that computers, rather than expensive staff, do the work of processing customers' business. This gives banks greater reach, lower fixed costs and increasing returns. The same is observed for all service industries from data processing to managing inventories. In essence, computers and networks greatly diminish variable costs when volume is important.

As much as intellectual property is marketed as a commodity, a fundamental paradox exists in determining the demand for information (Perelman, 1991). The value of information for the producer is not known until he has the information and, by then, he has acquired it without cost (Arrow, 1962a: 615).

As noted, the pricing of computer software defies microeconomics since the demand for computer software has a positive *price elasticity*, implying that the higher the price, the greater the demand for the product. Low prices seem to hurt credibility and it is even argued that higher prices ultimately benefit users since software products require a lot of support and many issues exist besides price. Low prices tarnish the image of the product and judging quality by price is not wholly irrational consumer behaviour. A new commodity that has no traditional price and no past reputation is likely to be appraised partly or wholly on the basis of its present price.

The logic comes from people's habit of judging quality by price, which is not irrational since the implicit belief is that price is determined by the competitive interplay of the rational forces of supply and demand (Scitovsky, 1945: 100). Moreover, there is Harrod's *law of diminishing price elasticity* where the rich are far less concerned with price than those less wealthy (Scitovsky, 1945: 103).

The anomalous pricing of computer software is related to a combination of incredible mark-ups with potentially enormous benefits, which may be promised but not necessarily met, superimposed on the relative ignorance of the software market (Perelman, 1991: 194). Even reviews of computer products are surprisingly divergent, particularly for specialised programmes that rely on the idiosyncratic needs of its users. There are costs involved in searching for the right software, trimming the potential savings from finding and buying cheap software, which is supposed to be more effective. In the absence of traditional price levels, software pricing is based on trial-and-error and is erratic. Thus, intensive promotion by software firms often pays off by riding on these special features of software pricing.

Since the marginal cost of an additional copy of software is zero, software is an ideal public good (see chapter 5). Perversely, pirated copies help to popularise the use of the software. But since marginal costs are really low or zero, original software sellers are able to offer upgrades and new versions to existing users at very competitive prices. This may reduce piracy if customers are locked into using a particular software package. *Software piracy* thus approximates the software vendor's price structure, marketing nothing more than the information contained in the programme (Perelman, 1991: 194).

Software companies willingly incur significant costs to send samples *gratis* to acquaint potential new customers with their product. Software pirates claim they save firms and developers such expenses by introducing the products into the market. Copy protection creates an artificial cost of transmitting information with the intent of making software unlike a public good. Ironically, from the vendor's perspective, copy protection makes software more like a public good because the extra programming involved in copy protection adds to the fixed cost of production rather than to the marginal cost. Copy protection schemes have disappeared as the utility of the programmes diminished for all users, legitimate and otherwise.

Software is also a meta public good, defined as having a marginal cost of zero and that each additional user confers a benefit or externality on other users (Perelman, 1991: 199; chapter 5). Consequently, the cost per unit of a meta public good does not merely decline, but declines exponentially as more users come aboard. The enlarged user base helps new users learn faster, discover bugs and new applications and, ultimately, improve the quality or effectiveness of the programme. Externalities are reaped from the cumulative spillover effects. Using the same logic, pirates perform a service in establishing a larger user base. Externalities created in the software market are not due to the firm's efforts or skills in creating a programme.

The Broadcast Industry

Transmission and delivery modes

Prior to the early 1970s, virtually all broadcast signals were delivered over-the-air from terrestrial transmitters for reception by individual homes. Cable systems then had limited channel capacity. Public control over the use of the radio spectrum sets limits on the maximum number of channels on private radio and television broadcasting that can be transmitted over-the-air. Each channel of traditional television and radio broadcast is allotted a specified range of radio frequency wavelengths. To avoid interference, only one signal can be transmitted over each channel in a particular area.

Due to a scarce transmission spectrum, the range of wavelengths allocated by the government limited the number of radio and television stations. The government controlled transmission by allocation or by strict licensing of private transmissions, limiting both the number of traditional channels and the division between private and public broadcasting.

Over the last ten to fifteen years, other technologically and economically feasible methods of signal delivery have loosened the binding constraint of limited spectrum. While the reasons for ending the public monopoly over broadcasting may be varied, the most prevalent is to improve efficiency through competition. Thus, new allocations have favoured private broadcasting. The challenge of alternative delivery methods is greater for television than for radio broadcasting.

Delivery over cables eliminates both the spectrum limitation on the number of channels and the requirement for public authorisation. Broadband cable can deliver fifty to one hundred channels of programming. Other new methods for delivering broadcast signals—direct broadcasting by satellite (DBS) and multi-channel multi-point distribution services (MMDS)—use spectrum to deliver signals but, because they use spectrum outside the bands allocated to traditional broadcasting, they add to the spectrum available.

Direct broadcasting by satellite involves radio signals transmitted from satellites for direct reception by consumers' antennas. The original DBS used satellites transmitting high signal strengths that could deliver four to six channels of programming. Medium power satellites new deliver more channels than high power DBS satellites. While DBS signals can be received directly by consumers, they are also received and distributed by cable.

Multi-channel multi-point distribution services are terrestrial video broadcasters using a different portion of the spectrum than allocated for traditional television channels (ultra high frequency (UHF) or very high frequency (VHF)). While MMDS can deliver twelve to twenty channels of programming, one limitation is that its reception is limited to antennas with a clear line of sight to the transmitting antenna.

Both DBS and MMDS are subject to public control over the use of the spectrum. Orbital slots for DBS satellites and spectrum are allocated at the international level. MMDS do not require new spectrum allocations at the international level since they operate within bands already allocated for a variety of microwave communications.

Cable systems do not use spectrum to deliver signals so they do not need licences to use it. Some control over the supply of cable services exists because of the public right of way.

The economics of supply and demand underpin the growth of cable, DBS and MMDS. The cost of supplying broadcast services, in terms of development and distribution, has fallen and is the most pervasive factor. Satellite technology not only distributes programmes directly to consumers but also distributes programmes to cable systems, traditional over-the-air broadcasters and MMDS systems. As cost of distributing the product falls, new networks become economically viable. Advances in electronics and growing experience in manufacturing further reduce the costs of receive-only earth stations. As interconnection costs fall, new networks can be viable even if they only reach small audiences. It also becomes economically feasible to distribute programmes to more distant broadcast stations. Technological developments have also lowered the costs of delivery to consumers. Receiving equipment has become small enough and cheap enough to be used by individual households or apartments. Both the strength of satellite signals and the number of channels transmitted have increased.

Technology has lowered the cost of delivering broadcast programmes by cable or MMDS less dramatically than DBS. The use of videotape rather than film has lowered the cost of producing some types of entertainment programmes. It has also made a substantial impact on the production of news programmes by lowering the cost of footage and quickly getting it on the air since videotape can be transmitted to the broadcast station, edited and prepared for broadcast much faster than film.

Home videotape technology has changed the home environment for video broadcasting. The ability to record and playback has had a mixed effect on the broadcast delivery of programmes. This technology provides an alternative to broadcasting as pre-recorded videos are used in homes. They increase value to consumers since it becomes easier to get full value from multiple channels.

Payment and revenue modes

Tapping increased demand from viewers and advertisers has supported private broadcasting. *Pay television*, the sale of access to channels of programming though the sale of individual programmes known as pay-per-view, is also developing.

Before the mid-1970s, the sale of advertising time was crucial for private broadcasting. With transmission over traditional broadcast channels, broadcasters found it costly to scramble signals to limit consumption to only paying households equipped with decoders. The development of cable, DBS and MMDS broadcasting made it considerably easier to charge consumers rather than advertisers for broadcast services. Newer addressable equipment reduces costs, and consumers can be connected or disconnected to different groups of channels without changing the customer's physical connection. Unlike the radio and television, which households own, DBS and MMDS require special reception equipment that can be charged and descrambling circuitry that can be added at a relatively low cost.

The ability to charge consumers for broadcast services changed the demand upon which broadcasters draw on. The demand for advertising time depends on the willingness of advertisers to pay for the time during which they can broadcast commercial messages to viewers. The demand for pay television services depends on the willingness of consumers to pay for broadcast programming. In principle, advertisers might be willing to pay either more or less for additional viewers of their advertising than viewers would themselves be willing to pay for the programmes. In practice, consumers may have a greater willingness to pay—which broadcasters exploit.

Broadcast Television

Origins

Mechanical television, using a series of holes on a whirling disc to scan an image several times a second to give the illusion of motion with each hole passing at a different position over the image, made its debut in the mid-1920s (Walker & Ferguson, 1998). The more holes and the faster the electric motors that drive the disc to scan the image, the clearer the picture but, paradoxically, the less reliable the motors. In the later half of the 1920s, converting the light scanned into electric impulses to be transmitted over wire, or by radio waves, came with the invention of the more reliable cathode ray tube. But it was not until after the Great Depression of the 1930s that mechanical television gave way to electronic television with an electronic image system or an electronic gun that replaced the disc scanning system.

Hollywood, where entertainment production gravitated to, resisted television until the mid-1950s. Broadcast television was caught between an imitation of radio with pictures and low budget movies for television seen as more commerce than art. It reached stagnation by 1960 and colour television succeeded—but slowly—with three-quarters of American households converted to it by 1976 (Walker and Ferguson, 1998: 17). In the 1980s, with regulatory change and cheaper satellite distribution, cable television took over a third of the television audience.

Broadcast television uses scarce public resources: namely, airwaves that are almost perfectly reliable, universal and accessible with all standard receivers. Electromagnetic radiation in the form of radio waves is also cheaper than cable transmission, which requires the installation and maintenance of coaxial or fibre optic cables to transmit signals from the hardened or main operational facility of the local cable system to each customer's home.

Because television involves both video and audio information, or two-carrier waves, it requires enormous electromagnetic spectrum space, limiting the number of possible channels that can be allocated. Spectrum space has to be shared by the government, the military, two-way radio users, cellular telephone users, international short-wave radio users and many others.

Communications satellites, starting with Telestar in 1963, recast the technology and economics of television networking. At the heart of modern television networking is the geostationary satellite, which rotates at the same speed as the earth. A *satellite dish*, called an uplink, sends a super high frequency electromagnetic signal to the satellite where it is received, amplified, returned to earth and received by another downlink satellite dish. A huge *footprint* in which the satellite's signal can be received is the central efficiency of satellite distribution since one uplink and one geostationary station satellite can replace thousands of miles of coaxial cables or hundreds of microwave relay stations. Satellites can carry many transponders, each wide enough to carry broad quality television signals, further enhancing efficiency.

Organisation

The economic structure of the broadcast industry is affected by the different activities of firms, contractual relations formed between firms, different methods of delivering broadcast signals, differences in revenue orientation (by advertising or subscription), the size of markets and other historical developments. Underlying this diversity, a vertical chain of production made up of the same economic activities inevitably prevails.

The basic economic activities and transactions involving a vertical chain of production include the programmes to be produced, programming to be packaged into a schedule for viewing and listening, and programming to be delivered to consumers. This vertical chain stretches from the basic inputs used for creating programmes to the delivery of broadcasting services to consumers.

Producers of programmes sell the broadcast rights to other firms, called *programme networks*, or services that put together broadcast schedules. When the networks do not own the facilities used to distribute programmes to consumers, they sell their programme schedules to the actual broadcasters—that is, broadcasting stations, cable systems or other distributors. Alternatively, the networks buy distribution services. These three activities need not be done by separate firms. Many broadcast firms are vertically integrated to perform two or three of these functions. The extent of vertical integration is, however, rarely so uniform that one of these types of markets is completely replaced by intra-firm transactions.

A number of markets can be identified. First, markets exist for intermediate inputs to be bought and sold, including markets for inputs used in programme production, markets for the sale and purchase of programming rights, and markets for programme distributors to buy schedules of programmes from programme networks or, alternatively, for networks to buy distribution services. Second, there are also markets for final outputs to be sold including those in which broadcast services are sold directly to consumers such as pay or subscriber television and markets that sell airtime for advertising.

Programme production and the sale of broadcast rights

The production of programmes requires hiring or purchasing the necessary inputs including investment capital, production facilities, production personnel and creative talent. Programme production may be carried out by a single firm or by several firms. The producer may own the necessary facilities, have personnel on salary or contract and handle the distribution of programming. Alternatively, the producer may only be a contractor, arranging all aspects of the production including contracts for talents and renting or leasing production facilities. Programming rights may be sold to another firm that handles distribution, including the sale of specific broadcast rights, without being directly involved in the production.

Broadcast programmes may be produced for a single airing. More frequently, multiple releases are needed to maximise revenue since production costs are high. Releases are differentiated in time and location as well as the means of distribution so that the rights to different audiences are sold separately. These releases are called "windows" and a specific broadcast right and audience may be only one of many different windows.

The most extensive set of release windows is for cinema productions or movies. Starting with an initial release in home country cinemas, it is followed, with varying delays, by release to theatres in other countries, release on home videocassettes, release to subscriber supported broadcast channels or pay cable channels, release to advertiser-supported broadcast networks in home countries and then other countries. A second release to pay cable or DBS channels, followed by release for additional showings on advertiser supported channels, is possible.

Programmes distributed to broadcast audiences often have multiple releases, each with its own broadcast rights. The first rights sold cover a specified number of showings. Rights sold to other countries for broadcast, and additional later showings in the home country by a different network, are also possible. These different broadcast rights may be sold separately by the producer, or sold in a package to the initial broadcaster who in turn sells some of the rights to other networks or broadcasters.

Relationships between producers and programme packagers range from complete vertical integration to arms-length market transactions. Many programme packagers either own the production facilities used for most of their original programming or have ownership interests in the facilities. Producers and packagers frequently form contractual relationships that go beyond the simple purchase of broadcast rights for existing programmes. These contractual arrangements give packagers a degree of control over production decisions for programming intended for initial showing on their networks. Programme packagers may contract out the production of programming and acquire broadcast rights by virtue of having invested in the production. If the packager does not have a financial interest in the new production, paying a portion of the production costs would give them the exclusive option to purchase broadcast rights for the initial showing and to have a say in production decisions.

For arms-length transactions, packagers purchase programme rights from independent producers with no prior or direct involvement in syndicated programming. Sales are made to independent television stations not affiliated with a network and to affiliate stations for use during portions of their broadcast not scheduled by the network.

Often, an arms-length purchase of broadcast rights reflects patterns of multiple releases for programming. Packagers typically buy the rights to previously released programmes such as movies. Thus, even if programme networks are vertically integrated into programme production, they typically purchase some rights to programmes they did not produce. Conversely, vertically integrated programme producers and packagers typically sell to other broadcasters some rights to programmes they have produced and rights to later broadcasts or to broadcasts in other countries.

Production decisions are very much influenced by the fact that some programmes earn a substantial proportion of their revenue from releases subsequent to the original showing. Movies may be designed for—and financially justified by—later broadcast, video releases or foreign revenues.

Programme packaging

Programme packagers buy or acquire broadcast rights to programmes and assemble the programming into a schedule for broadcast. Programme packaging is a necessary step in the supply of broadcast services. It need not be developed as a separate activity since, in theory, each broadcasting or MMDS location or cable system could package its own schedules for the channels they cover. Programmers would have the advantage of following a pattern of local programming or matching programmes to the particular tastes of the consumers reached.

Television networks

Nonetheless, networks that package schedules of programmes for broadcast throughout the country, and to multiple countries, are pervasive. Networks first acquire the rights and put together the programming schedules. Often, they also arrange the interconnection of local terrestrial broadcast stations or cable systems that distribute the schedule to consumers. Even when they are not directly responsible for the technical networking, their activities presume this interconnection by creating a schedule of programmes intended to be shown in the same order and at the same times to consumers reached by different terrestrial transmitters or cable systems. Networks also sell advertising time and insert advertising into the programme schedule.

Networks enjoy economies of scale since the costs of arranging programme rights are significant, each typically involving negotiations over price, terms and conditions. The parties must decide on the bundle of rights (how many broadcasts over what periods) to be purchased, project the likely revenue to be generated by the schedule of programme broadcasts and agree upon a price within what may be a considerable range between the minimum amount the seller of the rights will accept and the maximum amount the broadcaster is willing pay. A network reduces the number of these transactions and their costs. A network acquiring rights to n programmes to be provided to m cable stations has a total of $n + m$ transactions, comprising n transactions to purchase the rights and m transactions between the network and individual cable systems. Without a network, each individual cable system has to acquire the rights directly and package their own programme schedule—at a cost of n x m transactions.

Networks also economise on the resources used to assemble a programme schedule with the greatest net revenue potential. The information needed to determine the revenue potential of different combinations of programmes requires audience research, particularly where advertiser-supported programmes are involved. Networks can pool rating information to measure the size and demographic composition of audiences. It would be more costly for individual broadcast outlets to acquire and analyse the same information independently.

Networks also contract for original programming to influence the production design in order to generate maximum revenue. Syndicated programming can be produced for individual broadcast outlets such as television stations that are not part of network schedules, but these outlets would not have the same amount of influence as networks over production, or it would be more costly for them to try to exercise contractual control.

Networks economise on the cost of selling commercial time to national advertisers. They can improve on the quality of the product sold. Since advertisers care about both the size of the audience and its composition, the audience reached by advertisements put in a particular spot in the network's schedule can be more predictable and uniform in composition than audiences generated by a heterogeneous mix of programming by individual broadcast outlets.

The delivery of programmes

The ownership of various means of programme delivery may be public or private. The vertical relationship between the activities of programme packaging and signal delivery can be variously organised, ranging from vertical integration within a single private firm through a variety of contractual relationships between private firms, to arrangements that allow a private programmer to use a publicly owned means of signal delivery.

Networks often own at least some of the broadcasting stations distributing their programmes, but are rarely vertically integrated with all the stations broadcasting their programmes. Where cable systems are privately owned, there is a trend toward increased ownership ties between them and cable networks, but vertical integration is far from complete. Cable system owners frequently own partial minority interests in programme networks rather than operating both cable systems and programme networks from a single vertically integrated firm. Cable networks are generally distributed by at least some cable systems with which they have no ownership links. Owners of broadband cable systems generally do not have ownership interests with a sufficient number and variety of cable networks to fill their channel capacity.

Market transactions and contracts between networks and delivery services take a variety of forms depending on who is buying or selling or which activity is input into the other. Firms providing delivery services may purchase a programme schedule as an input and sell the delivered programme or advertising in one variant. Alternatively, the programme network may purchase delivery services as an input and sell the delivered service. In other cases, both the network and the delivery service collect revenue from the sale of delivered broadcast services, which makes the identification of buyer and seller somewhat arbitrary.

Contracts between networks and delivery services can cover a variety of terms besides price. Networks may be contracted to programme part, but not all, of a station's schedule. The network may wish to specify its rights or, conversely, the station or cable system may wish to spell out theirs. Where delivery services are publicly owned, networks have to pay for the service. Public policies may affect the choice of programming or the sale of advertising.

Cable and Satellite Television

Origins

A recurring theme across all information technology and media industries discussed thus far has been the interaction between economics, technology and policy. In cable and satellite television, technology takes second place to economics since the search for business opportunities and profits provides the driving force, albeit enabled by technology.

Historically, the cable and satellite television industry has had eight phases of growth, with the pre-history stage as early as 1947 (Parsons & Frieden, 1998: 20–21). After some intervening phases (dubbed as "pioneers", "mom 'n' pop", "freeze" and "thaw"), the industry took off between 1975 and 1984 when a new satellite broadband system was spawned with the launch of satellite distribution to cable systems. Following that, expansion with deregulation took place until 1992, when the industry entered the most recent phase of control and competition, due to the entry of direct broadcast satellite services and telephone companies.

Technology is moving the distribution system from telephone lines and coaxial cables to fibre optics, and from analogue to digital communications, which only suffers from its voracious appetite for broadband. Satellite systems using an orbital location far from earth can cover more of the world with a weak but usable signal that creates an expanded signal "footprint" as noted previously. The geographical area covered by a single satellite is large. The incremental cost of each new communication stems primarily from additional receiving equipment, and is borne by the receiving party. The satellite footprint and point-to-multi-point service have effectively changed the calculus and economics of video programme transmission.

Distribution, convergence and competition

Distribution, in terms of the manner in which technologies are organised into coherent systems, falls essentially into wireline and broadcast platforms (Parsons & Frieden, 1998: 118–119) as shown in Fig. 4.2.

As traditional broadcasters are likely to become multi-channel video service providers using digital broadcast technologies, they will compete with local wire-based services. Cable and satellite television will not cause the demise of broadcast television since over-the-air television will continue to serve those who cannot or choose not to subscribe to cable television or other paid,

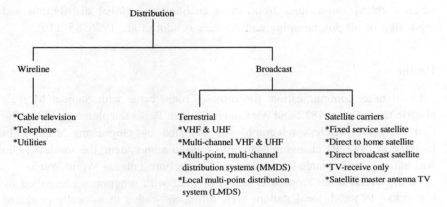

Fig. 4.2. Distribution systems
(*Source:* Adapted from Parsons & Fried (1998: 119))

multi-channel programme services. Broadcast television will remain an important content provider since government and public agencies require these services. Universal access and service may break down if public broadcasting is completely substituted with fee-paying distribution services or charging by market-based distribution services; this will be discussed further in chapter 11.

But subscribers will be increasingly willing to subscribe to basic and expanded services that are supported by advertising, or to pay for services like pay-per-view or video-on-demand. *Pay-per-view* charges customers for each programme selected, with different prices for different programmes ranging from films to sports. *Video-on-demand* (VOD) is a fully interactive system, which requires a digital system that connects the viewer to a server containing the video or film of choice. The individual subscriber has VCR-like control over the programme selected. Pricing structures are yet to be worked out, though it will likely be per-programme based. *Near video-on-demand* for films, which is more practical currently, offers greater viewer choice in terms of the selection of films and the flexibility of the viewing times. Essentially, a given film is run on three or four channels at staggered times such that the subscriber need not wait more than a few minutes before a film starts.

Niche networks thrive with cable television (eg, general entertainment, news and current affairs, sports, children, women, disabled or other groups defined by demographic characteristics, speciality entertainment, information and education, religious, self-improvement, shopping, special interest and others). Television without frontiers is enabling the global distribution and marketing of all programming and services (Cadot et al., 1996: 85–116).

Radio

Like all mass communication, the roots of radio came with Samuel Morse's electric telegraph in 1832 and Alexander Graham Bell's telephone in 1876. The first workable wireless telegraph was patented by Guglielmo Marconi in England in 1897. By changing Marconi's transmission system, the wireless radio was initiated by Reginald Fessenden and Lee de Forest during World War I.

Commercial radio broadcasts began in 1922 with programmes supplied by networks—to which local stations were affiliated—rather than locally produced (Martin, 1998). The programmes were produced largely by advertising agencies, networks for the sponsor or the sponsor itself. Programmes with musical content were the most popular. Educational stations flourished in the US until the stock market crash in 1929. Radio regulation, in existence since 1912 in the US, was expanded in 1934 to cover both wire and wireless communications.

Frequency modulation (FM) radio, which produces greater fidelity of sound compared to *amplitude modulation* (AM), was invented and patented by Edwin Armstrong in 1933. *Short-wave broadcasting*, available since 1923, spans incredible distances by broadcasting at higher frequencies, where radio waves are shorter, to enable international short-wave broadcasting.

By the mid-1950s, with the threat of television and the introduction of the cheaper and faster 45 RPM (revolutions per minute) record in 1949, which had higher fidelity than the 78 LP (long-playing) record, the radio became mainly a music medium. This change in format (a formula to appeal to a particular audience segment by age, socio-economic factors, gender or ethnicity) to music bolstered the recording industry.

The broadcasting of news from radio's earliest days was reflected in the fact that many newspaper publishers started their own radio stations. As radio turned commercial, competing for advertising revenue proved more threatening. Since radio was speedier, it regularly scooped newspapers in airing news and stories long before they were printed. Broadcast journalism created a new breed of electronic journalists. *Broadcasting for a fee*, or toll broadcasting, allowed anyone to use a station's studio and transmitter for a fee.

As it competes with television and other audiovisual entertainment, radio listening as a backdrop that stimulates the imagination and blends fantasy with reality is its strength. But the future of radio depends on government deregulation as well as on how other media affect radio listening. The medium is fully matured in terms of its product life cycle and radio stations are becoming part of larger corporate entities.

Recording and Motion Pictures

Recording

The recording industry owes its growth to technology. On the input side, musicians and writers can make high quality recordings, reproduce and distribute them at lower costs and get further dissemination through cable television and video cassettes. On the output side, high quality, lower costs and affordability stimulate demand. The electronic revolution has also made a significant impact on the creative inputs of this industry with the advent of home recordings.

Recording qualifies as a mass medium since its primary component is popular music, which is a form of communication. Various bits of information get across subtly, setting moods and emotional associations for many life experiences. The activity of recording merely sees to the production and distribution of the content to heterogeneous audiences using several technologies including digital, analogue or video recording and reproduction.

The recording industry is characterised by several unique features including multiple technologies for recording and transmission, a low degree of regulation, a high degree of internationalisation, younger audiences, subversive potential, organisational fragmentation and a diversity of reception possibilities (Hull, 1998: 18). The three income streams in the industry are live appearances, recordings and song writing.

Motion picture

The first motion picture camera, called a kinetograph, and its viewing machine, the kinetoscope, originated in 1894, but it was not until 1905 with the nickelodeon theatre that the movie industry stood on its own in the entertainment world. In terms of distribution, the industry is dominated by a handful of major companies in the US with high barriers to entry. Some economies of scale are required in order to enjoy declining long-run average costs. Vertical integration to studio ownership has to be weighed against high overhead costs.

Cinematography is the art of making motion pictures where the motion picture camera takes the pictures and projects them on a screen. The production sector of the motion picture industry is monopolistically competitive with a large number of firms and substantial barriers to entry (Litman, 1998: 37). A production company may even be created around a specific film project with a major film star or director, a handful of writers and other technical personnel. Under a complex union system, these personnel can be "rented" for the period of time to complete the picture, obviating the need to retain a large permanent staff.

Demand in the film industry has been stagnant for some time during the last two decades due to competition from cable television, VCRs, pay-per-view and other forms of entertainment. But movie attendance has a similar demographic profile to television: that is, more female viewers/patrons over the age of thirty. The encroachment of television in the 1950s was severe. Initially, movie makers were complacent in their thinking that television's smaller size and lower quality were factors in their favour. But changing technologies and the more contemporary and intimate nature of television persuaded the film industry to produce and distribute programming for television.

The film environment has also expanded with novelisation of film scripts and movie-related merchandise such as toys, clothing and other paraphernalia. Even video games and attractions in theme parks were created. Marketing and advertising strategies have become more important since branded goods and products featured in movies sell well.

Newspapers

English historian Thomas Babington Macaulay dubbed the press the *fourth estate;* the other three estates or important classes during feudal times being the nobility, the clergy and the bourgeoisie or commoners of substance. The press can influence the monarchy while the peasants cannot utilise the fourth estate. The forerunner to the newspaper in the US was the newsletter, a short, periodic report for business and government to keep them informed of vital economic and political events. However, early newspapers were far from objective since partisan journalism preceded objectivity.

A definition of newspaper is nebulous, with variations in publication frequency, the size of the pages, the average number of pages, content, format and others. For legal and regulatory purposes, a *newspaper* is defined as a publication, usually in sheet form, for general circulation, published at regular intervals and containing intelligence of current events and news of general interest (Picard & Brody, 1997: 7). Many types of newspapers exist, including religious and other speciality papers.

Expensive newspapers were replaced by the penny press, which had newspapers sold per issue to the general public in the US. A shift to human interest stories, rather than politically partisan reporting financially aided by political factions, took on the excesses of sensationalism or yellow journalism. Newspapers originally developed wire services, which are organisations that supply international, national, state or regional news stories and photos to newspapers, radio and television stations and cable systems, to save money and improve news coverage. Newspaper chains or groups of newspapers owned by one individual or corporation emerged between World War I and World War II. Regional syndicates, small town weeklies and dailies also developed. But newspapers declined in the 1930s, hurt by the Great Depression and competition from radio.

The five departments of a typical newspaper include editorial/news, advertising, circulation, production and business. For the average newspaper, between two-thirds and three-quarters of its income is from advertising. One-third of its operating cost goes for supplies, personnel and equipment for technical production. Modern technology facilitates writing, editing and layout.

Compared to electronic media, newspapers and magazines have certain advantages. They are at a low risk of loss or theft. They are disposable, portable, lightweight, detachable, flexible, offline (no battery or power), have high resolution (print and image quality) and are inexpensive (no upfront technology investment), sharable and easy to store. The merits of electronic media include currency, searchability, customisable, interaction, multimedia features, depth, hyperlinks, network storage, a communal feeling and ubiquitousness (instantaneous delivery everywhere in world).

The functions of a newspaper include a source of entertainment, news and other information that can affect socio-political systems, languages, reading ability and the democratisation of knowledge. Newspapers can be reader-driven by using market research to give readers what they want to read. But the responsibility of newspapers to inform and prod public opinion and thinking should not give way to the quest for better demographics and readerships.

Both technology and labour issues are vital since producing a newspaper is labour-intensive, including the intellectual skills of writing and reporting.

Computers and information technology have not only affected the production of newspapers, they have made the electronic delivery of papers over the Internet a reality. Computers may not cause of demise of journalism and newspapers, but the newspaper industry has to respond to market-driven, reader-directed approaches in order to appeal to younger, more technology savvy readers. The industry is faced, not only with mergers and acquisitions, but also with crossovers from related media industries.

Chapter 5

Government Intervention and Regulation

Introduction

Ideally, as stated by the *Coase Theorem*, with well-defined property rights, competition and negligible transaction costs, individuals and firms will find an optimum solution in demand and supply without government intervention. In reality, property rights are not easy to define and assign, and transaction costs are not minimal. Government intervention becomes inevitable. As noted in chapter 3, the government intervenes in the information technology and media industry by setting public policies regarding competition and regulation. This chapter describes the nature of private and public goods, externality and the government's role in taxation and subsidies. These economic principles provide an understanding of state-owned enterprises and state-controlled organisations in information technology and media industry.

The Theory of a Public Good

The government's role in a market economy is best seen in the context of its overall macroeconomic objectives to attain full employment, price stability and a desirable rate of economic growth. Real sustainable growth is necessary to generate a certain standard of living and welfare. The government must also view economic growth in the context of non-economic goals in social and political areas. Economic efficiency may thus have to be weighed or traded-off against socio-political aims.

The government has a wide array of instruments to achieve its economic goals, namely *fiscal policy*, pertaining to taxes and expenditures, and *monetary policy*, related to the money supply, interest and exchange rates. Other areas of public policies may range from wage policy in the labour market to telecommunications and broadcast policy in the information technology and media industry.

The most distinct justification for government intervention lies in the theory of public goods. A *public good* is characterised by non-exclusion and non-rivalry in consumption, with the price mechanism inoperative for indivisible and jointly consumed goods and services. In contrast, a *private good* can be excluded by price and its consumption is rivalrous. A *mixed good* has one but not both characteristics with respect to exclusion and rivalry in consumption. For pure public goods and mixed goods, the government intervenes when the market fails; that is, when the price mechanism does not work.

A *merit good* may be a private good for which market mechanisms have not failed but, because its consumption is of a meritorious nature, the government has taken it over. These goods usually display *positive externality* whereby consumption of the good has internal benefits for the consumer and external benefits for others. Left to the private sector, such goods (with positive externality) tend to be under produced and most people cannot afford the price. The reverse exists for goods with *negative externality*, that is, goods that are harmful to other consumers. To encourage goods with positive externality or discourage goods with negative externality, a subsidy or tax is imposed respectively.

The Principal-Agent Theory

Government intervention implies a collective decision on the part of the government that private sector market forces are unable to achieve efficient resource allocation. Democratic governments have the mandate to make such collective decisions. This principle of collectivism gives rise to the *theory of a principal-agent* relationship in which the government, in this instance, is the agent to whom the principal, or the people, has entrusted their well being. In the corporate sector, the board of directors is the agent and the shareholders are the principals.

So long as agents perform their functions faithfully—to attain the goals and objectives of their principals—the principal-agent theory works. Checks and balances, such as regular elections and annual general meetings for shareholders, help keep the principal-agent relationship intact. But when agents want to maximise their own agendas and goals, such as when civil servants as agents want bureaucratic control and large staffs, the asymmetry of interests may be harder to remove.

In principal-agent theory, two concepts have to be understood. A *moral hazard* occurs when the principals cannot observe the agent's behaviour, actions or decisions. The principals simply trust that the agent has the principals' best interests and welfare in mind and that the agent conducts its assigned functions on such an understanding. *Adverse selection* occurs when an agent is aware of some relevant information before signing a contract or agreeing to undertake functions on behalf of the principals, but the principals are ignorant of such information. In both cases, the principal-agent theory does not achieve its full potential.

Asymmetry in information exists in principal-agent relationship because the agent usually has more knowledge and information in order to perform its assigned tasks. By deduction, the principal knows less, or has imperfect information. This asymmetric information gives room for moral hazard and adverse selection behaviour.

The economics of information based on an asymmetry of information can also be seen in terms of contractual relationships. One party has an informational advantage over the other and various models can be simulated to show how agents and principals behave, how bargaining power is affected and so on. A theory of contracts under asymmetric information involves *signalling* when one party knows some important information which is signalled to the other party via the informed party's behaviour (Macho-Stadler et al., 1997).

Applied within the principal-agent framework with a contractor as the principal and a contractee as the agent, the principal designs the contract, which the agent accepts and carries out any necessary action on behalf of the principal. Outcomes and payoffs have to be studied since the agent may have objectives in conflict with those of the principal because the agent may have more information than the principal.

After the contract has been made, the principal has difficulty observing and verifying the agent's efforts; that is, the principal can no longer perfectly control the action. A moral hazard problem develops. An adverse selection problem also appears when the agent holds private information before the contract or relationship begins. Private information distorts the contract since the agent attempts to take advantage of it. He does not reveal it if he obtains greater utility by keeping it secret. The agent will only signal private information if the utility is greater after making the information public or revealing it in the contract, for example.

As an example of signalling, a technology-licensing contract can be established when it is the seller who has private information on the value of the patent. The buyer is a monopsonist in the industry. The seller, that is, the investigation laboratory or creator of innovations and creations of high quality, will always be interested in signalling and will do so by offering a contract that includes a greater royalty payment than the optimal symmetric information contract.

Approaches to Intervention

The government can intervene in the economy in a number of ways. A distinction is made between *direct government production*, where the government owns the factors of production for telecommunications services, and *indirect government provision*. The latter can occur through a subsidy. Two types of *subsidies* are possible for production or consumption. *Producer subsidies* can be in the form of explicit grants, tax breaks or cosy cost-plus contracts. They can be incorporated into private firms' pricing structures and other costs. *Consumer subsidies* can be in the form of cash grants or tax exemptions for the general public or targeted groups.

Even in situations where the government neither produces nor provides, it does regulate. As seen in chapter 3, *regulation* involves laws and rules to guide the private market to serve public interests. It inevitably influences the cost of capital and the level of profits that can be taxed. However, once a regulatory framework is in place, established firms can use it to protect their positions and make entry and competition extremely difficult. Conversely, with *deregulation* the government liberalises rules and regulations that may increase or intensify competition in an industry, such as when the telecommunications industry was deregulated.

The five traditional regulatory modes include public ownership, common carriage (ie, regulating the maintenance of competition and spectrum allocation), public trustee (ie, light regulation such as in entry) and *laisse-faire* (ie, minimal regulation of business practice) (Neuman et al., 1997: 26). The nature and scope of government intervention will, however, drastically change when technology, convergence and new developments (especially in digitisation, high definition television (HDTV) and others (see chapter 7)) are fully evolved. As seen in chapter 4, spectrum allocation becomes unnecessary, except for public broadcasting systems, as cable, satellite and other means of transmission take over. Such developments may also seriously hamper the current government's policies of universality and accessibility when marketplace provision and pricing take precedence (see chapter 11).

State-Owned Enterprises

A *state-owned enterprise* (SOE) is a company or corporation that essentially performs no differently from a private company in being subject to market forces and discipline with the only distinction that it is owned wholly or partially by the government. The funds to form such enterprises may come from budgetary surpluses. The *raison d'être* of state involvement is to combine the best of government ownership and control with production subject to private market criteria, including profit maximisation and efficiency. On the other hand, a state-owned enterprise may be inefficient and incur losses, in which case state funds may be channelled to subsidise the enterprise if its existence is deemed important, usually from a socio-political perspective.

Conventional motivations for state-owned enterprises include industrial restructuring and promoting certain industrial structures, such as when the state pioneers certain industries. The later falls under an *industrial policy* in which the government promotes industries deemed desirable, such as technological winners. High technology industries in defence and other sensitive areas may come under such consideration, together with a *strategic trade policy* to ensure that security-sensitive exports do not go to unfriendly countries. If they are natural monopolies (see chapter 3), such as in the telecommunications and broadcasting industries, the argument is that public monopolies under state-owned enterprises are preferred to private monopolies. High infrastructural costs, overlays and social capital, such as for goods and services that have externalities, are among other reasons leading to the formation of state-owned enterprises. The private sector may be unable or unwilling to commit to such industries. Without basic infrastructure, economic growth and development will not occur, or are stymied. Hence, the government traditionally undertakes projects requiring massive investment and expenditure, such as in transport, communications and telecommunications services.

Public ownership in state-owned enterprises may also be the ultimate means of the government playing the role of the custodian of public interest (Welfens & Yarrow, 1997: 434). Thus, nationalisation of public utilities and telecommunications is justified, especially if a socialist ideology is also endorsed.

Many state-owned enterprises are established to fulfil non-economic socio-political functions where subsidies are to be given, such as in public and merit goods. Public broadcast stations are an important means of communication for the government to convey national news and information to the population at large. Alternatively, programming in state-owned broadcast stations enables the government to ensure that certain public policies—such as in education, language, censorship and others—are transmitted. Content and censorship are other motivating factors for government regulation.

A global trend of *privatisation*, which involves the government selling off (wholly or partially) its shares in state-owned enterprises, started in the 1980s. Sometimes, privatisation may be initiated because the objectives of the state-owned enterprise have been attained and a return to market forces and private sector production is best. For inefficient state-owned enterprises that are a drain on state coffers, privatisation is aimed at improving profit maximisation, which forces management to attain efficiency and effectiveness.

Privatisation may also be forced upon by changing technology and the environment, such as in the telecommunications industry (discussed in chapters 3 and 4). The private sector broke the monopoly of state-owned enterprises by using technology that enabled private firms to supply telecommunications services more efficiently and cheaply.

By and large, a government that is beginning to have more faith in the private sector will privatise its state-owned enterprises by removing any protection from competition and by creating more competition among private corporations. The government may be content to regulate the industry and provide the framework for the private sector.

Recognising that market failures still exist, the government tries to be market supporting by removing or eliminating failures or deficiencies to help market forces perform better. Just as there is market failure, *government failure*, such as in the lack of information to operate perfectly and efficiently, corruption, bureaucratic red tape and inefficiencies may also prompt privatisation.

Cosmetic privatisation, in which ownership may change but not control, such as in the democratisation of ownership of telecommunications shares through public listings, may also occur. By owning a sufficiently large share, the government's hand in the industry may still be very visible and large even if ownership is diffused. In *rolling privatisation*, as the government privatises, it may form new state enterprises in other industries it deems worthy of promotion and nurturing. Thus, state-owned enterprises pioneer new, high technology or high infrastructural content projects, but are sold off once the tutelage effects are deemed unnecessary. A development-oriented approach to government intervention is one that does not compete head-on or crowd-out private sector initiatives. Ultimately, market discipline, market demand and choices may better reflect allocational efficiency and effectiveness.

One consequence of privatisation is regulation, as the government reconsiders its role in safeguarding public interest and competition (see chapter 3). As public ownership disappears, transforming public monopolies into private monopolies or oligopolies has potential damaging dangers. Thus, privatisation is usually preceded by pro-competitive restructuring, such as in *corporatisation*, which restructures the enterprise to run along the lines of a private company facing competition. If self-regulation by free market forces is unlikely to come about, a regulatory body is usually set-up with privatisation to ensure that competition is enhanced in a level playing field. It also ensures standard safety and other quality criteria as well as pricing and other issues of public interest.

Information as a Public Good

Information is deemed to be a public good, implying that it has the characteristics of non-exclusion and non-rivalry in consumption. Moreover, the more available and widespread information is, the better it is for everybody's welfare. Ideally, there should be an unlimited amount of information available and provided free except for any transmission costs (eg, costs incurred through information technology using telecommunications). But these characteristics do not make the production and processing of information amenable to the market forces of supply and firm theory (chapters 2 and 3). There is also a fundamental paradox in determining the demand for information when its value to the producer is not known until he or she has the information. But, by then, he or she has acquired it without cost (Arrow, 1962: 615).

Computer software qualifies as a *meta public good* in that each additional user confers a benefit on other users (Perelman, 1991: 189–201). Thus, more so than a pure public good, where other users simply benefit from the consumer using it, it is the presence of additional users in the case of a meta public good that confers the benefit. This is more likely when the marginal cost is zero such that, as the number of users increases, the cost per unit declines exponentially.

More people using the meta public good transmits knowledge about the good since users often help each other learn how to use a new software package in order to work with each other. The knowledge spreads and any bugs or problems in the new applications are duly found and rectified.

Moreover, new products and services may come about as books, simpler manuals, tips and other support services appear to serve a larger user base. In short, the more people adopt a software programme, the more valuable it becomes.

The enlarged and entrenched base of users may also cause some *excess inertia* as it becomes harder to get people to try alternative programmes. Once locked into a particular kind of software that is expensive, there is inertia to change from it since new software packages may entail hardware changes and upgrades. Learning costs are also high.

Consumers also logically deduce or expect that, given the very competitive software market, there is little true product differentiation among highly competitive products. The existing champion, such as Microsoft, will also ensure continuous improvement to maintain its market share and position.

The bandwagon effect of such externalities ultimately benefits producers. Taken to its logical conclusion, the standard economic prescription would be that subsidising users improves social welfare. The price may even be brought down to be in line with marginal costs. Thus, subsidies for computer software may be even stronger than those for pure public goods.

This argument of the meta public good is diametrically opposed to that of protecting *intellectual property rights* (IPR). Instead of producers demanding such protection to safeguard their high research and development (R&D) costs, the possibility of financing such R&D through taxes rests on the proposition that discoveries and innovations have externalities that benefit society as public goods.

Thus, technological progress and R&D need not be discouraged without protecting intellectual property rights if the fiscal system takes care of funding them. Instead of monopolies using their supernormal profits to finance R&D, they are taxed away and subsidies are given to fund R&D.

The flaw in this argument is that while the monopolist allocates funds from supernormal profits according to his risk-taking behaviour (with the incentive of more profits if his R&D hits a winner), the same incentive and risk-taking behaviour may be absent in a tax funded system. Going into welfare and altruistic grounds may conflict with market-based competitive principles.

Some externalities due to a large user base where dedicated users unravel bugs and suggest improvements *gratis* to producers cannot be attributed to the firms' skills and efforts in developing certain software programmes. They should thus not be allowed to collect excessive economic rents for these externalities.

An alternative to computer software firms producing public goods or meta public goods is to offer their products at marginal costs. While they cannot recover fixed or R&D costs from high prices, they should be able to do so from a higher volume in sales. Pirated versions will be priced out of the market. At the same time, companies can market other support services at much higher marginal costs and low fixed costs. Currently, with few notable exceptions, firms charge high marginal costs for software and leave users to source for support services in manuals and tips published by third parties. Worse is if they charge high fees for aftersales support services as well as sell the software at high prices.

The Role of Government in Information and the Media

Whether information is a public good or meta public good, government intervention and regulation in the information technology and media industry appear unavoidable. To summarise, apart from the public good theory and externality, reasons for the government's involvement include infrastructural development, regulation to safeguard competition and public interests, income distribution and equity such as to ensure accessibility and the universality of basic telecommunications services and other non-economic motivations.

Civil society

Some socio-political dimensions deserve elaboration before looking at governmental intervention in the media industry. Democracy, such as in the freedom of speech, the freedom to choose and other basic human rights, comes with the evolution of a civil society. A *civil society* refers to one that enjoys a set of relatively autonomous social relations (Splichal et al., 1994: 1). Traditionally, a civil society exists as a residual where the state is dominant. The line between a civil society and the state is a normative precondition for the emergence of pluralistic, parliamentary democracies.

A tension is perceived between a civil society and an information society (see chapter 1) for two reasons. With the increasing globalisation of capital, production and exchange (especially in information technology and services), the nation-state becomes an important boundary-setting mechanism, paradoxical and difficult as that may well be. So, if state and legal powers have to be wielded in a globalised information society, control such as in censorship and regulation are inimical to the development of a civil society.

The second problem in the global juxtaposition is that a civil society represents a political society, while an information society describes an economic system. Information is commodified, bought and sold subject to the market criteria of efficiency. In politics, information conveys power, as is necessary for a civil society to promulgate autonomy and self-determination. Yet, the information age proceeds like a steamroller and there is an inevitability of the technological and social trajectory rolled into one path. The information age and society delivers people from impersonal power, such as the rise of a *technocracy* where an educated professional-technical science class will emerge as the new breed of elites.

Logically, a civil society will lead to an information society enabled by technological innovations in tandem with the economic information sector. New theories, or transitions in mass communication theories, may emerge with new communications technologies and new media (DeFleur et al., 1987, 1989). From a humanistic, cultural-historic approach, communication theory has moved to a social scientific perspective as cybernetics and technology take over.

It is inevitable that both a civil society and an information society raise issues concerning individualism, privacy, pluralism, class relations, class equity and the role of the market and government in these areas. A convergence, rather than a conflict, between state and market is best, with growing mutual dependence overlapping and interpenetration of the two sectors in supportive rather than competitive roles. A mesh of these ideas to portray the civil society and information society as one is attempted in Fig. 5.1. The ultimate society must also be a sustainable one in terms of the environment, natural resources and intergenerational sharing of such resources.

The state is expanding into social spheres as an employer, regulator and manager of public services, if not producer, provider, consumer, entrepreneur, investor and a host of others. The distinction between a market economy and a public polity may become arbitrary and unnecessary except for pure ideological gratification. It is clear that the information technology revolution is changing the boundaries of a traditional control revolution. Even in democratic industrialised countries, the media were allegedly producing an "adversary culture" that undermined leadership, challenged authority and delegitimised established institutions (Crozier et al., 1975).

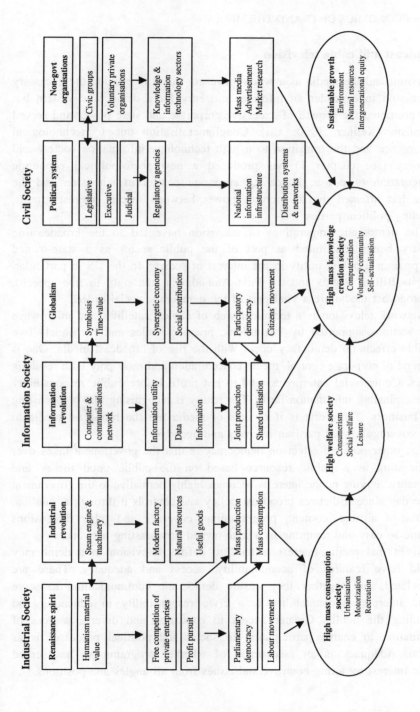

Fig. 5.1. From an industrial society to an information society and a civil society
(*Source*: Adapted from Masuda (1990) and DeFleur (1987, 1989))

Broadcast and cable television

Television and the media as a whole have not failed to provide the necessary information to engender an informed citizenry for a democratic system but have promoted the growth of excessive corporate and state power and served capitalism (Kellner, 1990: xiii). Conglomeratisation due to technological convergence and the transition to a high technology information society and economy (see chapter 1) has produced a new socio-political economic configuration of power. Increasing corporate control of television and the media has affected the division of power between special interest groups, including political parties.

The democratic imperatives of television have led to the broadcasting industry being constituted as part of the public sector as a state-owned enterprise or a public utility in the interest of society. In the US in particular, with its Bill of Rights and the First Amendment (the right to free speech), the broadcast media are a vital part of the democratic social order.

Network television is a technical web of cables, satellites and microwave relay stations supported by institutions, practices, rules and personnel. Two possible effects on democracy occur with the rise of broadcast media. One is the trend of corporate control, media concentration and monopoly with resulting abuses. Commercial enterprises tend to put profit before public responsibility in disseminating information fairly. The reality is recognising that broadcasting is a business. The worst is if owners of media use the broadcast media to slant coverage toward partisan interests and agendas.

The other possible effect on democracy is that the government takes over broadcasting as a public resource based on the public good theory and externality. Serving public interests becomes highly normative to the government of the day since it dictates broadcast policy and controls it through regulation. Control of airtime, content, programming, coverage and other dimensions become so easy and tempting in a state-owned broadcasting network.

Given that public interest is hard to define, television in a democracy should have features of accountability, access and adequacy. These are interrelated, and together they ensure democratic communication to serve public interest. Accountability is a civic responsibility in educating and informing the public. Greater access to education and diverse sources of information to enable participation in social and political processes is as critical. Adequacy is an assessment of whether programming has served public interest by airing controversial issues from all angles and positions.

In particular, the role of television news may be scrutinised. News by definition deals with what is new and current and should be a mirror or window of what is happening in real life. But with professional and skilful editing and reporting, television news, which is highly visual, can become an ideological construct rather than aesthetically packaged realism. Trade-offs occur between providing "hard news" or public information necessary for a democratic polity, attracting an audience for advertisement revenue or tampering news with editorial inclinations.

Like newspapers, the ethics of objective journalism and news reporting may play second fiddle to credit ratings of news with human touches or factual narratives. A sacrifice of probity or responsibility to drama and even fiction is inevitable when using a story format in television news reporting. By its nature, television news is superficial and telescoped in terms of meaning, interpretation and context to simplify and condense complex events.

Worst would be when an ideological bias is injected, disinforming rather than informing in a hegemony model or a propaganda model (Herman & Chomsky, 1988; Chomsky, 1989). Hegemony means assimilating the views, codes and practices of the ruling class, including the government if the broadcast station is state owned. Propaganda presupposes a conscious intent to deceive and manipulate to advance the views and interests of the ruling groups.

Telecommunications

Government intervention in telecommunications fits all the principles of public goods and externality. The political authority on telecommunications essentially oversees the system and comprises three main categories: users, manufacturers of hardware and software, and information and service providers and network operators.

The performance of national telephone companies varies across countries and time with sufficiently long time series for assessment (Duch, 1991). Market structure and political constraints also vary, but recent changes in technology and consumer demand have affected all regardless. In the initial stage, increasing returns to scale or telecommunications as a natural monopoly held true, leading to public or private monopolies imposing tremendous welfare costs on society.

But such blanket protection is challenged by the theory of *contestable market* where there exists significant scale economies and a monopolist is subject to competitive pressures so long as entry and exit are possible without a loss of initial investment. In the airline industry, a new carrier can compete on a route by undercutting the price of an established carrier, making a profit and then exiting without any sacrifice on initial investment.

A number of heroic assumptions of contestable market may be criticised. First, there is no significant sunk cost associated with entry and exit. Second, the monopolist with surpluses is unable to respond immediately by lowering prices even more than the contestant does. Third, there is a pool of potential market entrants with the resources to enter and exit quickly that pose an element of competition. Nonetheless, the potential threat of such competition is sufficient to ensure that the monopolist sets prices at marginal costs rather than what the market can bear. The government's role in such situations is simply not to block or regulate entry.

Most developed countries tend to assume a more liberal regulation and private ownership telecommunications policy (Shaw, 1998). The British Telecom case was puzzling: it remained a monopoly for a number of years after its privatisation in 1984. In the US, it was the converse in the break up the AT&T private monopoly (Davies, 1994: 156–165). But globally, national telecommunications is facing more foreign competition. With mobile capital, globalisation and shrinking product life cycles, the competition and urge to privatise and liberalise telecommunications have become more real and urgent.

Newspapers

Marketing news is torn between performing a public service in fulfilling people's right to know and making profits—a tussle between principle and finance. There are four arguments for marketing news. The first pedagogical argument is predicated on the belief that people learn from news (Norris, 1997: 52–61) The second is the enticement argument where editors are morally obliged to lure readers to buy newspapers that they will seriously read. The third democratic argument allows surveys and focus groups to produce newspapers that correspond to readers' needs and desires. But the libertarian model with press freedom requires no censorship and control that suppress falsehood. Fourth, the business imperative argument maintains that to be profitable, newspapers give people what they want. But when this happens, quality journalism is sacrificed.

A newspaper is a mirror to the culture of the country. Being affordable, portable and available, newspapers have some advantages over competing media such as television. How news is reported, packaged and presented can influence mass opinion and behaviour such that the governments of developing countries in particular would want to restrain press freedom. The socio-political impact of what is considered the wrong editorial line is tremendous if newspapers are indeed effective as the fourth estate.

In international affairs, the "CNN effect", "CNN factor" or "CNN curve" depicts the new global real-time media impact, which is substantial if not profound (Norris, 1997: 291–318). The accelerated, real-time effect is distinguished by its accelerant, impediment and agenda-setting effects on foreign policy. Media has shortened response time and is also a force and multiplier in sending signals and drawing attention. It can pose two types of impediments: emotional, grisly coverage that may undermine morale, and global real-time coverage that may threaten operational security. The media is powerful enough to set the agenda since coverage of an event and its priority in reporting may determine what becomes a crisis. The media's level of interest in a story and the potential consequence of that interest can be significant.

In developing countries where democracy and press freedom are not as sacred as in the Western libertarian model, government control ranges from subtle to overt such as in a state created private monopoly such as the Singapore Press Holdings. Press censorship is deemed more necessary in multi-ethnic sensitive settings. Whether newspapers are beholden to the ruling government varies from country to country, but government intervention in newspapers is part and parcel of an overall media policy. Given the relatively poorer and less developed status of developing countries, newspapers as the fourth estate will be subject to greater political scrutiny for a long time more.

Chapter 6

Information Technology, Labour and Employment

Introduction

The knowledge economy (see chapter 1), featuring intellectual rather than physical capital, and information technology, revolutionising production and exchange, are set to affect employment and the labour market as well. These new economic and technological trends and implications will first be reviewed to examine their effect on human resource development and management.

New Economics

New capitalism

As communism breaks up, unleashing economies transitioning towards market models, capitalism is undergoing further shifts in its tectonic plates (Thurow, 1996). Since capitalism emerged from feudalism, the world is in a period of punctuated equilibrium caused by the simultaneous movements of five economic plates. These are the end of communism, a technological shift to an era dominated by man-made brainpower industries, a demography never before seen, a global economy and an era where there is no dominant economic, political or military power. There is a new game with new rules requiring new strategies. Some of today's players will adapt and learn how to win the new game. Those who understand the economic tectonic plates will rise to the top of the food chain; they will comprise the "fittest" individuals, business firms or nations. The economic magma is a fluid mixture of technology and ideology.

The eternal verities of capitalism are growth, full employment, financial stability and rising real wages, which fluctuate and cause much volatility.

Capitalism is continuously challenged and threatened, cyclically and structurally. In all of Western Europe, the heartland of capitalism, not one net new job was created from 1973 to 1994. In periods of punctuated equilibrium, new and old technologies and ideologies do not match smoothly. Through a complicated process, beliefs filter experiences, condition visions of reality and alter technologies to be deployed.

In an era of man-made brainpower industries, capitalism will need some very long-run communal investments in research and development (R&D), education and infrastructure. Yet, capitalism's normal decision-making processes are usually not beyond eight to ten years. Developed countries, mired by budget deficits, cannot support long-term investments. Corporate downsizing is occurring when firms should be integrating their skilled workforce ever more tightly into their organisations. Brainpower firms must somehow hold on to and enhance their only strategic asset—their workers.

There is also an ideological conflict between democracy (equality of political power) and letting the market rule (great inequalities in economic power in practice). The egalitarian foundation of democracy and the inegalitarian reality of capitalism have been finessed by the grafting of social investments and the social welfare state onto capitalism and democracy. But the foundations of such social welfare policies are being rocked by financial, demographic and technological factors. As discussed shortly, employment and employability are called into the public-making arena.

Globalisation

Globalisation is broadly seen as an intensification of worldwide relations that link distant localities in such a way that local happenings are shaped by events in distant locations and vice versa. More narrowly, globalisation is a functional integration of corporate international operations. It is expedited principally by direct foreign investment (DFI) and multinational corporations (MNCs) that have woven a borderless, seamless global economy affecting employment, trade and exchange, including technology transfer and networking through information technology. Globalisation has intensified with the *internationalisation* of financial, capital and labour markets, which inevitably lead, in varying degrees, to the liberalisation of exchange controls and capital. The architects and beneficiaries of globalisation are global corporations, driven by the relentless logic of capitalism, owing neither national allegiance nor social responsibility in their dealings.

Expedited by new information and communications technologies, the global economy is more integrated and interdependent, but less stable and more volatile and uncertain. The linkages and dependence also mean more exposure to contagious downside effects. As the currency crisis in 1997 has proved, there could be sinister and far reaching consequences for East Asian developing countries, especially when their institutional frameworks are not adequately developed to shoulder the global pressure of competition and liberalisation.

The global economy makes everyone mutually interdependent and linked in vertically different patterns of supply and demand. Powerful institutions, such as world and regional banks, MNCs and other international institutions, also have vested interests in maintaining themselves and their environment. Supranational bodies, such as regional trading blocs with bodies that make trade policies and decisions in the interest of the group, are meant to be stepping stones from national economies to a global economy. But regionalism is a messy process since co-operative policies require the surrender of national sovereignty. Moreover, in a multipolar world with no dominant power since the end of the cold war—witnessed by the implosion of former Soviet Union and the end of American internationalism—it may be timely for the global economy to reinvent and rethink international and regional relationships.

Accompanying globalisation is a new *international division of labour* postulating that the development of global markets and firms causes companies to locate different technological levels in different centres according to local conditions (Driffield, 1996: 4). While high levels of technological activity linked to the activity of MNCs in the UK (eg, the Silicon Glen, Scotland) is observed, there is little evidence that this is part of a global strategy by firms to locate in such areas (Driffield, 1996: 137).

There are myths of globalisation with respect to global/universal products, borderless geography and giant firms. In essence, the transnational or multicultural multinational corporation that emerges is a cosmopolitan conglomerate diverse enough to respond to local tastes but united enough to amount to more than the sum of its parts. Marketing mantras such as "go global, act local" sound sensible but there are nuances that are easily overlooked in global strategies. These subtleties are crucial in misguiding some MNCs to not size up the competition and the challenge unleashed by globalisation.

An important consequence is that it is difficult for any country in the globalised world economy to institute an effective, long-run pro-employment policy on its own. Moreover, political considerations will become a decisive factor in coping with economic problems to combat joblessness and threats to social contracts which come with less work and greater economic insecurity (Simai, 1995). The public sector's role is being recalled as effective government interventionist policies have worked in Switzerland, Austria, Norway, Japan, South Korea, Taiwan and Singapore. These are, incidentally, all small but fast growing countries that have made a virtue and necessity of globalisation by integrating themselves effectively into the global grid.

Like labour, capital has become global and, in particular, can move frictionlessly in electronic form. The fluidity of digital capital flowing to the highest bidder at an unprecedented speed also affects the nation-states since they can no longer control the flow. Globalisation heightens economic promiscuity as multinational corporations colonise consumer markets and marry domestic firms. The nation-state, conjuring nationality and country of origin, gives way to regional and global units of account.

Instead of corporate giants, technology is spawning amoebas as corporations decentralise and fragment into individual pieces in new constellations of power to form alliances all over the world. Over and above alliances and joint ventures, outsourcing goes to subcontractors who can put together the most innovative technology at the lowest price for non-core competencies. Resculpturing into a modular form tears apart classical corporate structures. Companies are going topless as well as borderless (Browne et al., 1995).

Governance is eroded with global tribalism and eco-tribes replacing nationality. The emerging world order sees a demise of the nation-state, as much a product of amoeba-like organisations, global pollution and global communication. Trade blocs and possible intergalactic marriages occur despite the World Trade Organisation (WTO), which has exposed new imbalances in power as much as it hopes to free global trade.

Knowledge economy

In contrast to an industrial or even post-industrial economy, where raw materials and then man-made brainpower industries form the basis of production and exchange, a decoupling has emerged as knowledge industries become the focus in knowledge economies (see chapter 1). Return to a hunter-gatherer society is in tandem, since the hunt is for knowledge in the forest of information technology, global telecommunications networks and electronic highways. Taken to its logical conclusion, a knowledge economy and knowledge society is where all economic and social activities revolve around information. An era of skill acquisition and upgrading forms the only source of long-run sustainable growth and competitive advantage.

At the heels of the globalnomic and millennium fever are a number of technological trends. From the industrial revolution, which initiated the second wave with factory-based production, the third wave is de-massification with knowledge industries (Gibson, 1996, 1997).

Apart from infrastructure in new communication and information technologies, modern corporations can no longer be run along old lines of hierarchical chains of command. The trust between managers and employers has to be built (Horton & Reid, 1991). Values in an electronically interconnected global village move from the written word to visual-verbal media, which is more emotive, and not controlled by village chiefs. What sells is speed and instant gratification. The wired village leads to more direct, rather than representative, democracy.

Technological and employment trends

Consequent to the knowledge economy and the information and communication technology (ICT) revolution, new human resource development and management ideas revolve around paradoxes rather than simple right and wrong thinking. Principles such as the doughnut principle (Handy, 1994), where life is viewed as an inverted doughnut with the hole on the outside and the dough in the middle, an age of uncertainty—where life is best understood backward but lived forward—or an age of discontinuity (Drucker, 1992b) has emerged.

The factory is the organisational and economic core of industrialism but cybernation is changing that with the imminent "workerless" robotised factory (Jones, 1997). *Automation* refers to the age-old trend of replacing discrete human actions with machine operations by linking different machines with new controlling devices. More automatic control with broader execution, integration and control of entire functions and groups of functions such as material processing, assembly, testing, storage and others have occurred. Automation of automation is *cybernation* such as in a self-governing control and self-acting factory.[1] It converts entire productive functions into co-ordinated

---

[1] *Cybernetics*, as coined by Norbert Weiner in 1948, is the new science and technology of systems control. Its principles of information feedback and automatic controls extend back to the steam engine as the governor of initial mechanisation.

machinery or machine-like routines characterised by regularity, predictability and precision. The fusion of cybernetics as the technology of control with micro-electronic computing power is only the latest, most advanced attempt at perfecting this logic of factory production.

Fordism defines the twentieth century expansion of capitalism as a regulated co-ordination of mass production with mass consumption, eponymous with the Ford Motor Company. It stands for the large-scale standardisation of products and production methods. The economic effects of Fordism include making mass consumption affordable as workers' purchasing power increases with employment and rising wage levels. *Taylorism*, the scientific management of work organisation, complements the process of mechanisation and the institutionalisation of centralised and hierarchically simplified job tasks.

A distinction between Fordism and Taylorism is necessary so as not to efface their distinguishing features much as they work wonderfully together (Jones, 1997: 9–12). Fordism is distinctive in its advance specification of component production of product parts and production processes by standardised designs and plans and integration of the maximum number of processes on a flow of work principle. This lateral product-driven standardisation is distinct from Taylorism's scientific management, which is a discrete logic of vertical administrative controls focused on specific tasks. The computerisation of machining operations, transfer devices and inventory represents horizontal integration. On the other hand, hierarchical vertical controls over costing, staffing and production planning control functions, such as in lean production systems, is more distinctively Taylorism. Lean production organises consecutive operations so that one pulls the necessary supply from its predecessor just-in-time. It is aimed at shifting the initiative from the vertical to the lateral axis.

Computer technology has improved high level control over product design, planning and final production. Computerised centralisation improves control, precision and flexibility and, hence, efficiency and cost effectiveness. New production technologies involving computerisation include computer integrated manufacturing (CIM), the flexible manufacturing system (CMS), computer-aided manufacturing (CAM), computer-aided software engineering (CASE), computer-aided drafting and designing (CADD) and the like. As an illustration, CIM lowers overhead costs and, with a more capable work force, lowers direct costs per unit output and reduces lead times for implementing changes; all of which allow better time to market—from the initial design to a deliverable product in market. Computer-aided design (CAD) transferred to computer-aided manufacturing (CAM), or CAD/CAM, results in more satisfied customers. In turn, information technology allows newer and better ways of improving stakeholder relationships among customers, employees and investors. The ultimate computer-integrated factory with automation of all constituent activities of a manufacturing plant, or the cybernation of factory production, is the factory of the future.

If technology and a knowledge economy lead to reengineering and downsizing, such corporate anorexia may make one leaner, but not necessarily healthier. Greater emphasis is placed on leadership, stressing human relations and human management, and building competitive advantage based on strategic thinking and reinvention as the basis for competition with the changing nature of consumer tastes and empowerment.

The learning organisation invoking personal mastery, mental modes, shared vision, team learning and systems thinking (Senge, 1990) aims to control large scale human systems since it leads to a dramatic enhancement in productivity by people who feel their work environment is close to what they value (Winslow et al., 1994). The old contract of an implied promise of lifetime employment, a bankable career ladder and bureaucratic—as opposed to entrepreneurial—professionals have given way to downsizing as a way of life.

The information and knowledge economy has permanently eliminated jobs. Whole job categories have shrunk, restructured or disappeared. The growth of the new knowledge sector has redefined opportunities and responsibilities in the absence of mass formal employment as technological displacement is observed in the agricultural, manufacturing and services industries. Income inequality and social inequity may worsen with the end of work (Rifkin, 1995; Frank & Cook, 1995). Already, in advanced industrial economies, unfavourable demographic trends—such as older workers with old skills who tend to be more unemployable—worsened unprecedented unemployment. Global unemployment, at some 800 million, has not been higher since the 1930s.

The backlash on developing economies is simple. Faced with stubborn, longer lasting unemployment and discouraged workers (especially youth), industrial countries are forced to stop exporting employment abroad. Less DFI and fewer MNCs shift to developing countries as MNCs are urged to re-examine more competitive wage costs and productivity in their home economies. The trend is further heightened by regionalism and trade groupings in the North America Free Trade Agreement (NAFTA) and the European Union (EU).

The Economic Impact on Work

The most immediate impact of such new technologies and developments is on work and the lifestyle that accompanies work. In a job-fixated society, work represents not only income and a means of sustenance, but also self-respect, self-worth, hierarchy and the governance of individuals in a society.

In a knowledge economy, there must be new ways to attract, retain and motivate people as intellectual capital is owned and resides with people. The demands of a better-educated, more self-confident and independent workforce are such that they want empowerment, such as in more responsibility and authority. Recognition of the individual's performance and needs, with an emphasis on building their commitment to organisations, must come with greater worker participation rather than through the traditional management-labour divide.

In the service age, manufacturers and suppliers change from being purveyors of things to satisfiers of personal needs. The production aspect is only incidental. Quality rises to the fore and service in providing things implies the application of knowledge and ideas regardless of where the market is located. The successful company is one that develops a cosy and intimate relationship with customers. The service aspect of selling the product is a reverse process of just selling the thing. Such distinctive service quality is found in new industries such as health care, education, software, recreation, entertainment and lifestyle products.

In the post-business society, business is no longer the main avenue of advancement in society. In reaction to rising entrepreneurialism, jobs are redefined as a property right in the knowledge society. The right kind of education in the knowledge society is a new form of security. Educated persons who are effective in their organisations are those with the ability to present ideas orally and in writing, work with people, and shape and direct one's own work, contribution and career.

Industrial restructuring induces corporate structural and organisational changes. But the age of information and knowledge is one of uncertainty and discontinuity that has aided and abetted corporate unbundling as companies get smaller to be more focused. The unbundling is dictated by the need and ability to move ideas and information fast and cheaply. To avert uncertainty, the strategy is to husband knowledge by growing and nurturing it and handling people who possess it. The new company also has to cope in an environment of discontinuity. *Discontinuity* persists with the rapid emergence of new technologies and new industries, the emergence of a genuine world economy and a new pluralism of institutions that renders traditional theories of government and society obsolete (Drucker, 1992b, 1993).

In rethinking the company, both management and workers are aware of the forces of knowledge, learning and innovation and the need for strategy, vision and scenario planning to put it all together. Businesses will integrate themselves into the world economy through strategic alliances, joint ventures, research and marketing consortia, partnerships in subsidiaries, special projects, cross-licensing and so on.

More and more radical restructuring takes place following two rules: first, move to where the people are, rather than having people move to where the work is; second, concentrate on core competencies and farm-out lessor activities to outside contractors. Such contracting-out will squeeze out opportunities for advancement into fairly senior management and professional positions. Neither big nor small size preconditions restructuring but, as size follows function, paring down to core competencies does mean smaller organisations.

Thus, old assumptions about corporate size, strength and structure, such as in vertical integration, are changing. Old lines of command and control have evolved into inverted pyramids with workplace democracy and power back to frontline functions. From decentralisation to empowerment, the growth of alliances to gain outside expertise without takeovers are the emerging trends. The new building blocks comprise core competencies and corporate renewal. Core competencies are skills and capabilities that give companies their unique flavour based on their collection of knowledge. Renewal is vital to avoid sclerosis, with entrepreneurialism and networking as the means.

Production sharing and transnational integration, new consumer markets, the need for second careers as mandatory retirement ages end, job needs (eg, creating jobs in developing countries and job security in developed countries), redundancy planning as the new social policy, and the emergence of professional groups and business management in the modern organisation are juxtaposed with turbulent environments. The latter include the integrated world economy, transnational world money, the end of sovereignty, a fractured world polity, an employee society, the survival of labour unions and the rise of the business enterprise as a political institution.

Work rules and job descriptions will end with job restrictions by trade unions. Cutting job classifications will raise productivity. Organisations will restructure around information. More managerial and professional people will be in lower, rather than middle, let alone upper, level jobs; proportionately more of such people will be in operations, functional and technical work rather than in general management or staff work. More will be on their terminal job at a fairly early age, rather than on a promotion track.

It will not be middle management disloyalty if taking responsibility for one's family and career becomes a concern. Dual ladders of advancement means to reward people with pay and recognition, rather than promotion alone, and to compensate for performance, rather than rank. With rising property rights to a job, employers may have to institute due process to remove jobs. It is not just the information age, but also demography that causes such management changes.

The "unseen revolution" transforming corporate ownership is now visible (eg, in the US, where the twenty largest pension funds hold one-tenth of equity capital in America and where institutional investors control close to 40% of the common stock of the country's large businesses (Drucker, 1980: 235). The largest and fastest-growing funds, those of public employees are no longer content to be passive investors. As pension funds become premier owners of the country's share of capital, managers as trustees shift to owners as stakeholders to account for performance and results and to maximise the wealth-producing capacity of the enterprise.

Rethinking work

It is vital to discuss the impact of new technologies on the economy and to work to lead into the social impact. With automation and information technology, the knowledge economy spawns information workers with new attributes. As noted, a job is redefined as a property right in the knowledge economy corresponding to rising entrepreneurialism. The right kind of education and skills in the knowledge economy is a new form of security as employability is assured.

As new communication technologies impinge on work arrangements, a social effect includes that of deunionisation, since the physical platform for socialisation in the workplace disappears with telecomputing and the virtual corporation. Contingent and part-time labour further loosens bonds among workers. Work becomes more self-directed in knowledge and information industries, cutting down a layer of supervision and middle management. Strategic pay, rather than administered pay, also occur with flatter organisations and individualised work contracts (Murlis, 1996). Trade unions may be further marginalised when *differentiated work* based on creative qualities are more important than cognitive manual skills, such as in traditional supervised production jobs.

The shifts in thinking about work were noted ahead of massive downsizing, though they were not taken seriously then in a job-fixated society (Handy, 1984; Winslow & Bramer, 1994). Universally observed and recurrent changes bespeak the full employment society giving way to part-time employment as manual work yields to knowledge activities, and industry declines as service rises. Hierarchies and bureaucracies eclipse as networks and partnerships dominate.

The transformation in employment is hastened by a blurring of industry borders as evident in commercial banking, investment banking and brokerages, in computer hardware and software and in publishing, broadcasting, telecommunications and filming. A demarcation in specialised jobs is giving way to multi-skills and fluidity in job assignments. An entire career in one company has rapidly become a thing of the past.

Similarly, in the public sector, privatisation and corporatisation are spawning new theories of public sector management as governments are reinvented (Osborne & Gaebler, 1992; Hollings, 1996). Governments are no less affected by competition, technology and fiscal pressures. As cost-effectiveness and customer-orientation take precedence over traditional budgetary practices and allocations, public managers are learning about reengineering as well. The problem with implementing new management theories has to do with measurement and mindset realignment as bureaucrats turn into managers.

More specifically, three types of career paths begin with the demise of the bureaucratic-corporatic type, and the rise of professional and entrepreneurial careers (Kanter, 1990). The *bureaucratic-corporatic career* involves responsibilities, challenges, influences, formal training and development, compensation and assumptions of a steady, long-term rise up the job ladder. New economic realities and new expectations, long-term uncertainty, portable skills and employability have begun to alter these rigid modes.

The *professional career* is defined by a skill or craft, possession of valued knowledge and the promise of opportunity in the professional form in terms of the chance to take on ever-more-demanding, challenging, important or rewarding assignments. The professional career may not unfold in one organisation. Careers are produced by projects and the key variable of success is reputation or name rather than the anonymity of bureaucrats. In the professionalisation of occupations, name confers status and establishes value in the marketplace.

The *entrepreneurial career* comes with the formation of an independent business venture or the ownership of a small business. It is one in which growth occurs through the creation of new value or new organisational capacity. The key resource is the ability to create a product, service or value in contrast to a bureaucratic position in a hierarchy, or knowledge and reputation in a professional career. Instead of moving up the job ladder, the entrepreneurial professional sees the territory growing from below, and owning a share of that growth becomes the challenge. Entrepreneurs have only what they grow but they enjoy freedom, independence and control. Arguably, the risks may be lower for franchisee-entrepreneurs than for self-made entrepreneurs.

Less contentious is that risks are greater for professionals and entrepreneurial professionals than for bureaucratic-corporatic types. Skills or knowledge commanding the price in the marketplace operate instead of certainty and security in a bureaucracy. Post-entrepreneurial management requires three strategies: restructuring in search of synergies, increasing reliance on alliances with suppliers of labour substituting for permanent internal employees, and encouragement of innovation and entrepreneurship.

Similar to the concept of new professionals are *portfolio workers*, who are knowledge people with a portfolio of skills they can sell to a variety of different companies (Handy, 1994). The portfolio world is one where organisations buy the product or service, not the time. A portfolio is a collection of bits and pieces of work for different clients, and what matters is how time has been used, not how much of it was used.

The portfolio world is most feasible for people in their Third Age.[2] But, in some instances, portfolio workers may be people in their twenties who join the core of an organisation later. As technology frees people from routine and repetitive tasks, changing careers, and not just jobs, will be pervasive. The change may occur as many as three to four times during a lifetime with lifelong education as a certainty.

---

[2] When redesigned, life consists of four ages, each lasting about 25 years: a) The First Age is the time of preparation for life and work, such as in schooling, further education and qualifications, guided work experience and exploring the world beyond the home environment; b) The Second Age is the time of main endeavour, either in paid work, parenting or other forms of home work; c) The Third Age is the time for a second life that could be a continuation of the second, but might be more interesting or something very different, and to do nothing is no longer an option; and d) The Fourth Age is the age of dependency, that anteroom to or shortest interim desirable before death.

The growth of future employment lies in three areas. First, growth will still be positive for people who use and develop technology, instead of being displaced by it. Second, employment will grow in response to fundamental demographic shifts in industrialised countries that have dual-career families. Such families need domestic services such as cooking and cleaning. Those who marry late and start families late (possibly with some difficulty, biologically and physically) will need medical experts and childcare givers. Older persons require physical therapists and other health care workers. Third, employment will grow for people who can help society's organisations adapt to new operating rules. They include management consultants, human resource specialists, environmental engineers, lawyers, government administrators and such. Though employment falls in traditional areas, people will be redeployed if they have talents and extraordinary skills.

What is in consensus is that human capital and human resources are emerging as the determining factors in any successful enterprise. People are recognised as the most vital foundation for organisations to function and compete well. Hence, the measurement of performance of a human-centred technological future is of parallel importance (Winslow & Bramer, 1994).

The effect on productivity

The *productivity paradox* in industrial nations is where huge amounts of investment in technology have resulted in a tailing off in productivity increases after 1973 (Brooke, 1992). One explanation is that as large as such investment has been, it remains small compared to the total capital stock.

Another explanation is that much of corporate spending on information technology may have been wasted, either because workers waste time with computers (eg, surfing the Internet) or because they have more computing power than they really need. Also, while computers save time in some functions, such as in ticketless travel with bar coding and laser scanning, time still has to be expended in travelling and queues.

A third explanation is that a significant amount of time is needed for a generation to learn a new technology or attain a critical adopting level before producing effects. Finally, the lack of productivity increases may be a measurement problem, especially when new goods and quality improvements are not fully taken into account. Productivity in services is particularly difficult to measure, both for the output in service that is intangible (unlike physical goods) and for quality improvements. With the government as the largest producer of services, public sector productivity is traditionally problematic because cost effectiveness and profit are not usually motivations in social services such as education and health.

Outsourcing

Two trends in management thinking—first, that size is no longer a source of competitive advantage, and, second, focusing on core competencies—have resulted in *outsourcing* work to outside contractors. The net outcome is that big companies hand over jobs they destroyed to other contracted groups. Two sorts of companies are spawned as a consequence: small consultancies that provide specialist services to larger ones, and large companies operating on a wider front by providing temporary workers.

Outsourcing is an outcome of concentrating on core competencies and leaving non-cores to external contractors. A *core competence* is an integration of skills and technologies, rather than a single discrete skill or technology, representing the sum of learning across individual skill sets and individual organisational units.[3] A core competence is unlikely to reside in its entirety within a single individual or small team. To be a core competence, a skill must meet three tests: namely, customer value or benefit must be delivered, competitor differentiation must be uniquely different, and the core competence must be extendible to be gateways to tomorrow's markets.

The rise of outsourcing in the context of knowledge industries, globalisation, restructuring and reengineering supports the emergence of contingent labour and fertilises a new social compact between labour and management. The uncoupling of clerical work or contingent labour results in *temporaries* who actually hold down full-time, permanent assignments in client companies (Drucker 1992a). New types of office parks provide a trained clerical force and supervision for it, and provide work rather than office space and are located where the demand is. Corporate condominiums and virtual corporations are the new tenants in such parks.

---

[3] Motorola's competence in fast cycle-time (minimising the time between an order and fulfilment of the order) rests on a broad range of underlying skills including design disciplines that maximise commonality across a product line, flexible manufacturing, a sophisticated order-entry system, inventory management and supplier management. Federal Express possesses competence in package routines and delivery based on an integration of bar-code technology, wireless communications, network management and linear programming.

The need for blue collar workers will decline as the demand for knowledge workers rise. Technicians, professionals, specialists and managers of all sorts must have formal schooling in their qualifications. The decline is structural and irreversible, in tandem with the shift from labour-intensive to knowledge-intensive industries.

The redeployment of labour is not just within national borders. With training and management, an underdeveloped economy can attain within a short period the productivity of a fully developed one. Bangalore information technology specialists redesigning General Electric's internal software system for one-fifth the cost is more than what meets the eye. Manufacturing in developed economies will survive only if they shift into knowledge-intensive industries. This also fits with the demographics since the young now stay in school longer and are not available for blue-collar work. In other words, outsourcing is globalised.

As tempting as outsourcing is, the line between essential and peripheral services is not easy to draw. Being put on the queue of contractors may adversely affect costs and competitiveness. Stability has its virtues when special efficiencies come with giving workers a unique set of skills and a feeling of belonging. Teams work best based on familiarity, chemistry and a division of skills and competencies. Labour does not harmonise so quickly and is not as homogenous toward a task as desired.

Contingent labour

Pushed by globalisation, industrial restructuring, reengineering and business process reengineering (see chapter 8), contingent work and subcontracted work are further enabled by virtual work or telecomputing. A just-in-time *contingent* workforce, characterised as being fluid, flexible and disposable, is changing the sociology of work and fertilising a new social compact between labour and management. Outsourcing, contracting out or the externalisation of employment means contingent rather than permanent employment. Companies substitute supplier alliance for permanent employment and the phenomenon is more amenable in producer service industries.

Contingent work creates more uncertainty and less security, but it has a creative contribution since traditional, bureaucratic, managerial jobs are eliminated. The fee-for-service or contribution-based pay system does away with the need for promotion to increase pay, and enables jobs to be created rather than inherited as a pre-determined set of tasks defining a hierarchical position. A career now means formal movement from job to job and a change of title, tasks and work groups. It is generally in line with advancement and growth in the new environment.

The post-entrepreneurial blend of professional and entrepreneurial careers is another form of contingent jobs that weaken hierarchy and loosen the employment bond. The new security is employability security, which is the knowledge that today's work will enhance a person's value in terms of future opportunities. It comes from the chance to accumulate human capital in skills and reputation, which are invested in new opportunities as they arise. Companies no longer guarantee lifetime employment but *lifetime employability* in ensuring opportunities to challenging jobs and continuous training. One career in one organisation is rare and job mobility and career changes become as fashionable as they are necessary.

Employability as security is an appropriate career foundation since it depends on continuing hard work and growth in skills and security, and on the ability to generate income regardless of the fate of the employer. An attractive company is assessed on its ability to provide learning opportunities, chances to grow skills and improved capabilities to enhance a person's ability to be kept employable.

What is considered proper full-time work is also debated. The proportion of people who are unemployed or on short-term contracts is about 35% in the US, or one quarter if part-time, leased employees and the self-employed are added (Micklethwait et al., 1996: 223). The biggest employer in the US is no longer General Motors but Manpower, a temporary agency employing some 600,000 people. There are some 6,000 temporary companies in the US, double the number of a decade ago.

Part-time employment

Part-time employment has increased as business adapts to increasing global competition. Part-time employment has increased globally by around a quarter over the last fifteen years and it is estimated that 45% of all employees will be working part-time by 2003 (Briley, 1996: 3). There are five times as many full-timers who wanted to be part-timers as there were part-timers who wanted to be full-timers in the Organisation for Economic Cooperation and Development (OECD) (Briley, 1996: 4). Most of the part-timers were women facing pressure from family responsibilities.

Out of 25% of the US workforce identified as contingent, roughly four-fifths are accounted for by part-time workers, in addition to 40% of temporary part-time workers (Tilly, 1996: 1). Over the last forty years, between 1968 and 1992, the temporary workforce grew fifteen-fold while American labour as a whole did not even double. While not new, since 13% of the workforce worked part-time in 1957, the long-term expansion of involuntary part-time workers has existed since the 1970s. In 1993, almost as many Americans (6.1 million or 5.5% of workforce) worked part-time as those who were unemployed (6.5 million) (US Bureau of Labor Statistics, Employment and Earnings, January 1994).

Involuntary part-time employment is not a transitory but a prolonged predicament, and it feeds into the rising inequality of income. The quality of work suffers since the greater flexibility of work arrangements is associated with low wages, precarious jobs, poor social protection, dead-end jobs and poverty. The upward trend is not simply due to demographic changes, such as a higher female participation rate in the labour force, higher unemployment or a widening differential in wage and fringe benefits between full-time and part-time work. Two major reasons are noted (Tilly, 1996: 6). First, the industry mix in the US has tilted toward trade and services, which traditionally depend on part-timers. A secondary labour market is created, characterised by low wages, low skills and high turnover. Second, there is a conscious trend for businesses in virtually every industry to switch from full-time to part-time workers.

In effect, there are "good" and "bad" part-time jobs. A secondary worker's part-time job is truly half a job marked by low pay, low fringe benefits and low skills. It is founded on the distinction between the main breadwinner and secondary workers; managers like the later for their low compensation and scheduling flexibility. It includes *involuntary part-time* jobs and frictional unemployment. It is different from *retention part-time* jobs, which are created to retain valued workers whose life circumstances prevent them from working full-time. Retention part-time jobs belong to the primary labour market and involve high compensation, high productivity and low turnover; they are not half jobs.

Four policy concerns regarding part-time employment must be noted. First, low wages and benefits contribute to polarisation in the distribution of earnings and income. Second, they contribute less indirectly to lower productivity growth. Third, the low wages and terms of employment raise equity and efficiency problems. Fourth, that, in turn, leads to lower worker participation through trade unions. By the time economic forces have worked to create the flexibility to solve these issues, politics have come into play and complicated the solutions.

Job sharing

Job sharing as an alternative to temporary layoffs appears more acceptable in the US than in Germany and France where it is used as a means of job creation (Tilly, 1996: 129). Longer working hours do not necessarily mean more competitiveness since what matters is not the number of hours worked but how productive the individuals were. Worksharing is perceived as a threat to living standards when overtime is cut. Linking reduced work time to productivity gains—not wage cuts—would be more promising.

Voluntary arrangements have to be made among the individuals involved to allow working hours to be reduced without lowering real earnings. Ways to strengthen job attachment and motivation while creating a better understanding of the possibilities of job sharing are important. As such, not all jobs are amenable to job sharing, especially in service and customer-oriented services.

Displaced and discouraged workers

The US Bureau of Labor Statistics defines a *displaced worker* as one who has lost a job held for three years or more. This tenure restriction is intended to focus attention upon experienced workers whose skills may not be transferable to other jobs and who are likely to have reemployment difficulties. The restriction is criticised for using the length of time spent on a job as a measure of the time invested in acquiring skills, which may be more appropriately measured as time spent in an occupation or industry.

Similarly, *long-term unemployment* of three years or more affects discouraged workers who are essentially the victims of *technological unemployment*. Given their educational level, skills and age, these workers are not as easily retrained for new high technology or knowledge work. Since they continuously face negative responses from potential employers, discouraged workers may give up looking for employment and resign themselves to be welfare recipients. The destruction of the self-esteem and self-worth of discouraged workers, who cannot find reemployment through no fault of their own except being in the wrong time and under the wrong circumstances, can be profoundly debilitating.

More critical is the use of tenure criterion to implicitly equate the costs of *technological displacement* with the loss of specific skills. More than displacement, jobs are eliminated and people are shifted down to lower wage jobs regardless of their skills and experience. Where opportunities for high wage employment decline, the social costs of displacement are reflected less in the loss of specific skills than in the inability of those displaced to find jobs offering comparable pay. The measurement of social costs should include anyone who has lost a job due to a plant closing, slack work or abolishment of a shift or position.

The *risk of displacement* is the percentage of pre-retirement age workers within an industry, occupation or labour force group who have lost their jobs due to employment shifts. In the 1980s, the brunt of displacement was borne by the manufacturing sector producing goods, but displacement in the 1990s is more even across industries and occupations (Tilly, 1996: 25). At risk are workers in the financial, insurance or real estate (FIRE) sectors.

Downsizing

The change in employment pattern starts with the downsizing of companies in both manufacturing and services. The concept of a job for life declines as contract work and self-employment grow, allowing a greater enjoyment of autonomy and independence by workers. Virtual corporations change the nature of worklife and the relationships of workers with clients, colleagues and employers, as well as with family members and others.

Companies become amoeba-like, constantly repositioning and reconfiguring to suit projects. In computer literati, they *morph*, which means they transform and change all the time. Companies have to engage in continuous, lifelong learning and upgrading to compete in the context of ever-changing and new technology. Businesses will have to take into account manpower training and upgrading as part and parcel of operating costs and as a competitive strategy. Workers are no longer passive production digits as worker participation is invoked.

The amoeba-form of organisation is amorphous, changeable and conforms in shape to its environment. It is difficult to distinguish between where one form ends and another begins. Once past a certain size, an amoeba bifurcates and each part goes its own way. Resources are mixed and matched in an infinitely dynamic and *ad hoc* way to create economic wealth in a manner superior to ossified bureaucracies. Amoeba management begins with *decentralisation*, with less emphasis on titles and positions than on skills to get the work. The emphasis shifts from the motions of work to its result. Workers whose service adds value to a physical product are valued and compensated on the quality of their output.

The most immediate impact of restructuring and reengineering (see chapter 8) is the future shape of work and the diminution of it, such as in *downsizing*. Between 1979 and 1995, 43 million jobs were eliminated in the United States, though as many were created in new knowledge industries (Micklethwait & Wooldridge, 1996). Downsizing through reengineering has pushed up unemployment to as many as four million in Germany by 1996. In all of Western Europe, not one net new job was created from 1973 to 1994.[4] Over the same period, the US generated 38 million net new jobs even though it has one-third the people. Europe's unemployment rates, which had been about half those of the US throughout the 1950s and 1960s, rose to twice that of the US by the mid-1990s (Thurow, 1996). Temporary and part-time workers account for one in four of the workforce in Japan where lifetime employment was an institution. In the UK, as many as 6.6 million men (44% of the male labour force) and 3.9 million women (33% of the female labour force) have been unemployed, at some time, since 1990 (Micklethwait & Wooldridge, 1996).

Despite excuses about global competition and the job-destroying impact of productivity-enhancing technology, in large US firms, most of the employment contraction caused by foreign competition is not as simple as claimed. That they were undermanaged or mismanaged is closer to the truth (Hamel & Pralahad, 1994: 7). Failure to reinvent and regenerate the industry has caused the brutalisation of labour and resulted in the need for organisational transformation. Big, failing companies, such as IBM, have surrendered leadership in the task of industry transformation. As a counter example, AT&T and Hewlett-Packard moved more quickly than IBM to adapt their organisations and skills to the changing industry environment. The outcome is nonetheless the same: downsizing.

In the case of Europe, some responsibility could be laid with politicians and their overgenerous social security spending. But much of the problem remains mismanagement and protectionism. Low growth, ballooning overheads, diversification into unrelated activities and paralysis imposed by conservative

---

[4] Quoted in the Council of Economic Advisers. *Economic Report of the President, 1995.* Washington, DC., Government Printing Office, p. 314.

managers brought about the inevitable restructuring that practically destroyed lives, homes and communities. The loss of vision and leadership among top corporate executives imposed a heavy price on the dependent rank and file.

The seduction of downsizing lies in denominator management as the accountant's shortcut to asset productivity. This relies on the *return on investment* (ROI)—computed with net income in the numerator, and investment, net assets or net capital employed in the denominator—to steer the downsizing. Under intense pressure, the quickest and surest improvement in the ROI is to cut the denominator instead of growing the numerator. Clearly, such restructuring is a deadened solution, while reengineering is smarter and more sustainable.

While similar in having downsizing as a consequence, the difference between restructuring and reengineering is that the latter reinvents, regenerates and creates emerging opportunities. The reengineered company is changing the rules of engagement in a longstanding industry, redrawing industry boundaries and creating entirely new companies. Creating opportunities is more than catching up, since competition for the future involves staking out new competitive space (Hamel & Pralahad, 1994: 22).

Quality, time-to-market and customer responsiveness require smaller, better and different organisation to attain a competitive advantage. Some unlearning of the past is necessary to find the future that is so different. This concurs with the call of reengineering to obliterate, not automate. Strategies and thinking are changing from market share to opportunity share, from business units to corporate competencies, from stand-alone systems to integrated ones, from perseverance to speed and others.

Being contrarian in going beyond customer-led, more in empathy with human need will help companies gain industry foresight and craft strategic architecture with a sense of discovery and destiny. Thesis and antithesis as stark contrasts may help in viewing organisational choices, but creating a synthesis of the antithetical choices is more important to creating the future (Hamel & Pralahad, 1994: 288).

A number of lessons can be drawn from downsizing in America where the shrinkage has been unprecedented, though, by the early 1990s, downsizing was as inevitable in Europe as in the US. Masquerading under names such as refocusing, delayering, decluttering, rightsizing and downscoping (Hoskisson et al., 1994), the result of restructuring is the same: fewer employers. Large American firms in 1993 announced layoffs of some 600,000, 25% more than in 1992 and 10% more than in 1991, which was technically the bottom of the recession in the US (see Table 6.1 and Hamel & Pralahad, 1994).

Table 6.1. Companies reducing their headcount in 1993*

Between 5% to 10%		10% or more	
BASF	8	JE Seagram	17
Data General	8	Owens-Illinois	16
Westinghouse	7	Monsanto	11
Borden	6	Union Carbide	13
Dresser	5	IBM	13
Bethlehelm Steel	7	Digital	17
General Motors	5	Amdahl	30
Honeywell	6	Kodak	17

*Includes headcount reductions through divestment
(*Source: Fortune 500* (18 April 1994: 257–280))

General Electric removed 104,000 of its 402,000 workers between 1980 and 1990. Compaq cut its workforce by 10% in 1992, despite healthy returns, and Goldman Sachs twice reduced its workforce by 10% to increase productivity. The best performing company, Proctor & Gamble, laid off 13,000 workers and AT&T sacrificed 40,000 workers as it divided itself into three smaller, sharper companies. AT&T's dismissal of 40,000 workers in January 1995 occurred even though the company was prospering; its share price rose after the slaughter. Other gigantic layoffs in 1995 include Sears (50,000 workers), Xerox (10,000), Delta (18,000) and Eastman Kodak (35,000) (*The Economist*, 21 December 1996).

Two types of companies downsize. Apart from those that are desperate, others do it as a calculated choice to pursue a wider purpose. Downsizing as a consequence of reengineering is less virulent, shocking or contradictory. It lowered, rather than exacerbated, the unemployment rate from 7.1% in January 1993 to 5.1% in mid-1996. The American economy continued to create more jobs than it destroyed, providing 8.5 million new places between 1992 and 1996. Over half the jobs created during this period paid the top third of wages, implying that America generated more decent jobs than Europe, where loyalty to jobs for life was more sacrosanct.

The three biggest downsizers over the past decade—IBM, General Motors and Hughes Electric (a division of General Electric)—have also been upsizing. Between 1987 and 1995, IBM slimmed from 406,000 employees to 202,000, but recruited 21,000 new staff in 1995, which was more than in the successful

1970s. General Motors cut its force down from 450,000 in 1979 to 450,000 in the early 1990s, but recruited 11,000 employees in 1995. Similarly, Hughes Electronics added 8,000 new employees in 1996 after reducing its workforce by a quarter in the past decade.

One clear lesson was that most of the early downsizing was not successful. A 1990 survey by the American Management Association found that fewer than half the firms that cut jobs actually improved their performance (*The Economist*, 21 December 1996). A 1991 study of stock market reactions to downsizing found that, after the initial increase in stock prices following downsizing, companies performed below the market average three years later. The incentive and morale effect of profit sharing is similarly destroyed by downsizing. Only recent, better-planned downsizing did better, such as for AT&T, Proctor & Gamble and Goldman Sachs. Studies have shown that even the reemployed earn an average of 10% less than before (*The Economist*, 21 December 1996).

Another lesson is that a self-selection process in downsizing means that better workers, confident of getting jobs elsewhere, are the ones who leave. Where companies do the selection, their criteria are crude, such as in last-in-first-out (LIFO) policies that cost them bright young workers or weed out middle managers, representing a loss of experience, institutional memory and connections.

Downsizing is an art and a science, a mix of pseduoscience and euphemism with the same wrenching reality. Downsizing nicely and humanely involves bringing in professional outplacement services, keeping work teams intact to minimise disruption and demoralisation, asking those who survived the downsizing to help others who have to leave, and helping survivors tackle survivors' guilt. It is best for employees to update their skills and keep their options open.

In contrast, the US is short of high technology workers, especially in Silicon Valley, where companies are urging a relaxation of immigration laws to attract foreign talent (*Singapore Straits Times*, 18 April 1998). The US benefits, even if unfairly, from a scientific drain of students from developing countries such as China, India and Russia. Such students have put the opportunity for economic improvement above any moral obligation to return home.

Sufficiency of jobs

As muscle jobs disappear, finger and brain jobs grow into skill-based and knowledge-based jobs respectively. Though more personal services (eg, domestic work, eating, drinking, business services, craft work, education, tourism, health services) are created in information and knowledge-based activities, a resurrection of *Luddism*, marked by the union-led destruction of machines in England in the wake of the Industrial Revolution, is imminent in tandem with the shift away from labour-intensive activities.

Moreover, with jobs shifting south to lower wage countries and to areas inside and between countries, which are less expensive locations, there may not be enough jobs. As labour becomes more expensive, productivity measures are invoked, forcing pacing rationalisation and rightsizing. Even the public sector has shifted gears into management thinking. One consequence is that governments are not taking up the slack in unemployment, but are adding to the layoffs.

A rise in involuntary leisure results from the diminished creation of new jobs, the reduced demand for jobs and the search for the optimal employment size. Keeping people in school longer and encouraging older workers to retire earlier may deploy some of the extra leisure time. But, since income in pecuniary form, rather than in-kind as in time, is still necessary for livelihood, work-sharing and gradual retirement (Delsen et al., 1996) become inevitable consequences. Longer life spans, higher medical and old age costs and even the higher costs of consuming leisure, portend longer—not shorter—working life spans.

As jobs scale down in the marketplace and state economy, the informal economy grows with professional careers, entrepreneurial careers and service, knowledge and information activities. It may be the black economy, or legitimate voluntary and household parts, that pick up the residue of jobs as unpaid work because leisure hours loom large and people need activities to pass time. The mauve economy for personal services and home businesses range from the bizarre[5] to mundane (Handy, 1984). The grey economy for domestic and voluntary work grows with free time and the incentive to save expenditures.

To drive home the idea of sufficiency of work, the hypothetical example of cutting a 100,000-hour job (ie, 47 hours per week, 47 weeks per year, for 47 years) to a 50,000 hour-job (ie, 32 hours per week, 45 weeks per year, for 35 years) and a principle of half by two or three, have been propounded

---

[5] As people become busier in the complex industrial society, forgetfulness of personal events such as birthdays and anniversaries has provided a profitable business for entrepreneurial reminding.

(Handy, 1994). Essentially, the proposal is for half the people to be paid twice as much for three times the amount of work. The innovation would not create new jobs but would share it around. However, shared income may be only a compromise.

A diametrically opposite idea is that, in the post-entrepreneurial workplace, people actually work more and longer hours leading to an overload (Kanter, 1990). A shift from intellectual absorption to emotional absorption, wherein personal relations suffer, is a usual occurrence. The new workforce has a higher proportion of educated women who have heavier outside-of-work demands centring on family responsibilities. As workers become more participative and hold increasingly more responsible jobs that absorb emotions and energy, they need more time.

Social contract and class distinctions

The unfinished agenda of capitalist organisation is the minimisation of the use of human labour (Rifkin, 1996). Current downsizing, reliance on temporaries and the expansion of time presage the eclipse of jobs, careers, benefits and advancement as an economic expectation. Many social conflicts will implode within the realm of culture as class distinctions sharpen.

The impact on the moral contract and social equity also has to be reconsidered. Those who survive downsizing are the winners, or "haves", remaining as "symbolic analysts" who form a rising elite of highly skilled knowledge workers (eg, scientists, engineers, lawyers, investment bankers, management consultants) who are the creators and controllers of intellectual property (Reich, 1992). The losers are the low skilled service workers and blue collar workers. Even lower down are the unemployed, the marginalised and crime-prone individuals who lack the basic qualifications to operate in the new economy.

A vicious cycle of poverty and crime produced in America's inner cities and ghettos is thus worsened (Wilson, 1996). Class distinction is reinforced as the symbolic analysts who have global links, good education, comfortable lifestyles, excellent health care provisions and an abundance of security, withdraw into their enclaves and get blamed by the losers and underprivileged for their deprivation. The *nouveau riche* enjoys expanded leisure, a shift from achievement to enjoyment and from rational work goals to pleasurable play goals. The possessing class and Veblenesque display of status may be increasingly admired by peers, but condemned by the impoverished. The logic of the consumerist good life will form a new kind of society that, ironically, undermines the work ethic of the old (Browne et al., 1995: 79).

Less pessimistic are Frank and Cook (1996), who see increasing pay differentials among members of the knowledge industry rather than a monolithic class of symbolic analysts. Taxing the few in highly skilled professions who make astronomical salaries and fees would prevent the emergence of winner-take-all markets in various professions. Both Reich and Rifkin have similar thoughts for more resources to be diverted to retraining "losers" and for companies to share the fruits. A new *social contract* is imminent to preserve human dignity and sustain the new economy.

Employability, rather than employment for life, also implies that employers bear some responsibility for promoting a learning culture and learning organisation. Besides being part of the new contract, educating the workforce for tomorrow, as knowledge and skills for capability become driving forces, is also a form of competitive strategy for capital owners and managers.

Enslavement in employment is further decimated with the shift to investment in reputation to produce more skilful and self-directed business contributions (Kanter, 1990). As lifetime employment gives way, loyalty is a burden, not a virtue. It is best to invest in oneself; self-promoted networks become valuable. Career management is geared to the individual's resume. The careerist is no longer handed tasks but provided tasks by consumers.

But as contingent labour is prone to fluctuating income and may lessen economic well-being, the social contract is, paradoxically, more important for the employee, but less obligatory for management. The *trust gap* has ruptured the covenant between management and employees since what had once been guaranteed job security, promotion and annual raises for loyal employees has gone out of style (Horton & Reid, 1991). Restoring trust and teamwork to create an honest and desirable work environment should be in the new covenant and social contract.

While more discretionary time and energy is released with changes to self-directed employment, productivity may be lowered or improved with non-permanent jobs. More important in the *sociology of work* is the change in relationships, status, stature, belonging, shifting loyalties, trust, and teamwork among contingent workers.

Taken into the global context, anti-immigration and anti-free trade sentiments reflect the larger growing class conflict between the new haves and have-nots. Arguing even further, Rifkin (1996) foresees that the current winners may lose their jobs to automation and low wage economies unless industrialised societies move quickly to suppress the forces of the new economy and the power of information technology. The consolation is that transformational technology has created new industries with positive employment effects outweighing negative ones (Heilbroner, 1995: 103).

Unionisation

Humans work only in what engineers have not yet automated. Therein lies the danger of recurring Luddism. Even information workers are at risk. They replaced blue-collar workers under an industrial system with traditional factors of production (ie, labour, capital and raw materials), but more real time from computerisation, which enables independent, self-assessed work, and direct access to information have marginalised supervisory and middle-level management staff in the information technology age.

A new moral contract between employers and employees affecting unions and stakeholders is also implied. As employees have a "property right" in their jobs, the challenge to management is governance redefined as accountability and legitimacy, rather than self-perpetuating hierarchical management (Drucker, 1992b). Absentee capitalist owners do not own the brainpower of workers as they did manual workers in agriculture and manufacturing.

The impact on organised labour is thus another rude awakening. In the first place, unions, which have existed in the wake of the Industrial Revolution in reaction to gross abuses and inequities, have generally not kept pace with the expanding labour force. Labour membership has dropped around the world with improved government labour standards, more part-time workers and the rise of service workers. With industrial restructuring to servicisation, service workers in virtual environment are not amenable to unionisation.

Deunionisation will become more accentuated with contingent labour and wherever labour does not have a shop floor or some physical platform for socialisation to take place. As workers become more self-directed in knowledge and information industries, issues raised under the new social contract (eg, employability rather than working under one organisation for life) will adversely impinge upon union membership. Lines dividing industries will blur, rendering the organisation of unions by industry, craft, skills, occupations or company highly tenuous and unstable. Downsizing arising from technology, restructuring and reengineering is eroding union power. Flexible personnel (eg, core, peripheral and external workers), numerical flexibility (eg, overtime, part-time, flexible time) and functional flexibility (eg, multiskill, expanded process work) are changing industrial relations.

Contemporary labour-management relations based on more collaborative and participative models cast an ambiguity on the role of the shop steward. Equity shares and stakeholdership as a means to raise productivity and commitment make wages as an incentive less direct. Where industrial democracy (ie, where employees are involved in the decision-making process of the organisation) is practised, collective bargaining as the *raison d'être* of unions has to change. Processes such as computer-aided and design manufacturing, just-in-time manufacturing and flexible manufacturing permeating into service industries have even more wide-ranging effects on work, job security, employability and relevancy of skills and experiences.

While higher productivity and capabilities are undoubtedly beneficial, until mankind adjusts to take full advantage of the increased time and resources released by microelectronics, a resurrection of Luddism may occur. Governments are hard pressed with fiscal deficits, ageing demographics, declining industrial relations and the anachronistic welfare state, as opposed to workfare state. These slower changes make industrial nations the laggards in skills upgrading to keep pace with industrial restructuring. If they chose to battle with lower costs and more efficient developing countries through protectionist measures, there will be no net gains for the world from the new technology cycle. The techno-economic paradigm may well aggravate international relations, the division of labour, specialisation and productivity gains if socio-political dimensions are not well handled.

With global labour and the decentralisation and globalisation of manufacturing, labour unions' efforts at organising industries will be futile and frustrated. The traditional function of unions to bargain for high wages is already being frittered away by global competition. Alternative sources have cheaper labour, especially in developing countries where labour is not unionised. The efficacy of unions at home declines further.

Spatial issues

Information technology has created the *virtual corporation* (an alliance of independent companies brought together to capitalise on rapidly changing business opportunities based on their different but complementary skills), virtual networks and virtual production connectivity for MNCs across borders. Whether within national borders or spanning across countries, teams of people can work together without being physically together in geography or even time dimensions.

Telework is defined as work delivered to the worker via telecommunications, as opposed to the worker going to where the work is (Olson, 1989: 129; Jackson et al., 1998). Telework is further distinguished from more specific telecommuting, which refers to the individual worker who does not have to commute (Olson, 1989: 130). *Telecommuting* is the use of computer and communication technology to transport work to the worker as a substitute for the physical transportation of the worker to the location of work. This means that telework and telecommuting become interchangeable (Olson, 1988: 81).

Home-based work recognises that some types of telework do not take place in the home (Gattiker, 1994: 165). The politics of "private women" and "public men" and feminist theory entrap women in home-based telework since women are more vulnerable to traditional work-family conflicts. But there is a dark side to flexibility as subcontracting, flexible staffing and work-on-demand often mean part-time temporary work and marginalised wage workers. Women attracted to be home workers become a reserve army of the precariously employed and "disposable workforce" (Lipseg-Mumme, 1983: 559).

The implications of saving office space and costs, allowing flexible work arrangements that override spatial constraints and time constraints, and other benefits of virtual connectivity are enormous. City-states like Singapore and Hong Kong also exist as virtual states since they serve as the brain and nerve centres to production bases located offshore. The tyranny of time and distance is broken, though the sociology and physical merits of face-to-face contacts may be compromised.

Gender issues

From extensive empirical data of a sample of nearly 34,000 employees in American local government, three alternative conceptions of the possible linkage between gender and the impact of computing on white collar work is found (Gattiker, 1994: 33). Three broad white collar roles—namely, managers, staff professionals and clerical workers—shows one clear overall finding: women experience more favourable impacts on work from information technology than do men for similar categories of white collar work (Gattiker, 1994: 33–34). A second general finding is that there are many instances where there is no direct link between gender and computing on work. Third, there are substantial differences in the impact of computing across roles, although few of these eliminate the gender differences identified.

The three alternative conceptions of the gender-computing linkage are technological gender discrimination, technological gender empowerment and technological gender neutrality (Gattiker, 1994: 34–36). *Technological gender discrimination* refers to job control, deskilling, work degradation due to computing, greater time pressure, more intrusive monitoring of job performance and greater job stress. As women are disproportionately found in clerical and less professionalsied white collar work and are also found in job categories most susceptible to direct and indirect negative effects associated with labour reductions due to information technology, they suffer a higher incidence of negative effects.

On the other hand, if information technology is a liberating force that expands job skills and provides more information power, *technological gender empowerment* is the outcome. If neither technological discrimination nor empowerment is dominant, the third alternative is *technological gender neutrality*.

Modest results are found for technological neutrality and the data seems inconsistent with the hypothesis that women experience technological discrimination. Instead, the hypothesis of technological empowerment has more support. Women are more positive than men regarding the impact of computing on their information, interpersonal relations, work effectiveness and work environment. Men are more uneasy about being "glorified clerks" in computer-mediated work.

Managers thus have less to worry about female workers who are more positive and amenable to computing and information technology. If women are generally deemed less competent in technical skills and computer utilisation, they might benefit more from training opportunities.

It is nonetheless important to realise that technology in the workplace is shaped by gender issues more than it shapes such issues. Moreover, technology does not cause social change as much as it is an enabling force that opens the door for human innovation. Thus, women will continue to assess their work situation pragmatically and shape their behaviour and response in ways that take advantage of available computing opportunities.

The gender issue disappears with network technology usage when the contextual factors of occupational field, training and experience are taken into account. With no difference in network usage between men and women, the use of technology is driven by factors other than gender, such as training;

incentives become more important in encouraging usage. But women perceive themselves as more obsolete and less involved in updating activities (Gattiker, 1994: 150), which may be situation-centred or person-centred.

Family responsibility may mean women use less of their private time for updating or that less support is given by the organisations. On a personal basis, women's obsolescence may reflect low self-confidence in terms of technical expertise though there is no gender difference in general self-confidence and self-efficacy. That women's confidence in their updatedness resonated with their perception of the organisational environment implies that women need more help. Accordingly, women who intend to stay at home invest less in human resource development and human capital, and thus voluntarily put themselves in a less superior position relative to their male counterparts.

Impact on older persons

Older workers have a distinct handicap in new skills involving information technology and computers. Apart from educational qualifications and skills, they are more set in their work and attitudes compared to more technology savvy youths. Thus, older workers may be easily *marginalised* if they cannot learn, cope and upgrade to the necessary skills and aptitudes to work in a knowledge economy.

Employers also consider the higher costs of retraining older workers and fitting them into the restructured corporation. Older workers, based on seniority scales, higher medical costs and other benefits, also add to the wage burden. Some companies may thus use information technology as an excuse to trim older staff to save on costs and increase efficiency and productivity by hiring younger workers where experience is not the issue.

On a more positive note, information technology may have greater potential for old age care. In demographically ageing societies, there is a shortage of health care givers, which traditionally are women. But, as female participation in the labour force rises, more women at work will impinge on household production, including caring for the young and old.

Where older persons are still ambulant and independent, well-designed housing with hotline facilities and others using information technology for quick assistance and monitoring may be extremely useful. In hospitals and other institution-based care for the aged, information technology can be harnessed to perform tasks that save labour.

Other social issues

The commodification of labour, weakening of trade unions, erosion of social protection, withdrawal of welfare entitlements and widening of equalities are outcomes of a more deregulated, *flexible labour market* in a new knowledge economy. But the market forces unleashed are associated with the degradation of labour (Peck, 1996: 2). Labour cannot be commodified as in the real world labour market.

Wages as prices do not equilibrate demand and supply in the labour market as they do in other product markets. Wages tend to be sticky downward since they are equated with certain expectations and standard of living. Neither do workers enter as equals or pass from seller to buyer in the sense of legal ownership like commodities. The social nature of human labour is ignored and it has to be politically mediated. The price mechanism alone cannot regulate the labour market as social regulation, which unfortunately varies enormously, is also relevant.

The sociology and *socialisation of work* has traditionally given workers some identity and self-worth by what they do for a living. The importance of one's work role in the temporal organisation of daily life and the social and psychological effects of long-term joblessness must be noted more than mechanistic labour market concerns. Leisure is not defined by the absence of work, but in relation to work. The loss of work disorients habitual time structure and time becomes undifferentiated.

Besides structuring time, work is a source of contacts and personal networks and basis of social interaction. The loss in social standing and self-esteem leads to cynicism and the loss of trust regarding the motivation of others, weakening social integration. From disbelief and anxiety, many workers who have lost their jobs go through the emotional phases of grieving, denial, anger, bargaining and depression. Unremitting stress takes a toll on physical and mental health. Apathy, passive resignation, a loss of faith and an inability to control one's life reinforce the stigma of joblessness for the job seeker.

There is a growing shift from the welfare state to the *workfare state* that withdraws universal rights of access to welfare and asserts the primacy of the market as an allocative principle. The Schumpetarian workfare state in East Asia makes a clear break from the Keynesian welfare state as full employment is downplayed in favour of international competitiveness (Jessop, 1993, 1994; Peck, 1996: 199). Redistributive welfare rights take second place to a productive reordering of social policy. The marketisation of work-welfare is as much a political-economic tendency toward workfare consensus as is the moral, political and economic desirability of moving welfare recipients back into the workforce. All these boil down to continuous training and reskilling to keep employability high in a technology-driven industrial economy.

The concept of job security is embedded in cultural assumptions about what society owes workers for their labour. But these assumptions are changing as stable jobs, job security and progressive pay and promotion under seniority-based job ladders are threatened by displacement and the contingent nature of work (Moore, 1996: xvi). The mutual obligation or social compact between employee and employer has broken down and, with it, the shared experience and social interaction that connects people. The primary labour market, or the *internal labour market*, is a set of jobs within a firm linked by common features such as breadth of job definition, level of skill and responsibility, connection with job ladders, amount of compensation and expected tenure. As noted, these features are eroded, if not eliminated, in an information economy and society. The challenges become more stark with international trade and a global labour market implying an integrated labour force faced with international competitiveness.

Human Resource Development

In the light of the above trends, the logic of relying on human resource development as the basis of long-term sustainable growth remains true and relevant in the Asia Pacific and in developing countries in the Association of Southeast Asian Nations (ASEAN). Table 6.2 provides some indicators from the education and human development index in ASEAN economies, which generally show a need to catch up with other Asian newly industrialising economies (ANIEs) in human resource development. Through DFI and MNCs, ASEAN workers are part of a global labour force competing in an integrating world (World Bank, 1995).

With the emphasis on science and technology, results from the Third International Mathematics and Science Study of the average scores of 13-year olds is enlightening (*The Economist*, 29 March 1997). Based on an international average of 500, the scores in mathematics of students from 41 nations showed that Asian nations took the top positions. The first position was for Singapore (score of 633), second was South Korea (607) third was Japan (605), fourth was Hong Kong (588). Belgium (Flanders) (565) came in fifth position. Thailand was ranked in the 20th position (522) while the US was in 28th place (500).

Table 6.2. The education and human development index in the Asia-Pacific

	School enrolment			Adult illiteracy*	HDI 1994
	Pr*	Sec*	Tertiary		
Vietnam	na	na	2	4	0.557 (121)
Cambodia	48	na	na	20	0.348 (153)
Myanmar	na	na	na	na	0.475 (131)
Lao PDR	123	31	2	31	0.459 (136)
Indonesia	116	48	10	10	0.668 (99)
Philippines	na	na	10	5	0.672 (98)
Thailand	98	38	19	4	0.833 (59)
Malaysia	93	56	na	11	0.832 (60)
Brunei	na	na	na	na	0.882 (38)
Singapore	na	na	na	4	0.900 (26)

* Figures are for males; female rates are generally lower
(*Source:* World Bank (1997) and UNDP (1997))

The pattern is more or less the same in science with first place going to Singapore (607), second to the Czech Republic (574), third to Japan (571) and fourth to South Korea (565). As developed countries, such as the US and UK, perform at mediocre levels, it is heartening to know that the good grades of Asian countries is neither a matter of time (teaching hours) nor education expenditure. Common factors include banning calculators, spending more time on arithmetic basics (eg, handling data, doing mental sums in the head before doing them on paper) than on general mathematical topics, using standardised teaching manuals that are tested extensively, whole-class interactive teaching and extra coaching to ensure that students do not fall behind.

Undoubtedly, education and the wealth of nations are intimately correlated. A new and growing intensity of global economic rivalry among schools and education system is healthy. With rising globalisation and interdependence, national education systems must recognise the effects of global competition on the quality of education and training (Green, 1997). Moreover, besides fulfilling the requirements of the economy, national education systems have become more porous (Green, 1997: 171) and internationalised, partially through student and staff mobility and partially by widespread policy borrowing and imitation to enhance the international dimensions of curricula, especially in secondary schools and higher levels of education.

More computer-based interactive learning is another growing trend in human resource development. ASEAN countries may also consider some regional mobility programmes as found in the European Union (EU) such as Erasmus, Socrates and Leonardo (Green, 1997: 172). However, differences in systems and quality in national education systems would be problematic.

More private sector involvement in providing human resource development and education is another rising trend (Bridges et al., 1994). More and more national education is being privatised as public education shifts to the marketplace. In some systems, the inefficiency of public school systems have been identified as well (Chubb & Moe, 1990).

Areas identified in training for women, for instance, include career planning, confidence building and assertiveness skills, organisational politics and stress management (Briley, 1996: 17–18). Restructuring at both the workplace and home and the relation between the two should be at the heart of conceptions of the labour market (Briley, 1996: 153). The blurred boundary between home and work is not coterminous with either the equally blurred boundary between waged and unwaged work, or between production and reproduction.

Lower earnings when workers are retrained and reemployed may be due to specific skills lost, superfluous skills, non-unionisation and the internal organisation of firms. Firms in high wage industries are characterised by internal markets (ie, administrative rules and procedures that govern wage rates and the use of human resources). These firms usually hire workers into entry-level jobs and promote them along well-defined job ladders. Displacement generally means downward mobility.

Chapter 7

Technology and the Market

Introduction

The future society, as a dynamic society, will have each wave of civilisation tending to increase freedom and choice sets (Snooks, 1996). Timescape changes are most readily evident in the size of and changes in the population and accompanying material living standards. More existential dynamic changes involve the competitive driving force of the materialist man. Dynamic strategies cover family multiplication, technology, commerce and conquest.

The future revolution will release the population from its present natural resource limits. As the world population levels off, the fourth revolution involves the substitution of solar energy for fossil fuel energy (see Fig. 7.1). It will concurrently resolve the problem of increasing entropy, which is the outcome of the depletion of natural resources and the accompanying generation of waste. Wider choice sets have progressed over the first wave, which used human energy in combination with tools. The second wave used partial substitution of animal, water and wind energy for human labour and the third wave substituted fossil fuels for human and animal energy.

Reflecting the same time-dimensional concept of the world, the zero dimension of dot cultures started with no freedom and a minimum of social interaction when people lived in isolated packs (Knoke, 1996). People came together in the first dimension to live in permanent settlements and began to interact on fixed trade paths with neighbouring villages following river-banks and mountain passes. Dots of humanity connected, such as in the "silk route", making it possible for ideas and knowledge to be traded. As trade tracks grew, the second dimension saw imperialism seizing territory to consolidate power. The enabling age of discovery allowed maritime technology to cut the umbilical cord to land. In the third dimension of freedom, conquering airspace has happened in both aerial warfare and commercial aviation.

Each dimension lasted over progressively shorter periods, the first for 5,000 years, the second for 500 years and the third for 50 years. The fourth dimension in the new millennium may herald global government in a world of electronic neighbourhoods as humanity turns footloose in the ultimate dimension of freedom. A further dimension of freedom is effected by global migration through porous borders ranging from travel to the new detached labour, which is mobile. While not exactly coincidental in timing, Fig. 7.1 is a summary of various cycles of technology and their main features.

	Zero	First	Second	Third	Fourth
Dimension	Permanent settlements	Neighbouring villages trade along rivers and mountain passes	Territorial imperialism with marine technology	Aerial technology and warfare	Electronic technology and a borderless world
Duration		5,000 years	500 years	50 years	Ongoing
Energy	Human	Animals Water Wind	Fossil fuels	Solar energy Nuclear energy	Solar energy Nuclear energy
Industries	Cotton	Steam engine Railway	Automobile Steel Engineering	Electrical Aerospace	Microelectronics
Leading industrial nation	Great Britain	Great Britain	Germany	United States	Japan

Fig. 7.1. Various waves/cycles of progress and technology
(*Source:* Adapted from Snooks (1996) and Knoke (1996))

Instead of the world running out of raw resources, man-made resources have augmented supply—from plastics and synthetics to material science—as scientists experiment with the atom in biofabrication. But in its tow are new challenges such as pollution and how capitalism can survive the rising tide of eco-regulations that limit corporate and individual freedom in favour of communal well-being. As the environment, free global trade and other international public goods come under threat, global government intervention is becoming increasingly necessary.

Over and above demographic size and composition, the new generation in the coming millennium has already witnessed, and may be products of, sex decoupled from natural procreation, such as with in-vitro fertilisation

(Browne et al., 1995). Increasing domestic equality, feminism asserting itself in the workplace and the further disappearance of economic bonds has led to a collapse of family hierarchy. New familial structures include gay and lesbian unions, complex stepfamilies, communes and single living. Even children in the complete family set-up may be raised by foreign maids, displacing the traditional family structure and neighbourhood. The family is redefined as new bonds are formed in a new moral relativism where diverse notions of right and wrong have evolved.

Technology has so leveraged individual action and behaviour that ethical standards have been compromised. *Technocracy* favours rule by science rather than rule by man. Taken to its logical conclusion, a subtle shift from democracy to technocracy may be imminent (Rifkin, 1995). Witness genetic engineering with its associated ethical and moral implications, even as it confers expanded choices in life preservation. Even small breaches can potentially multiply many fold as social trust fails. Nonetheless, a renaissance of ethical standards and spirituality will come as religion has proved to be remarkably resilient and adaptable. With such varying opinions, a polycentric culture may generate more tolerance or clashes, but a common-sense approach, through altruism, civility, integrity or respect, will preserve the human race.

From such abstracted settings, this chapter explores the role of new information technology, new media technology and market-driven innovation in launching mankind into the next millennium. Starting with an overview of new technology, the rest of the chapter will consider the product cycle, the architecture of information and the economics of information networks.

Technological Trends and Developments

The evolution of the industrial, information and knowledge economy was presented in chapter 1. This section serves merely to specify the technological trends that parallel that evolution. The interest is not so much in technical specifics as it is in how technology affects the economics of production and exchange.

The term information technology is preferred to media technology in recognition that significant modifications in information management do not always involve mass communication (Couch, 1996: xvii). The term media may be too confining to only students of communications insofar as modifications in the techniques used to preserve information are as significant as modifications in techniques used to transmit information. Mostly, information technology has expanded human experiences and enlarged human arenas. Reciprocally, information technology has been used as an instrument of exploitation.

Most communication, both that which employs a technology and that which does not, is contextualised by social relationships (Couch, 1996: 1). The development of a comprehensive theory of information technology requires that attention be given to social relationships as well as to the technologies used to preserve and transmit information. Information technology can shorten and improve business cycles as the needed market information gets across effectively and in time (Vincent, 1990: 20–21).

Essentially, *information technology* enables data creation, organisation and handling, while *computer technology* enables data storage and processing and *telecommunications technology* allows the transportation of data over larger distances. *Telematics* is the integration of computer, information and telecommunications technologies to improve commercial performance and social cohesion through the enhanced potential of information handling and manipulation (Turner, 1997: 92). *Technomics* is the economics of technology and computing (Inmon, 1986).

New technology in the information sector promises improved productivity, a higher competitive advantage for manufactured products, a reduction in inflation and sustained economic growth resulting from the creation of new jobs and high employment. On the social front, the information sector facilitates a better organisational ability to manage the inevitable changes in society and to minimise hardship, such as in taking care of older people in ageing demographics. On the other hand, there is the threat of technological unemployment as noted in chapter 6.

The euphoria with new technology is marked by gross overestimates of market size, market share and profitability as industry lines are blurred and measurement of the information sector proves difficult (see chapter 1). New investment is inevitable in a growing industry, and the expansion is marked by the building of production facilities to fulfil projections.

Because the product cycle is short, there is a constant shakeout in the industry marked by the appearance of many vendors, price instability, competition for market share, the emergence of technological and pricing standards, and the dropping out of weak competition with inferior products. The *product cycle* is the length of time a vendor actively markets a product, beginning from the initial stage of a prototype to a mature product and ending with the announcement and delivery of a new family of products.

Twelve themes have been identified surrounding the inextricable links between the points of a triangle formed by a new economy, a new enterprise and a new technology (Tapscott, 1995). These are knowledge, digitisation (instead of analogue), virtualisation (instead of physical), molecularisation (instead of mass), integration/internetworking, disintermediation (instead of middlemen), convergence, innovation, prosumption (a cross between production and consumption), immediacy, globalisation and discordance. Many of these trends have been identified in the preceding chapters. Consolidating them in this chapter casts a holistic net across the emerging digital economy.

Converging technologies form a triangle involving content, computing and communications (see Fig. 7.2). The enabling technologies include networks, inter-enterprise computing, enterprise infostructure (ie, information infrastructure), workgroup computing and personal multimedia. The intended outcomes are to create wealth and social development, recast external relationships, transform organisations, achieve business processes, redesign jobs and improve task and learning efficiency at each level of the enabling technologies.

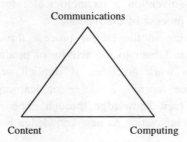

Fig. 7.2. Converging technologies

Ten technology shifts drive the convergence of content, computing and communications (Tapscott, 1995; see also chapter 1). These are shifts from analogue signals to digital signals, semiconductors to microprocessors, host-based systems to client server systems, garden path bandwidth to the information highway in network capacity, dumb access service to information appliance, separate data, text, voice and images to multimedia forms, proprietary systems to open systems, dumb networks to intelligent ones, craft computing to object computing software development, and graphic user interfaces to multimedia user interfaces.

A distinction is made between some aspects of technological change (Antonelli, 1992: 35–50). An effective state of technology uses all scarce and abstract resources in the economy to produce technology and technological information. Technological information is knowledge that enables economic production. In contrast, technological artifacts are physical or abstract products that result from the application of technology.

Invention is the necessary first stage of development of all new technological artifacts, whether techniques, processes or products. *Invention* is the process by which new technological information is created; a necessary part of that process is the embodiment of new information in scarce physical forms. A conventional but restrictive concept of innovation requires an invention to be subject to at least one exchange transaction before it becomes part of the stock of technology available in the economy. This fails to take into account a firm's in-house technological development, which has become an important contribution to technological change. *Innovation* involves the realisation in practice of the potential value of inventions, or is the process by which inventions are implemented such that they affect production activities in the economy. Every invention presents a possibility for innovation in the future, making every invention a technological information resource to be exploited through the process of innovation.

Innovation, occurring in the labour process through the application of knowledge embodied in labour to the activity of production, involves explicit or formal changes in work practices. If implicit or informal changes are involved, they become *learning-by-doing* or learning-by-using. Individuals can also create new tacit knowledge through experiences such as personal invention. This is also innovation as new knowledge is applied or implemented in practice.

The *diffusion* of technological information need not involve economic transactions, but more information or communications transactions. The diffusion of new technology can be in physically embodied forms, and there are some inherent public good characteristics (see chapter 5). A lot of basic and generic research and development is publicly funded or undertaken by institutions in the public sector in pursuit of overall technological upgrading and part of a science and technology policy. Assisting small- and medium-sized (SMEs) local enterprises in manufacturing and information technology is an important adjunct of those goals. As such, some national institutions and processes by which technology is effectively diffused are also critical, and the state has to be the agent.

Technologically speaking, the most significant trend is digitisation. *Digitisation* turns more and more analogue transmissions in "waves" into a version of electronic Morse Code composed of dots and dashes, or ones and zeroes for transmission through telephones, televisions and radios (Miller, 1996: 37). Digital transmission is crisp, clear and precise compared to fuzzy analogue transmissions. *Analogue* derives from the idea that carrier waves resemble or are analogous to the audio wave it carries. Unlike analogue signals, digital signals can be copied, compressed and combined with other digital signals.

Digital compression is a necessary part of *high-definition television* (HDTV), which offers substantial increases, over the existing standard, of the amount of picture information possible. As a comparison, an analogue HDTV signal requires ten times more bandwidth than traditional analogues, and a digitised HDTV can require transmission rates of a full gigabyte per second.

In the 1980s, the Japanese public television broadcaster, NHK, led the effort in concert with Sony, CBS and the US Department of State to get international acceptance of an HDTV standard. The public-private partnership broke down as Europeans and Australians united in opposition to a US–Japan standard (Neuman et al., 1997: 211–214). Despite two decades of debate, digital television has yet to evolve and HDTV remains a Gordian knot in which concerned parties jockey for market share in the evolving digital marketplace. Existing broadcasters are concerned with getting free spectrum to protect free television with crystal clear pictures and CD-quality sound.

Technology in the electronics industry

Because the electronics industry underpins much of the new technology and its applications to the information technology and media industry, a discussion of its technology trends is germane. The precursor of the modern electronics industry was the invention of the transistor in 1947 by scientists at Bell Telephone Laboratories. It was the transistor's replacement of the vacuum tube in radios that revolutionised the industry and spawned others. Functioning as an amplifier and switching element, the transistor enabled other complex functions to be constructed from silicon, which is an effective barrier or conductor of electricity, and hence birthed the semiconductor.

The vacuum tube, which spawned the microelectronics industry, suffered from high power consumption, its large size, heat dispersal and inherent unreliability until the semiconductor came along. A *semiconductor* can act either as an insulator or a conductor, and it can modulate, rectify or amplify electrical currents. Vacuum tube technology gave way to the transistor as the speed, size, reliability and costs of semiconductor materials improved. The semiconductor transistor is more reliable and efficient than the vacuum tube. In the 1950s, a major innovation was that a single silicon chip could hold more than a single transistor. So began more research and the development of capabilities with the design and manufacture of integrated circuits (ICs).

By 1982, a microprocessor developed by Intel made mainframe computers extinct as personal computers took over. Individual consumers and the non-corporate world have since latched on to electronic highways and information technology with fast high-capacity chips, such as Intel's Pentium chip, which contains 3,100,100 transistors. The diminution in size and fall in costs and prices that makes electronics products more affordable and accessible and improves performance by shortening switching time and the time needed for higher speed operations have transformed the world in more ways than one.

Thus marked the entry of *microelectronics* as a branch of the information technology industry devoted to the design and manufacture of circuitry devices constituted of extremely small electronics parts. Broadly defined, *electronic technology* embodies a set of human knowledge that makes possible the production of a wide range of electronic goods and services. By this definition, information technology is a subset of electronic technology.

From one million instructions per second, the Pentium chip allows one hundred million instructions per second. More amazing was the high speed achieved at reduced levels of power consumption. Chip miniaturisation and enhanced performance are embodied in the new field of microelectronics. Together with equally fantastic leaps in science and technology, many industries, applications and processes in telecommunications, broadcasting and information technology have merged, combined and synergised (see chapter 4). The digital age, knowledge economy and information society have further profoundly impacted governance and other socio-political structures (see chapters 1 and 5).

The electronics industry can be divided into three components, variously labelled as semiconductors or electronic components, consumer electronics and industrial electronics or electronic equipment (Dicken, 1992; UNCTC, 1986; Lim & Pang 1982) as shown in Fig. 7.3.

The electronics industry is simply too heterogeneous and diverse: even semiconductors can be further divided into a family tree of technology and applications starting with integrated circuits and discrete devices (eg, transistors, diodes and others) as shown in Fig. 7.4.

Semiconductors or electronic components	Consumer electronics	Industrial electronics or electronic equipment
Passive: resistors, capacitors, inductors, relays Active: semiconductors, discretes, integrated circuits, vacuum tubes	Computers and peripherals, telecommunications, industrial control equipment, testing and measuring (eg, office equipment, military, aerospace, automotive)	Televisions, radios, video equipment, audio equipment, electrical appliances, video games, watches

Fig. 7.3. The electronics industry

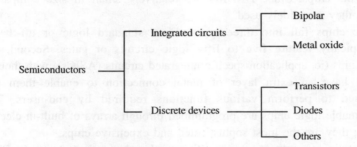

Fig. 7.4. The family tree of semiconductor technology and applications

Integrated circuits have eclipsed discrete devices and can be further differentiated into bipolar and metal oxide semiconductors as alternate methods of fabricating. Bipolar semiconductors are superior to metal oxide semiconductors in operating speed, but consume more power and generate more heat. They are more costly per circuit function and hence unsuitable for densely packed circuits. Metal oxide semiconductors are thus more commonly used in fabricating digital memory, microprocessors and speciality devices.

Both bipolar and metal oxide semiconductors are found in linear integrated circuits and digital logic circuits. Linear integrated circuits process electrical signals over a continuous voltage range and are more suitable for consumer electronics applications such as analogue computers, radios and televisions. Digital integrated circuits process information only in binary digits corresponding to high and low voltage electrical impulses. They can be further subdivided into memory chips, microprocessors and logic chips and are used in watches, games, calculators and others.

Memory chips store data. *Microprocessors* perform various arithmetic or calculating functions on data stored in memory chips. *Logic chips* perform functions such as control by steering data to its destination. Memory chips are either read-only memory (ROM) or random access memory (RAM); they respectively store operating instructions or information for processing by the instruction sets. Information stored on RAM is volatile since it can be erased by interrupting the flow of electrical current to the circuit's memory cells.

There are two main types of RAMs: static random access memory (SRAM) and dynamic random access memory (DRAM). The main difference is that DRAMs need constant "refreshing" during operation to prevent data loss; this involves a short (lasting a few microseconds) surge in electrical current through the chips. Since DRAMs are relatively small in size compared to SRAMs, they are widely used.

Logic chips fall into three types. First, standard logic or off-the-shelf chips typically feature five to fifty logic circuits or gates. Second, semi-custom chips (ie, application-specific integrated circuits (ASICs)) with thousands of gates have an extra layer of metal connection to enable them to be customised to perform various functions required by end-users. Third, programmable logic chips are programmed through arrays of built-in electronic switches; they are the most sophisticated and expensive chips.

The technology chain corresponding to the electronic industry in Fig. 7.3 is shown in Fig. 7.5. A *cluster* is defined according to its technological background. Clusters provide close linkage between the industries; this linkage is called a *technology chain*. The electronic technology chain begins with the production of electronics components that materialise electron movement in vacuum gas or semiconductors. The advanced materials industry is the foundation of the electronic technology chain. The electronics industry thus refers to the clustering of industries closely linked together within the electronic technology chain.

The technology chain can be divided into four layers of technology applications for production, support and consumption. The top upstream layer has primary products functioning as input factors to other industries of which the electronic components industry is a principal one. Its range of electronic devices varies from the simplest resistor to the most advanced microprocessor. The four segments of the upstream sectors are noted in Fig. 7.5. They are TV tubes, special electronic tubes, integrated circuits and transistors. Integrated circuits include three kinds of chips—memory, logic and microprocessor—all of which are widely used in many downstream industries.

Branches	Products
Upstream sectors	Advanced materials: TV tubes, special electronic tubes, ICs (eg, memory, logic, microprocessor), transistors
Industrial end-user sectors	Telecommunications equipment, computer systems, software engineering, industrial instruments (eg, optical, medical, measuring)
Consumer goods	Automotive industry, personal computers, cellular phones, TV sets, radios, audiorecorders, videorecorders
Extensions	Multimedia information systems, flexible manufacturing systems, management systems, industrial robots

Fig. 7.5. The electronic technology chain
(*Source:* Adapted from Kozmetsky & Yue (1997: 7))

The second layer of the electronic technology chain includes branch industries that function as industrial end-users or support sectors to other industries. Software engineering and computer manufacturing are the most important industries in this layer. The telecommunications industry is included because of its role in facilitating the flow of information in other manufacturing and service industries. Only three segments of the industrial instruments industry are indicated in Fig. 7.5, namely, optical, medical and measuring segments in which electronic technology is combined with optical, mechanical and biological technologies to produce sophisticated instruments and systems for specific applications. Except for industrial usage, a large percentage of products in this layer also apply to final consumption such as personal computers, cellular telephones and pagers.

The third layer relates to final consumption goods and services. Three segments are shown in Fig. 7.5, namely, TV sets, radios and audiorecorders and videorecorders (VCRs).

The fourth layer of the chain denotes the level of electronic technology chain that links many innovations in multidisciplinary fields, including multimedia information systems, flexible manufacturing systems, management systems and industrial robots. Rapid technology and innovations have led to the expansion of the electronic technology chain into many different industrial and commercial applications including those related to automobiles, petrochemicals, food processing, medicine and entertainment.

Artificial intelligence

Artificial intelligence programming enables a computer to work out simple logical theorems or principles of valid reasoning, hence developing logical skills of computers. *Artificial intelligence* refers to computer-based technologies that replicate behaviours associated with human thinking such as making decisions, evaluating options or developing new ideas. *Expert systems* computer programmes are designed to capture human expertise, combining the common sense of human beings with a machine's memory and logic skills. Intelligent machines can help make people work more intelligently, but as computers mimic human decision-making, they may transform abilities that are valued and rewarded in people. Highly professional skills and knowledge can be packaged and made accessible.

Computer vision in artificial intelligence requires three different, but not necessarily distinct, abstract techniques (*The Economist*, 14 March 1992). The first group, with humanist inspiration, comes from psychology in wanting to discover how people think so as to simulate those processes on a computer. But it is still hard to predict when humanist programmes break down or succeed. To ensure greater predictability, the second group, the logicists, uses formal scientific, mathematical logic to create non-monotonic forms of logic. Chains of reasoning based on traditional logic fall apart if an assumption on which they depend on turns out to be wrong. A non-monotonic system of logic is built precisely to recover and cope with the necessary adjustments. The third group, the structuralists, believes that the best way to simulate the workings of the mind is to recreate the information-processing capabilities of the brain. Structuralists (also known as connectionists) thus build interconnected networks, or neural networks, of artificial neurons using silicon.

Virtual reality

Virtual reality refers to the use of computer-based systems to create an environment that seems real to one or more senses (usually including sight) of human users. The computer-generated environment represents an amalgam of technologies, notably, a digital computer, software capable of processing visual and auditory information and a means of presenting the information to the user.

Applications of virtual reality range from entertainment to military training. Wherever a laboratory, clinical, pedagogic or simulated situation or event is required, virtual reality is ideal since the necessary simulation can be very real. It is useful for medical exploratory tests and scans, industrial designs, engineering, scientific visualisation, safety testing, teaching, rehabilitation and job placement as well as for venturing into areas where human testing has to be moderated or controlled. It is role playing to a higher power, one that allows measurement and all sorts of laboratory and clinical control to be exercised. While virtual reality is not real, it has a relationship to the real and is an exemplary evocative medium. Virtual reality is still in its infancy and its potential is yet to be.

Technological Convergence

Technological convergence is further removing borders across information technology segments, first linking telecommunications and computers, and then using multimedia to link to broadcasting and other media industries as well. Distinct trajectories in technology are coming together through digitisation, which is broadening the technology base and facilitating the emergence of large-scale communications networks.

Industry Feature	Print	Film	Records	Radio/TV	Telecoms
Production technology	Paper	Film, camera	Recording apparatus	Video, microphone	Telephone
Carrier material	Printing press	Film	Vinyl tape	Radio waves	Wire, switches
Production systems	Publishing companies	Film companies	Record companies	Broadcasters	Public telecoms operators
Distribution technology	Wholesale, retail	Projector	Road, rail	Transmitter, receiver	Networks
Distribution systems	Road, rail	Cinema	Wholesale, retail	Broadcasters	Public telecoms operators
Regulation	Competition	Licence	None	Regulation	Regulation

Fig. 7.6. The pre-digital media industry structure
(*Source:* Adapted from Dutton (1996: 105))

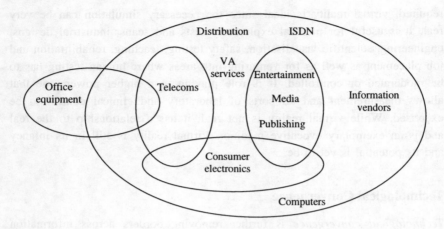

Distribution
Telecommunications
 Video conferencing
 Voice & video electronic mail
 Digital & cellular telephones
 International, long-distance & local telephone services
Office equipment
 Telephone
 Facsimile
 Copier
 Printer
 Scanner
Consumer electronics
 High-definition TV
 Two-way television
 Video printer
 Electronic photography
Computers
 Mainframe
 Minicomputers
 Personal computers
 Information appliances
 Operating systems
 Virtual reality
 CD-ROMs
 Interactive, entertainment and education
 Interactive news
 Custom software
 Transaction processors

ISDN
 Cable networks & operators
 National data highways
Entertainment, media & publishing
 Video games
 Cartridges
 CDs & video discs
 Film, TV & video
 Records & cassettes
 Custom publishing
 Newspapers
 Newsletters, magazines & journals
 Books
Information vendors
 Information-on-demand
Value-added services
 Voice mail
 Electronic mail
 Data storage & retrieval

Fig. 7.7. Merger mania of information industries by the new millennium
(*Source:* Adapted from *The Economist* (27 February 1993))

The blurring boundaries and core competencies of traditional suppliers are further breached by the lateral entry of firms from adjacent markets abetted by deregulation and liberalisation. In the future, the information technology industry will provide a continuum of products that cannot be categorised as telecommunications or computer products, in contrast to the five segments of the pre-digital media industry structure, as shown in Fig. 7.6.

With digitisation, Fig. 7.7 shows the possibilities of overlap between information technology and media industries such as in the production of hardware and software products and their distribution. *Value-added services*, such as enhancing the content and delivery of database services (eg, voice mail, electronic mail, data storage and data retrieval), are further facilitated. Megamergers have increased the degree of broadcast television, cable and non-television media integration.

While the average prices for both hardware and software fall with larger quantities due to economies of scale, this is not so for professional services that rise with quantity (Ahamed & Lawrence, 1997: 21). The converged hardware market will link up end-user devices with backbone network equipment. The integration of end-user devices in personal computers, smart televisions, cable set top boxes, network computers, smart telephones, personal digital assistants, VCRs, CD players and stereos is already happening more than in network equipment.

The converged transmission services market and network-centric power will transform bandwidth from a scarce to a surplus commodity, as in what the microprocessor did for computer processing power (Moschella, 1997: 120). Internet access providers, online service companies, cable companies and regional and long-distance phone companies will begin to overlap as these vendors begin to carry voice, audio, video, graphics and text-based information. Competition varies by country and is further complicated by unresolved regulatory environments in many countries. One certainty is that since bandwidth is the critical industry bottleneck, telecommunications companies will move to centre stage in terms of moving the industry forward—a rude awakening for computer companies in the context of Fig. 7.7.

Synergy, convergence and multimedia

Synergy means the co-ordination of parts of an organisation or company so that the whole actually turns out to be worth more than the sum of its parts acting alone. With technologies converging, there is the corresponding need to link activities involving the movement of completed material, or people representing that material, from production firms in one mass media industry to another.

The rise of the fragmented audiovisual mass media world begins with the splintering of channels so as to theoretically make each channel's percentage of the audience pie smaller. The increase in audiovisual channels tends to decrease audiences for most individual channels as viewers take advantage of expanded menus. It would be advantageous if narrower slices of the population were targeted with messages specifically tailored for them. New windows of distribution would emerge.

Synergy across borders has practical implementation problems. Across organisations and countries, strategic partnerships or joint ventures are formed. Synergistic link-ups occur in services such as advertising, promotion and direct marketing.

The Architecture of Computer Technology

The vision of the future involves a physical/hardware environment (eg, mainframes, minicomputers, microprocessors and fourth generation language software geared for flexibility and direct use by end-users), modes of operation, organisation and data. As an important component of developing, organising and managing information systems, it is vital to have information vision and architecture (Martin et al., 1994: 457). *Information vision* is an expression of the desired future for information use and the management of an organisation. *Information technology architecture* is the way information resources are deployed to deliver that vision. The architecture provides the grand scheme within which individuals make decisions in a decentralised information system. It is the rationale or glue to help communicate the future to others.

Components of the technical aspects of architecture comprise hardware, software, data, communications, management controls, personnel and user elements. In specific terms, an *information technology platform* is the hardware and standards used to build an information system. The technical design of computing architecture involves dealing with processors, networks, services and standards. The software resources of the system include local area networks, workstations and others.

Technical infrastructure has to have a parallel in management system architecture that embodies values and beliefs as well as managerial concerns (see Fig. 7.8). *Value architecture*, specifying the moral fibre that sustains a

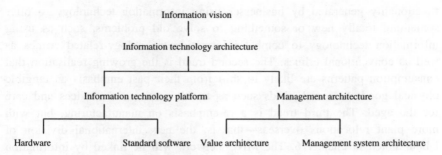

Fig. 7.8. Information vision and architecture

technical system, should emphasise productivity, quality, service orientation and professionalism as well as support diversity and achieve integration. *Management system architecture* is concerned with the role of the information system in the organisation, the breadth and scope of media and media applications, linking the architecture and the system with a business plan, and identifying commodity vendors (based on prices for supplies) and strategic vendors (for partnership), funding, planning and control.

Starting from the architecture of information based on how its form (ie, the shape and structure of the information) and function (ie, its actions or activities) may be portrayed, the matrix in Table 7.1 is instructive. Computer architecture started with processing telephones at the transmission stage.

Three emerging trends are perceived in terms of this information architecture framework (Davis & Davidson, 1991: 196–198). The first trend is a new

Table 7.1. The architecture of information

	Generation	Processing	Storage	Transmission
Data		*		
Text				
Sound				+
Image				

* Computers started here
+ Telephones started here
(*Source:* Adapted from Davis & Davidson (1991: 25))

functionality generated by businesses using information technology to offer something totally new or something to solve old problems, such as using information technology to combat information technology-related crimes as well as conventional crimes. The second trend is the growing realisation that consumption patterns are likely to shift from their past emphasis on tangible physical goods to social goods such as health care, social services and care for the aged. The third trend is a re-emphasis on manufacturing, but with more plant relocations overseas—that is, the new international division of labour noted in chapter 6. The MNC network will be linked by information technology.

Six relationships are discerned in information technology architecture as involving the team of architects; the frameworks, rules and principles to be applied; the models, standards and guidelines to be delivered; the components to be defined; planning to establish the basic requirements and constraints; and the interrelationships to be resolved. The planning process, for instance, involves establishing and maintaining the architectural framework; determining the current baseline; determining the target, direction and standards; developing migration plans; measuring results; and updating the architecture.

The Economics of Networks and Social Capital

The network has made a pervasive entry into economics literature due to a couple of processes (Antonelli, 1992: 5). The first is the ubiquitous revolution of information, communications and technology, including telecommunications networks, which provide the enabling capabilities for all inputs, including information to be effectively and efficiently transmitted. The second is the increasing rediscovery of both static and dynamic externalities, especially where information is concerned. Chapter 5 considered information in general, and computer software and networks in specific, as public goods and even meta public goods. More than pure competition and market forces, information technology and media firms and the industry as a whole are beginning to realise the intricacies of co-operation and co-ordination, such as in architecture and network protocols. A middle-of-the-road approach is co-operative competition or "co-option" where externalities and interdependence are recognised. *Co-option* involves co-operating and competing within a business in an attempt to improve the performance of all parties.

As the age of networks emerges, *social capital*, wherein trust is accumulated, will grow. Trust must exist in teams, corporations, communities and nations. With more trust, more business can be conducted and more wealth is generated. Community-states, such as existed in Athens and other Greek city-states including Florence, Venice, Bologna, Genoa and Milan, thrived on mutual-aid associations. With the invention of credit, savings and investment become linked and enabled more economic growth to take place as wealth is mobilised globally to create more wealth. Credit is the quintessence of trust and, the more trust exists, the more credit is available to propel growth and wealth creation.

Conversely, when confidence and trust break down—such as in the currency and financial crises that erupted in East Asia and Southeast Asia in 1997— growth plummets. Information and communications technology became a bane as it expedited capital mobilisation for speculation, spreading the dreaded contagion effect as well as information that profited speculators. Weak regulatory and supervisory structures proved ineffectual as networks turned perverse. Instead of civic communities where people engage in horizontal relationships, responding to reciprocity and co-operation to give better performance in terms of civic culture, which is all about trust and equality, the government and regulatory authorities had to step in, even if futilely.

Relationships reinforce social capital, which is jointly owned. As more and more relationships are created, transactions costs are lowered and opportunities for productive co-operation rise. Like physical capital, social capital has to be maintained and renewed. The open-loop future (Dizard, 1989) posits four dimensions involving society, technology, economics and politics (STEP) as the ultimate integration.

Social capital accumulates in a virtuous circle as trust develops with reciprocity among people in horizontal networks. When people benefit from an exchange, they continue to contribute to the network in anticipation of more benefits among people whom they now know they can trust. While being selfish is logical and rational, once the fruits of trust based on co-operation have been experienced, co-operation becomes practical and rational too.

All that has been said for civic communities applies just as well to organisations and corporations. Trust in an organisation is built by equalising perks and symbols, and improving the team reward system. Trust across companies—even traditional arch rivals such as Apple, IBM and Motorola that got together to develop a new computer chip—has brought about results that essentially increased social capital. Networks and teamnets create extra value when people get together with a common goal. Information-based co-operation, stakeholder economics and technology investment are the motivations behind teamnets (Vincent, 1990).

A *network* is an agreement to use a common set of standards or protocols (Miller, 1996: 42). *Protocols* are agreed upon ways to control the flow of data through a system, to format data so that zeroes and ones can be translated into meaningful messages to pass instructions from one piece of equipment to the next, and to perform other tasks needed to send communication from one place to another. Examples of networks include the *broadcast network*, a one-way system designed to distribute a single message to a large number of destinations (eg, over-the-air television, radio, cable television), and the *telephone network*, a two-way switched system that allows anyone connected at any point to connect with anyone else.

Intranets on intra-sites allow managers to organise and distribute work across departments, regions and projects, to implement technological change, to monitor employees and to generally connect sites, or even different organisations, through the Internet. Extending the system to branches and partners or communicating with suppliers, distributors and customers create *extranets*. Inter-organisational networking represents a particular form of organising, governing and exchange relationships among organisations (Ebers, 1997: 4).

Such connections also give rise to organisational changes and transformative social effects. With work groups widely distributed geographically, the traditional command hierarchy and culture of organisations inevitably change. Organisations become flatter, with less supervision and greater participation by peripheral employees with access to, and ease of, communication (see chapter 6). The international mobilisation of resources would speed up turnover, innovation and change.

The resulting teamnets and networking join other management buzzwords such as reengineering and the learning organisation, and megatrends such as the global paradox and holonomy (see chapter 8). In each of these, teamnets are an inevitable feature. Reengineering to attain higher quality requires teams to be formed and to implement changes. Networks complement and enhance the concept of reengineering; they do not replace it. A variety of networks exist, including vertical, horizontal, regional, out-of-necessity and self-promoted networks.

The learning organisation, which shows how groups of people use and process information and convert it into knowledge and wisdom, underpins the information age. Senge's five core principles of a learning organisation (personal mastery, mental models, shared vision, team learning and systems thinking) requires teamnets to build the intelligence of a network (see chapter 8).

A *holon* (coined by Arthur Koestler, see chapter 8) is a whole as well as a part. Inevitably, holons lead to systems and networks. In turn, complementary relationships are generated when groups, hierarchies and bureaucracies evolve. In the final analysis, networks provide the bridge between individuals and the group. Mistrust increases transaction costs and, when trust diminishes, prices go up. Trust, reciprocity and networks go up or down together in a mutually reinforcing manner. Trust in organisations between suppliers, customers, competitors, regulators and special interest groups is as equally potent and desirable as it is in nation-states.

ISDN

The *Integrated Services Digital Networks* (ISDNs) is the most important network because it provides integrated service facilities for plain old telephones (POTS), facsimiles, personal computer (PC) connections (eg, local, long distance and global via bearer- and packet-switched channels), local area network (LAN) services, and low-rate telemetering and premises security services (Ahamed & Lawrence 1997: 185). An ISDN may also be connected to mainframe host computers and private branch exchanges (PBXs) on customer premises. Wireless ISDNs—current and future intelligence networks that communicate, control and carry out computations—all have the ultimate goal that any information is available to anyone authorised to receive it at any place, any time (Ahamed & Lawrence 1997: 5). From narrow voice, non-voice, the shift to broadband ISDN for video services, electronic banking and shopping, electronic mail and newspapers, and videoconferencing has been amazing.

The convergence of communications and computation expedited by digitisation using ISDNs will be the wave of the new millennium. However, since it was developed in 1982, the ISDN is more widespread in Japan and continental Europe than in the US (Cairncross, 1997: 53). But Japanese industrial policies for both high definition television (HDTV) and ISDN have not been successful, just as Japan's position in the global information economy has not. There are too many entrenched interests that limit the ability of Japanese policies to adjust to user demand and competition.

Internet

The *Internet*, which stands for inter-network, as an electronic technology that makes connections between people is an extraordinary example of networking. No one controls it, there is no formal management and it is a co-operative effort where anyone with a computer can connect to it. It started as an academic network for exchanging information and data for research, rather than for commercial ends. Users access the Internet via a local area network (LAN) via the telephone network or a dedicated higher-rate circuit with an ISDN connection to their Internet service provider's router (Heldman, 1995: 159–60).

The Internet has grown exponentially since 1983, with an average 10% increase in the number of users each month (Heldman, 1995: 160). By 1995, while long-standing use of the educational (edu) domain has continued to grow, use of the commercial (com) domain has overtaken it to become the leader in the number of hosts, followed by the government (gov) domain in a far third position, then the military (mil) domain and the domain for other organisations (org) (Kiesler, 1997: 23). More than 51% of the 118,000 Internet domain names have been assigned to commercial businesses, with five million servers and ten million people connected to the Internet in 1995 (Bollier, 1996: 2).

Table 7.2 shows the number of Internet users in terms of core Internet users (ie, users of computers that can distribute information through services such as the World Wide Web (WWW)) and consumer Internet users (ie, users of computers that allow access to information through services such as the World Wide Web).

Table 7.2. Internet hosts and users

	Jan 1990	*Jan 1997*	*Jan 2000 forecast*
Internet hosts	188,000	18,000,000	254,000,000
Core Internet users	725,000	36,000,000	438,000,000
Consumer Internet users	1,120,000	57,000,000	707,000,000
E-mail users	3,400,000	71,000,000	827,000,000

(*Source:* Adapted from Cairncross (1997: 88))

Conceptually, the Internet backbone supports databases, stock prices, access providers and users, software, games, movies, news and others. But the Internet is not just making technological connections. More important are the relationships built between people around a shared purpose engendered in Internet culture (Kiesler, 1997; Rosston et al., 1997). Electronic groups, electronic brainstorming, electronic social support groups and the like can be as focused and bounded or as sparse and unbounded as the groups choose to be. Being online is, paradoxically, not abstract and virtual since it can become very personal as well as practical.

The Internet as an economic system is a network of computers and an infrastructural highway of information paths with no usage-based fee and only a connection fee for a server (Cooper et al., 1997: 55–75). A free and open environment policed by the users themselves in enforcing established norms of behaviour is one of its greatest strengths. But there is a growing debate on whether to charge for network services and whether a flat fee incorporating seasonal changes in prices should be considered. No network survives without gateways or connections and network managers or co-ordinators. While people are willing to pay for technology network managers and infrastructural support, the practical question of whether they should remains unanswered (Lipnack et al., 1994).

The economics of the Internet is successful because the Internet is free and cheap. But cyber growth has caused congestion, from academic traffic to commercial traffic with companies setting up intranets within single locations and extranets with branches and partners (*The Economist*, 19 October 1996). The Internet was originally built to avoid the complex accounting and time-and-distance charging of telephone networks, but some charging may be necessary to regulate the huge growth in flows.

Suggested models range from building a second Internet II distinct from the academic Internet I to implementing charges either by use or by flat fees. Comparing the costs of telephone companies and the Internet, which performs the same digitised electronic transmissions as the telephone, would reveal the fundamental reason why one is regulated and the other is not. However, the two are not really competitive as substitutes. The Internet encourages telephone use, which brings in more revenue based on time use and for installing extra telephone lines for surfing.

Nonetheless, the Internet helps bring prices down to reflect their true costs, although the Internet itself does not reflect social costs. The public good and externality features of the Internet suggest market failure but, as congestion rises, pricing will inevitably enter to regulate demand and supply. Congestion occurs, not along the Internet's highways, but at their intersections where routers direct data toward their destinations.

Two laws (as noted in chapter 1) may operate. The first states that the value of a network increases by the square of its users (Metcalfe's Law) and the second states that computer chips double in speed every eighteen months (Moore's Law) (*The Economist*, 19 October 1996). While there is a conflict in the laws, the eventual problem is the same. The very popularity of the Internet means that computer companies as routers will be unable to keep up. With Internet traffic growing three times faster than companies, collisions become inevitable and surfing must slow down to a crawl.

Most specialist Internet services providers are facing financial losses as a result of price wars involving a flat fee pricing system (*The Economist*, 8 March 1997). The overwhelming rise in demand strains capacity, with the added buffet syndrome of overconsumption as users simply stay online permanently. Virtual communication is not that virtual in the final analysis.

The congestion problem is made worse by customers churning around for the current internet service provider of choice. One in seven customers abandons his or her internet service provider, a turnover five times higher than for mobile phones in the US (*The Economist*, 8 March 1997). Industry shakeouts will be particularly savage because of fickle, price-competitive consumer markets. The companies that survive have to be able to combine steady telecommunications revenues with higher margins of media and advertising. This implies more convergence and alliances since current Internet service providers are good at only one of the two areas.

Requests for user services based on the transaction priority is one possible model of pricing. Like any utility, prices act as a congestion toll in which each service requesting to enter the system pays the incremental delay cost imposed by it on all other users. The system reaches an equilibrium in which user expectations are fulfilled on average and demand is equal to the net benefit-maximising level. Logically, the economics of a pricing scheme compared to a free access scheme should show that pricing provides much higher net benefits as the exogenous arrival rate of service requests increases. Net benefits decline under free access due to negative externalities and forecasting errors in predicted waiting times. Optimal pricing reduces such negative externality and forecasting can always be improved.

The Internet is mostly software driven. Today's digital machines, from the personal computer to telecommunications networks, can project an enlarged shape when they are colonised by a new code. The Internet offers a new platform as a fundamental technology to build a new market. The consequence is a booming industry for software, presently controlled by giants. But the Internet, which is both cheap and open, is changing that to favour the small and nimble (*The Economist*, 25 May 1996).

With growing commercial Internet use such as in electronic commerce (see chapter 9), other challenges emerge. The Internet must offer security for banking, financial and credit card information. Privacy is a related issue despite the Internet being on an open environment with messages forwarded through the network. Its capacity is strained by its exponential growth and the network is vulnerable as the type, frequency and duration of use increases. Finally, the survivability of the Internet, since it is no longer an academic network, means that there must be full-time interoperability as new uses grow.

New uses, such as in multimedia, videoconferencing, voice and many others, are very different from the requirements of applications involving data. Being connection-oriented, the new uses are sensitive to delays and tend to have long holding time. As a packet connectionless network, the Internet is presently incapable of supporting such applications.

The free and open Internet is cluttered with users from diverse backgrounds, with disparate and conflicting views regarding appropriate Internet usage. Proper Internet language, etiquette and courtesy have to be consciously developed and self-regulated. Abuses may destroy the Internet since it lacks effective management and structure. The paradox is that the Internet cannot be effectively managed and controlled as a simple store-and-forward packet network. As a precursor to a public data network, the Internet must become the right network with the right capabilities to enable the continued dynamic growth of voice, data and video services.

The unifying purpose that keeps a network together has a number of requirements. First and foremost, as a meta public good (see chapter 5), independent members who stand on their own must realise that they benefit as part of the whole network. Thus, voluntary links, which increase and develop relationships, to reduce costs and generate opportunities must evolve. Also, multiple leaders in a network must emerge to increase resilience and provide *de facto* management or self-regulation. Integrated levels and co-operation on the Internet has the virtue of marrying hierarchy with various levels of small groups and coalitions.

To reiterate, a fundamental ingredient in networking is the concept of trust and social capital, which must be built up and used to generate more prosperity such as other forms of physical capital. Making everyone feel that they are part of a team and leaders in their own right would generate more holistic, integrated views and solutions.

Electronic commerce

New ways of reaching customers started with the telephone or telemarketing, via toll-free calling, and moved to television marketing as broadcasting advertisement by satellite television augmented sales of hotels, airlines, credit card companies, mail-order firms, vehicle-recovery services, call-back services and many others (Cairncross, 1997: 126–153). The Internet provides a wider global marketplace, expanding the narrow market of television marketing. Two tools of global commerce, namely, on-screen advertisement and toll-free numbers to the Internet, have become one under *electronic commerce* or online commerce. Internet users are wealthy, intelligent individuals, especially young males who are professionals, managers and executives and, most of all, technologically savvy.

Distance shopping evokes a culture, economies of cost and convenience. Electronic commerce is infinite in providing an assemblage of information to be winnowed and packaged, and yet it connects people in intimate ways (Bollier, 1996; Rosston et al., 1997; Dorn, 1997). More specifically, the advantages of electronic commerce include lower entry barriers as the Internet cuts costs, in terms of marketing (with better customer information) and distribution. Some goods are delivered electronically such as in computer games, software and newspapers. Online delivery is also an inexpensive way to test the market for new products. Outside the technology sector, electronic commerce is making a large impact on financial services, travel, retailing, music, cars, advertising and marketing (*The Economist*, 10 May 1997).

Better customer information comes with improved communication as customers are alerted to new products and product changes. In fact, the customer contributes to production and innovation by providing invaluable feedback and sharing some of the product tracking information available within a company. They become quasi-collaborators in product development and improvement. A new consumer sovereignty comes with the shift of bargaining power from the supply side to the demand side as consumers are empowered to seek out a large universe of sellers.

The costs of distributing information in catalogues and postage are reduced by online delivery. Small companies appreciate these cost reductions most;

they can be global niche players since there is equity in this respect regardless of company size.

More efficient markets are created by electronic commerce since, where prices are available, buyers can search easily for the lowest price. In auctions, the Internet widens the number of bidders. For customers who do not necessarily want the least expensive price and who consider quality, proximity, servicing and delivery dates as more important criteria, online trading is no less useful.

Electronic commerce may cut down on the need for agents and intermediaries if buyers have access to online information. But agents can reengineer themselves to play a different role to take advantage of the new way companies are formed or to help individuals faced with information overload. Specialist, customised advice will always be on demand as sellers compete, not on price, but on convenience, quality of service and comprehensiveness. Intermediaries will remain in demand if they realise that success is no longer premised on accessibility to information but on the skills to interpret and market it. New intermediaries will arise in the form of navigational tools and aids or software to locate information. Moreover, the subtle way in which an intermediary or agent also acts as a guarantor between buyers and sellers should not be underestimated, especially in more complex and new transactions.

Lower distribution costs for many products are enjoyed such as in financial services, computer games, software, gambling, adult entertainment and pornographic products, videos, airline tickets and all sorts of electronic publishing. In areas where piracy is a problem, such as in the music and recording industry, companies may be more reserved in using electronic distribution to save costs.

Electronic commerce promises global reach with toll-free numbers and the Internet. An unprecedented range of choices and level of price competition is offered to customers. Technical, but not insurmountable, problems such as culture, language, standards (eg, voltage, sizing), servicing and the need for local distribution will, however, not stop electronic commerce.

The value-added features of electronic commerce include a reduction in navigation and search costs, an "economising of trust" as Internet-mediated commerce is viewed as safe and easy for strangers to conduct transactions, collaboration that goes beyond episodic transactions, the creation of user-friendly interfaces, an increase in the value of time and ubiquitous access (Bollier, 1996).

Problems do exist regarding customs controls and taxation. With over-the-wire transactions, tangible inspections by customs for illegal exchanges and transactions, such as pornographic materials, is restricted. Cyberlaws have to be enacted as noted in chapter 11.

Tax collection becomes difficult if sellers and buyers cannot be identified and has to be voluntary. A physical presence has to be established for out-of-state vendors and one possibility is to make the local server somehow accountable. Whatever the future tax regime, it cannot be burdensome; complicated accounting requirements add to costs and impede transactions. Barter trade, underground transactions and evasion are better fended off with a simple system that attracts taxpayer compliance.

Regulators also worry about consumer protection, global advertisement and distribution, privacy, intellectual property rights, competition, censorship, health standards and fraud. Buyers may eventually have to protect themselves by signing up with national consumer protection groups and schemes. Reputable companies would see such protection as a value-added service and consider it voluntary, necessary and even a competitive advantage. Regulators should devise consumer protection schemes at reasonable costs without restraining consumer choice.

Electronic payments, including the use of credit cards, are subject to security concerns, but these concerns have largely been dispelled with the development of encryption techniques. However, the use of credit cards for micropayments in small amounts may not be ideal for online sellers. New forms of electronic currency to reduce the anonymity of transactions and minimise record keeping are sought to make electronic currency universally acceptable, secure and untraceable. Microtransactions may be compared to the telephone billing system, which is optimised to process high volumes of small specific transactions.

Corporate structures and corporate employment policies and practices will be affected as electronic commerce catches on. The way companies define their relationships with suppliers, distributors and customers affects how they communicate with branches and offices, monitor sales and replenish stocks. Intranets with the same software and network equipment run on private networks within companies and allow employees to break down communication barriers. Business decisions accelerates and management culture changes with the Internet.

As the culture of the virtual marketplace and issues concerning security and congestion remain to be smoothed over, sales using electronic commerce is dominated by business-to-business transactions. They are followed by computer, book and music sales.

The globalisation of technology

Information technology is a prime candidate for techno-globalism, which encompasses three categories in taxanomy. They are the global exploitation of technology such as in the extension of patents into foreign markets, global technological collaboration such as in inter-firm R&D agreements, and the global generation of technology such as patents granted in the US to foreign forms (Archibugi et al., 1995). While the third, lending legitimacy to inventions originating from less credible countries for production and exporting purposes, may be a bit questionable except in advanced countries such as the US, the results from the first two are very significant. Techno-economic networks belong to a category of meso-systems or intermediate systems that are neither local nor national.

Crossborder networks in informational technology are where the globalisation of technology challenges national systems of innovation. At the same time, each actor in such a network can contribute to various networks or meso-systems while remaining an actor within its nation or societal system. In crossborder techno-economic networks as shown in Fig. 7.9, the innovation process results from interactions between people, firms and institutions with citizens in their own countries. This is where globalisation is challenging national systems of innovation. Leading industries that are information technology-intensive with crossborder networks tend to be oligopolistic. Through direct investment, international alliances and agreements, they are in countries where governments are also acting to boost their technology scales. Whereas such industries form meso-systems at a global level, shaping the world's technology and industrial trajectory, national societal systems involved in the techno-industrial trajectory may not fit that of the world.

Various national, societal systems may have differences. For example, a developing country may be keen to get industrialised with technology but may not want the democracy associated with the capitalist sources of such technology (Nielson et al., 1998: 101). On the other hand, technology is neutral and need not be nation-specific except where the institutional set-up may hinder technology transfer or absorption.

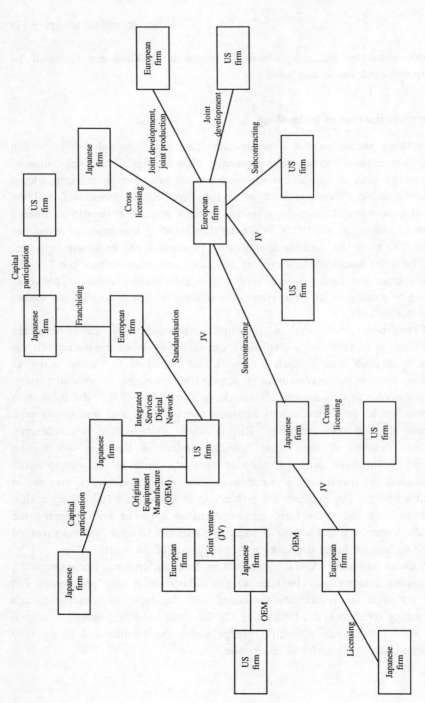

Fig. 7.9. A hypothetical crossborder technology network

Chapter 8

Information Management

Introduction

Having established in preceding chapters that information is a valuable but scarce resource and asset, it is logical that information has to be effectively and properly managed. Moreover, with the convergence of technology and the growth of networks as noted in chapter 7, information management becomes imperative as users and producers wade through the labyrinth of systems, networks, media and languages. Change management revolves around three distinct but related concepts: reengineering, business process reengineering (BPR) and the learning organisation. These will be explored in detail as they provide the basis and *raison d'être* for information management.

This chapter will also present tools for information management as in benchmarking, information and communications audits, total quality management (TQM), business process reengineering and others. Strategic information management to maximise the synergy and strength of multimedia is a concern at both micro (corporate) and macro (national) levels.

The Nature of Information Management

Concepts and definitions

Information is an asset and a resource. Information as a resource is a public good (see chapter 5), which presents difficulties of appropriation and ownership. To ensure a continuous supply of information, its value has to be maximised, its cost minimised and it must be made accountable. Information as a resource covers all expenses which go into establishing and operating information resource entities such as libraries and statistical offices. In contrast, information as an asset depicts the content of the information or the value obtained from using the information.

Management is a process of achieving organisational goals through others, emphasising resource acquisition and co-ordination. Human resource management has moved to the frontline of management, as people must be imbued with strong cultural values of honesty, trust and respect. Open communication and knowledge sharing are cornerstones of human resource management. The idea is for *human resource management* to be based on an appreciation of human potential, a conviction that when people are freed from the limitations of narrow, fragmented jobs, they are capable (with education) of full ownership of the new work. The first managerial revolution is about the transfer of power. The second is about freedom. Free enterprise is really free: markets are wide open, anybody can participate. Customers with purchasing power and choice, resulting in consumer sovereignty, are free to pick and choose. Businesses are free from shackles of government control, regulation and protection.

Information management is the stewardship of an organisation's information resources and assets in pursuit of its aims and objectives. This involves inventory, defined requirements, accountability for safe keeping, costs, value and results. *Strategic information management* involves corporate executives, information technology managers, business and human resource managers and users of services. A *strategic information system* comprises vehicles to implement business strategy using information, information processing, and/or the communication of information to compete. The aim is to maximise intelligent use of information to achieve cost minimisation, quality improvement and customer responsiveness. *Information value management* highlights the importance of shifting from a perspective based on costs and cost control to one based on realising the value of an organisation's total information assets. A wider approach to assessing the rate of return (ROI) is to justify expenditures, including qualitative and intangible factors.

Information technology management skills include: the development of reliable, timely and cost effective applications; the management of reliable and responsive data-processing operations; the appropriate management of human resources in information technology; the integration of long-range and tactical business and information technology planning processes; the ability of senior management to value information technology activities and initiatives; and cultivating harmonious and trustful relationships among business and information technology managers (Sauer et al., 1997: 144). *Management competencies* are defined as unique skills and knowledge which a firm possesses and its rivals find difficult to imitate and replicate. Product-market strategies are a reflection of a firm's manoeuvres to enable its most valued competencies to exploit market opportunities and influence competitive terrain (Sauer et al., 1997: 146).

Managing change

Information technology specialists refer to themselves as *change agents* by virtue of their identification with the technology they create, implying a belief that technology creates change or that technology is imperative (Sauer et al., 1997: 118). Having created change-producing technology, they deem themselves as having no other responsibility for organisational change. The ability of technology, rather than people, to cause change is obviously a one-sided affair no matter how powerful the technology.

The change agent may have designed and built the systems which enable organisations and people to do things previously thought unattainable, but the goals and outcomes of change remain to be set by managers who can incorporate the technology into business and behavioural regimes. Technical, organisational, managerial and human resource specialists must come together to make information technology work.

Change advocacy is different from change management. *Technology advocacy*, in terms of the promotion of technology and technological solutions to organisational problems, is tolerated so long as advocates or champions do not venture outside their spheres of influence. But boundaries of influence are bound to be crossed in major change efforts. An inevitable clash may occur between information technology specialists on the one hand and management and executives on the other if line managers, for instance, want to continue doing business without interference from other functions and staff groups. Here, the will to collaborate is more vital than the means of collaboration.

Change management involves the sponsoring manager acquiring the necessary resources, managing the project, providing the vision, defining the requirements, implementing the system, obtaining business benefits and championing the system (Martin et al., 1994: 442). Familiarity, while not necessarily breeding contempt, symbolises comfort and acceptance. Changes in attitude and feelings take time, requiring some sort of unfreezing when a felt need for change is established, moving the change and refreezing to fix the new behaviour and routine. Trial and evaluation can come in between, before the final adoption.

But, as with all changes, barriers include: breaking down human resistance; setting standards; providing interfaces between new and existing hardware, operating systems and data structures; and resolving issues such as security, integrity and ownership, financial justification and politics (as political power and interests come with information).

Change and progress

Change enables progress and prosperity. Initiating change to create wealth is a moral act. Seven ways of wealth creation are identified (Hampden-Turner & Trompenaars, 1993: 6–9).[1] Each process represents a tension and dilemma: universalism versus particularism, analysing versus integrating, individualism versus communitarianism, inner-directed versus outer-directed orientation, sequential time versus telescoped time, achieved status versus ascribed status and equality versus hierarchy.

In a study of managers from twelve countries on time-as-sequenced and time-as-telescoped, Americans were the most sequential of the cultures surveyed. In contrast, Japanese managers were synchronised, had more condensed time than any other group and maintained a direction toward the future (Hampden-Turner & Trompenaars, 1993: 76–77). A sequential approach to time reflects a country in a hurry: time management is crucial and views are short term rather than long term. Nonetheless, Japanese managers were strongest in long-term thinking; the Japanese hold a consistent competitive advantage in this area. South Koreans and Germans followed next to Japan in synchronous thinking. Managers from the UK, Belgium and Italy had the past and the present telescoped to some extent, as did Singapore managers, but the spatial distance between present and future is nearer for the three European

---

[1] The seven ways to create wealth are: 1) to make rules and discover exceptions, universalism reconciled with particularism; 2) to construct and deconstruct in order to examine for defects and improvements; 3) to manage communities of individuals by harnessing their initiative, drive and energy needed by the community; 4) to internalise the outside world, inner-direction reconciled with outer-direction; 5) to synchronise fast processes to do tasks swiftly and at the same time create an integrity of sequential time and synchronised time to get to the market first; 6) to choose among achievers, recognise what is worth achieving and recognise persons setting these goals and 7) to sponsor equal opportunities to excel (Hampden-Turner & Trompenaars, 1993: 6–9).

countries, denoting some telescoping. This implies that while the Singapore managers' thinking about the past and the present was synchronous to some extent (though not as deeply as the Japanese), they were more sequential with respect to the present and the future.

Reengineering

Definition

A quick definition of *reengineering* is starting over, not tinkering for incremental changes that leave basic structures intact. It means abandoning long-established procedures and looking afresh at the work required to create a company's product or service and to deliver value to the customer.

Formally defined, "reengineering is the *fundamental* rethinking and *radical* redesign of business processes to achieve *dramatic* improvements in critical, contemporary measures of performance, such as cost, quality, service and speed" (Hammer & Champy, 1993; see also Champy, 1995; Hammer et al., 1995; Hammer, 1996). The key words by the authors have to be emphasised.

Reengineering has to be fundamental. Why do we do what we do? Why do we do it the way we do? Reengineering begins with no assumptions, no givens. The first task is to determine what a company must do and how to do it. Reengineering ignores what is and concentrates on what it should be. Reengineering has to be radical; it must get to the root of things. The key is business reinvention, not business improvement, enhancement or modification. It is dramatic, not marginal or incremental in its improvement. It is about achieving.

Reengineering and work

In economics parlance, the world is no longer ruled by traditional economies of scale and Adam Smith's division of labour and specialisation applied in scientific management under Taylorism (Giodarno, 1992) and mass production under Fordism. Instead, economies of scope, reengineering and business process reengineering (see Chawla et al., 1995; Wheatley, 1992 and others) predominate. As discussed in the foregoing chapters, the catalysts for such change include globalisation, competition and international competitiveness which have both perils and promise. Current restructuring and employment trends are epitomised in new management techniques, the most dramatic of which is reengineering.

In reengineering terminology, three C's (ie, customers, competition and change) separately and in combination render Adam Smith's world and its way of doing business a bygone paradigm. Customers have to be treated individually as they have higher expectations, access to more information and communications technologies and can be choosy as they know what they want, what they will pay and how to get it on terms they demand. Competition is not only of greater intensity. *Niche competition* to sell similar goods in different markets on disparate competitive bases (eg, price, selection, quality and service) is another new trend.

Technology changes competition, merges distribution and inventory systems and forces the development of new service techniques. Change becomes constant, pervasive and persistent, accelerated by globalisation, competition and rapid technological change and innovation. Technology, product and service life cycles are shortened or diminished as just-in-time production is in vogue with time to market practices.

Some corporations will not survive but their failures cannot be blamed merely on closed foreign markets, the low cost of capital, predatory pricing by foreign companies with government subsidies, federal mismanagement of the economy, government regulations, poor husbandry of natural and human resources, poorly educated and unmotivated workers, unions or other causes. The responsibility rests squarely on corporate strategies, not just management deficiencies. Management theories including management by objective, diversification, Theory Z, zero-based budgeting, value chain analysis, decentralisation, quality circles, the pursuit of excellence, restructuring, portfolio management, intrapreneuring (Dance, 1994), one-minute management and such have only distracted managers from the real task of treating symptoms rather than causes.

In moving away from task-oriented jobs, companies must organise work around processes. Reengineering is not downsizing or restructuring, not automation or software reengineering, not reorganising, delayering or flattening an organisation, not quality improvement, not total quality management (TQM; see later section) or any manifestations of contemporary quality improvement.

Themes in all cases of reengineering include process orientation, ambition, rule-breaking and creative use of information technology. Other recurring themes in reengineering involve work and workers. Several jobs are combined into one and workers make decisions. Work is performed where it makes the most sense; this involves shifting organisational boundaries. Checks and controls are reduced and reconciliation is minimised. A manager provides a single point of contact and a hybrid of centralised and decentralised operations is prevalent.

Reengineering begins with the strategic imperative to anticipate—or better yet—to initiate the currents and cross-currents of customer demands, needs and wants. The market may be market-driven but customers may not always know what they want until they see it. The chief executive officer's (CEO's) task is to re-examine and restate the business purpose and decide when to reengineer (usually when pushed by greed and fear). Everybody must be told, including managers, non-managers, vendors, investors, customers and the surrounding community.

The leader in reengineering is one who can compel compliance from all parties and who has authority over the entire end-to-end process to be reengineered. The chief operating officer (COO), not the CEO, is usually the leader. The CEO typically deals with issues relating to external constituencies, the COO with internal operating issues. The leader can also be a divisional general manager who heads a business unit or an executive vice president with responsibility over a broad area of the organisation. Reengineering cannot be led by staff executives like chief financial officers (CFOs) and those who have no line responsibility or full control over major processes. Likewise, sectional functional heads such as senior vice presidents will not have the leverage to lead.

The decision to reengineer comes from a leader who is basically self-anointed, based on personal experience, intuition and wisdom. But reengineering is not a one-person show. The leader must enlist a team of process owners, team members and staff assistants, and create an environment to transform the mindset and attitudes of the people.

Three types of companies need reengineering. Those in deep trouble have no choice. Those not yet in trouble, but whose management has the foresight to see trouble coming, reengineer proactively. Even ambitious and aggressive companies in peak condition would have management think about reengineering. Companies in the first category have started reengineering and are injured as seen in chapter 6. The second category of companies cruise at high speed but see something rushing towards them. The third type drive along with no obstacles but are wise to stop and build a wall for others in competition.

Reengineering also applies to government and other public agencies. The bigger challenges include measuring performance, breaking down departmental barriers and politics. Also, managing a country is different from running a company, and government heads are often policy people with little experience with operations. Socio-political considerations are not amenable to profit maximisation as the sole criterion and, if it is not to abnegate its mandate, the government is the provider of last resort to the community at large.

In the new world of employment, jobs are evolving from narrow, task-oriented duties to multidimensional work. As jobs change along with the people needed to fill them, the relationships people have with their managers, their career paths, the ways the roles of managers and executives and even what goes on in workers' heads, will alter. Executives and managers must change from thinking deductively (ie, to define a problem and then seek and evaluate different solutions) to inductive thinking with information. Reengineering demands the ability to recognise a powerful solution and then seek problems it might solve as technology creates its own demand in a reinterpretation of Say's Law.

Reengineering and unions

Reengineering can succeed in an unionised environment as it is not organised labour which tries to scuttle reengineering but middle management whose power and turf are likely to be diminished. Bad industrial relations, a bad history or previous downsizing can sharpen people's sense of job insecurity. While some jobs may be lost, reengineering is for reorganising work, not eliminating workers, and it is best to get people engaged in the process as early as possible.

Unionised companies that have successfully reengineered themselves typically involved union leadership in the process from the outset. When union resistance develops, however, a strategy of firm commitment is a company's only choice while it continues to keep employees, unionised or not, engaged in the process. Union leadership that understands reengineering and why it is being done is less likely to call for a strike.

Management needs to abandon the old ideology and thinking about power. The democracy of customers voting with their money summons a meritocracy of people and producers. The hardest part of reengineering is living through change, getting people to let go of old ways and to embrace new ones. A set of principles and techniques to deal with the resistance to change is needed.

A business diamond

When a company reengineers its business process, a *business diamond* as shown in Fig. 8.1 depicts the relationships connecting the business process, values and beliefs, management and measure systems and jobs and structure. Changes from reengineering affect people, jobs, managers and values. These key elements are shown below.

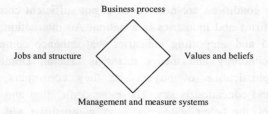

Fig. 8.1. A business diamond

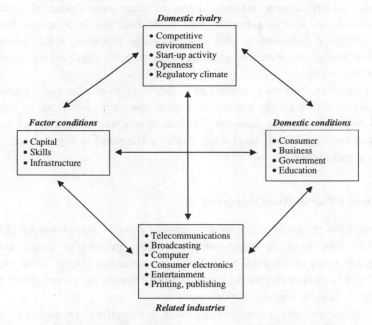

Fig. 8.2. Porter's Diamond in information technology and the media

Porter's diamond

The business diamond (see Fig. 8.1), depicting components of business process reengineering within a firm, has a parallel in the larger context of global competition. *Porter's Diamond* (see Fig. 8.2) uses the business diamond as a framework to analyse factors determining the competitive advantages of nations competing in information technology and the media (Porter, 1990).

Basic factor conditions are necessary but not sufficient competitive factors for successful firms and industries in a nation. An internationally competitive layer of related and supporting industries that enhance competencies in the information technology and media sector is crucial. Domestic conditions affect the sophistication of buyers—be they consumers, businesses or government—and education is key. The more demanding and challenging the domestic market, the better honed and more competitive will be the industry and the nation as they first cut their teeth at home before venturing abroad.

One crucial success factor in Japan's electronics industry is the intense domestic rivalry among Japanese firms in their export-oriented pattern of industrialisation. The oligopolistic system of keiretsus is a unique blend of fierce domestic competition and self-regulatory practices which manage to keep out foreign competition while Japanese exports aggressively invade the rest of the world.

Put together, Porter's Diamond of competitive advantage has an important implication: with the right national strategies, competitiveness can be enhanced on all four sides of the diamond. The business diamond in Fig. 8.1 forms a subset at the micro, firm level while Porter's Diamond in Fig. 8.2 reflects the industry and the nation.

Business Process Reengineering

Shifting from products to processes, *business process reengineering* (BPR) is a radical rethink of an organisation's business process to focus on value adding processes which deliver satisfaction to customers (Drew, 1994; McHugh et al., 1995). Business process reengineering focuses on a company's efforts relating to its core business processes.

Business process reengineering and information technology-enabled organisational changes may still founder on human aspects, notably in radical changes to the skills, training and jobs needed to reach across functional and organisational boundaries. Human resistance may threaten culture, resources, authority, power and shifts in knowledge and power as people's roles and skills become embedded in data and knowledge bases (Sauer et al., 1997: 116–117).

With respect to business process reengineering, total enterprise management has three features (McHugh et al., 1995). The first is virtual as teamwork crosses boundaries of functional departments and/or established companies. The second feature is the ability to respond rapidly, as everything becomes just in time. The third is holonic, involving autonomous distributed systems whether computer or human.

A *holonic network* is a set of companies that acts integratedly and organically; it is constantly reconfigured to manage each business opportunity a customer presents. Each company in the network provides a different process capability and is called a *holon*. Each configuration of process capabilities within the holonic network is called a *virtual company*.

A holonic business system is an extension of business process reengineering and thus goes beyond business process reengineering. The advantage of a holonic business system includes leverage, speed, flexibility, shared risk, independence, faster growth and increased profits, sustainable customers, less capital requirements, quick failure recognition and the increased ability to deal with inevitable change.

Learning Organisations

Inherent in reengineering and business process reengineering is an imperative to learn and change. Seven learning disabilities have been identified (Senge, 1990). The first is reflected by the statement "I am my position", implying a focus only on one's own position with little sense of responsibility for results produced when all positions interact.

The second statement, "the enemy is out there", is a by-product of the above and the non-systemic ways of looking at the world that it fosters. For instance, to American companies, the "enemy" has become Japanese competition.

Third is the illusion of taking charge, as proactiveness is simply reactiveness disguised as more aggressive fighting of "the enemy out there". True proactiveness comes from seeing how people contribute to their own problems. It is a product of a way of thinking, not an emotional state.

The fourth learning disability lies in a fixation on events, which is part of our evolutionary programming. But the primary threat today comes not from sudden events but from slow gradual processes. If thinking is dominated by short-term events, the best one can ever do is to predict an event before it happens so one can react optimally. But one cannot learn to create.

The fifth learning disability lies in the parable of the boiled frog. If a frog is placed in boiling water, it immediately jumps out. But if the temperature is gradually increased, the frog may not sense it in time to escape. A good example is the Big Three automobile manufacturers in the US. They did not see Japan's threat in 1962 when the Japanese share of the US car market was only 4%. By 1989, it reached 30%. The moral of the story is that learning to see slow, gradual processes requires slowing down and paying attention to subtle as well as dramatic changes.

Sixth is the delusion of learning from experience because one never directly experiences the consequences of many important decisions. There is an inherent difficulty in observing the consequences of actions. Once actions have consequences beyond the "learning horizon", it becomes impossible to learn from experience. The learning horizon is the breadth of vision and time within which one can assess effectiveness.

Finally, there is the myth of a cohesive management team, which in reality spends time fighting for turf, avoiding anything that makes them look bad. The team functions well with routine issues but not complex ones that may be threatening or embarrassing.

Being prisoners of systems or prisoners of one's own thinking can be explained at three levels. The first level, the most common in contemporary culture, is when reactive management prevails. The second level focuses on seeing longer-term trends and assessing their implications, suggesting how a response to shifting trends in the long term occurs. It is not merely reactive. The third level is the least common and most powerful. Its focuses on systems structure and on answering the question, "what causes patterns of behaviour?" It is generative, not reactive or responsive as in levels one and two respectively.

Systems thinking

Five new "component technologies" are converging to innovate learning organisations (Senge, 1990). The first is *systems thinking* which is a conceptual framework, body of language and set of tools developed over the past fifty years to make full patterns clearer and to help managers see how to change them effectively. Shifting the mind is a Galilean shift. Systems thinking is a discipline for seeing wholes, a framework for seeing relationships rather than things. It deals with both detail complexity and dynamic complexity. The essence of systems thinking lies in seeing interrelationships rather than linear cause-and-effect chains, and seeing processes of change rather than snapshots.

Personal mastery

The second technology, *personal mastery*, involves continually clarifying and deepening one's personal vision, focusing energies, developing patience and seeing reality objectively. Personal mastery is a discipline for personal growth and learning. Mastery is ground in competence and skills but goes beyond them and beyond spiritual unfolding or opening. It means approaching one's life as creative work, living life from a creative, as opposed to reactive, viewpoint.

There are two underlying movements: first, continually clarifying what is important and, second, continually learning to see current reality more clearly. The juxtaposition is between a vision, as in what is wanted, and a clear picture of current reality, that is, in vision being relative to the existing situation. This generates a creative tension as a force to bring them together to seek resolution. The essence of personal mastery is learning how to generate and sustain creative tension.

A basic characteristic of people with high personal mastery is a special sense of purpose that lies behind their visions and goals, where vision is a calling rather than simply a good idea. In addition, such people live in a continual learning mode, never having "arrived" but being engaged in a process rather than with something already possessed.

Mental models

Mental models are ingrained assumptions, or even general pictures or images, that influence how one understands the world and acts. The best ideas fail because new insights conflict with deeply held internal images of how the world works, images that limit managers to familiar ways of thinking and acting. Mental models allow surfacing, testing and improving internal pictures of how the world works. Nothing is right or wrong about mental models; they are all simplifications. One example is Shell's group planning method that developed scenario planning as a way to summarise alternative future trends. This method targets microcosms or mental models rather than a documented view of the future.

The elements of mental models are: first, to recast traditional planning as learning and to establish internal boards of directors to bring senior and local managers together regularly and, second, to develop skills of reflection by slowing down one's thinking and becoming more aware of the mental models formed and the skills of inquiry used.

Shared vision

Building a *shared vision* of the future involves people seeking to create. It stresses genuine vision (as opposed to vision statements) where people excel and learn not because they are told to, but because they want to. If an individual's or group's vision is imposed on an organisation, at best, it commands compliance, not commitment. A shared vision is one that many people are truly committed to because it reflects their own personal vision.

Shared visions are extrinsic (focusing on achieving something relative to an outsider such as a competitor) and intrinsic (uplifting people's aspirations). They are exhilarating, compel courage and foster risk taking, experimentation and long-term commitment. They emerge from personal visions; they are not top-down, one-shot, or solutions to a problem. Visions have to be infectious to bring about enrolment, commitment and compliance, and they must be spread with a reinforcing process of increasing clarity, communication and enthusiasm.

Team learning

Team learning starts with a dialogue, as opposed to a discussion. A dialogue is a free creative exploration of complex and subtle issues, a deep listening to one another and suspension of one's views. In a discussion, different views are presented and defended in a search for the best view to support the decisions to be made. Team learning is the process of aligning and developing the capacity of a team to create the results its members truly desire. It builds shared vision, personal mastery and camaraderie.

Three critical dimensions comprise the ability to think insightfully about complex issues: innovative action, co-ordinated action and the role of team members on other teams. Thinking creatively invokes and must be followed by innovative action. In turn, the process must be co-ordinated for maximum impact. Synergy between teams require a higher level of action and co-ordination, and that is the value of a team as a driving force. Though it involves individual skills and areas of understanding, team learning is a collective discipline.

Tools for Information Management

The foregoing described implicit tools and strategies for information management, including business process reengineering, the five principles behind a learning organisation and general information on how to compete in the rapidly changing corporate world. More detailed information on management tools can be found in management literature and only a selected few are highlighted in this chapter.

Information audits

Auditing is a combination of data processing and accounting where, in the process, tests are run to ensure that high quality systems and procedures are functioning properly. Electronic data processing (EDP) auditing combines data processing controls with classical accounting methods including compliance tests, statistical sampling and others.

Information audits use either a cost-benefit analysis (CBA), which is systems oriented, or a geographical approach, which identifies major components and maps them in relation to each other. A hybrid approach combines a cost-benefit analysis with the geographical approach. An operational advisory audit determines the purpose of a system and its success in meeting objectives. Communications audits facilitate comparisons of the state of communications within an organisation measured against a set of criteria of softer human variables.

A cost-benefit analysis attempts to assess in advance whether returns from a particular action outweigh all the costs. Both benefits (returns) and costs may involve tangible and intangible ones, externalities and opportunity costs; many of these are difficult to measure. Finding a right rate of discount to obtain the net present value for comparing benefits with costs is also critical. Other non-economic factors (eg, socio-political) may constitute the operating imperatives rather than a pure CBA.

A just-in-time (JIT) inventory system gets materials from a supplier exactly when they are needed to minimise inventory and holding costs and to increase product quality and plant productivity. While JIT pushes inventory costs to suppliers, the responsibility for inventory control is pushed up the whole distribution channel. The danger lies in times of rapid or unexpected production fluctuations where JIT can leave a company without sufficient capacity to maintain supplies to its customers.

Benchmarking

Benchmarking is based on the premise that customer satisfaction can be achieved by continuously improving processes that support customers. This is done by measuring and comparing the performance of an existing process with those of industry-recognised top performers. It is a search for industry best practices that lead to superior performances. Benchmarking involves learning from companies that are the best at something and emulating them. The problem is it predisposes reengineering teams to follow what has been done before and to aspire only to being as good as the best in the industry. It is a tool for catching up not jumping ahead, but it can spark ideas that create a new world-class benchmark.

Other tools

Business process reengineering as a management tool is the task of reconstructing processes in order to achieve radical improvements in business effectiveness. It is different from *total quality management* (TQM) which is characterised by commitment, ingenuity and employee empowerment linked to placing responsibility for improvements with frontline staff. In TQM, quality means meeting or exceeding customers' requirements. It combines hard statistical tools like flow charts and process controls with soft features such as teamwork and empowerment.

Reengineering and TQM are neither identical nor in conflict but complementary. Reengineering is dramatic. TQM is slower, involving incremental adjustments as it tunes up a company in between periodic process replacements that only reengineering can accomplish. But TQM for efficiency may have its shortcomings in destroying skills and contracts developed over the years, affecting innovation and institutional memory which resides in experience. Reengineering may have greater claims to new skills as old ones outlive their time.

Part III

Public Policy and the Global Economy

Chapter 9

National Information Policy

Introduction

This chapter looks at a national information policy and how it ties in with global and international policies on information and communications, which are discussed in the next chapter. Chapter 5 established a definite role for the government as a protector and provider of information for all citizens. Apart from technical and quality standards, national information policy also involves economic and other softer socio-political aspects. The marketplace will increasingly have a greater impact on such policy due to consumer demand and technological developments.

Thus, in all aspects of growth and development, a national information policy supported by a national information infrastructure (NII) is imperative. Not all developing countries will have the resources, wherewithal and priority to formulate and implement a national information policy and a national information infrastructure before other more urgent tasks are undertaken.[1] Physical infrastructure, rather than information infrastructure (infostructure), may easily take precedence.

A Framework for a National Information Policy

A *national information policy* is to ensure the effective and efficient flow of information for economic, social and political functions, and to ensure universality and access for all citizens. It means ensuring an open and competitive system and infrastructure for all. Whether the policy is for

---

[1] See Kahin et al. (1997) for country reports on national information infrastructures in Asia, North America, Europe and other developing countries.

traditional information, or electronic information to be communicated, the goal is immutable. Universal connectivity and operability, such as with the traditional postmaster general, is to ensure that all citizens are able to communicate with each other for commercial or social reasons. Postal rates are thus uniform with the same standards of service and a national distribution system assured. When telegraphic and electronic means of communication entered, the principles remain unchanged and immutable, extending services nationally and internationally with telephony, radio and television networks.

Common elements in any national information policy would thus include being open, accessible, universal and flexible. An open architecture, as discussed in chapter 7, allows digital networks to transport digitised voice, text, data and images with equal facility with two-way connectivity and interoperability. *Open architecture* is a prerequisite for a competitive information marketplace since flexible interconnection enables suppliers and customers to have a wide range of applications and functions performed through advanced networks.

Open access means interconnection and the elimination of regulatory barriers to allow as many competitive paths as possible to get into workplaces and homes. Competition, including contestable markets, would again help ensure honest suppliers and affordable prices charged close to marginal costs. Technology such as in wireless access will enhance personal communications services, which has become increasingly more mobile. Rationalising and revamping regulations is a necessary step to open access.

The principle of *universal access* for basic services entails cross subsidisation where necessary such that uneconomical low-density routes are provided for by creaming or skimming profitable high-density routes. Deregulation may threaten universal access since competition deprives more remote areas and those less privileged if they cannot afford market prices. But even where private provision or market-based organisations are involved, universality can be assured by user rate regulations and other stipulations of service. The emphasis is on universal access, not universal service, though the term universal is a very political one. The biggest test of universal access or service is getting on the Internet, or national information infrastructure.

Flexible access means an interconnected and interoperable network of telecommunications, broadcasting and electronic publishing possibilities. Bandwidths can be adjusted according to consumer demand and the medium of communication. Design and provision will affect flexible access; light-handed regulation can assure that a variety of services will be available whatever the configuration and specifications.

Regulation affects each of these four elements (ie, being open, accessible, universal and flexible) of a national information policy. It is argued either away totally or for a lighter, more sensitive touch to ensure that the goals are met. Each country will have its own set-up in terms of regulatory agencies, but it is recognised that strong, effective institutional support with the right staff are vital to the successful implementation of national information policy. Regulators will always be in a fight against time, scarce financial resources and vested interests in deciding what is the collective good and other considerations, as in all cases of public policy-making.

The government should further ensure the efficient use of the limited electromagnetic spectrum resource, domestic allocation of the spectrum to various types of services, technical standards regarding the use of the spectrum and the assignment of licences. Privacy rights and the ownership of information are also the government's responsibility, together with content regulation with an implied degree of public sanction and the trust of users.

Advances in information technology may have affected the dependence of citizens on governments for some of these prescriptions of a national information policy. In fact, it may even have enabled some governments to get around with strict censorship, for instance. Universal connectivity and operability requires less government intervention with the greater availability of computers, communications products and consumer electronics. But protecting communications and information as a universal basic service and ensuring no great disparity between information haves and information have-nots remains crucial.

National Information Infrastructure

All off-line applications that are supported by a nation's general purpose data networks and other communications services (eg, computerised telecommunications, customer interfaces and other applications) are collectively referred to as the *national information infrastructure* (NII) (Branscomb & Keller, 1996: 3; Drake, 1995: 1, 4–5). The term can be inchoate and multi-dimensional for the "emerging global broadband digital meta-network" (GAO, 1995: 72).

Key elements identified include technical systems such as the Internet, landlines, satellites, telecommunications systems, networks, architecture and connectivity, economic sectors supplying information technology goods and services, government policy covering generic and industry-specific interests, institutional structures, sub-national groups and individuals, culture, communications and the media (Kahin et al., 1997). Digital network services consist largely of unregulated value-added services built on the largely digital national telecommunications infrastructure. The most ubiquitous of these networks is the Internet (see chapter 7).

Alternatively, national information infrastructure is also termed *infostructure*, comprising electronic highways and other infrastructure necessary for information technology to be transmitted, distributed, received, processed or stored. Figure 9.1 shows the two major elements of infostructure encompassing the technical links between telecommunications and broadcasting.

Apart from a *telecommunications infrastructure* of physical lines and switches, there must be a knowledge infrastructure and an integration infrastructure (Branscomb & Keller, 1996: 5). *Knowledge infrastructure* is comprised of content or digitised information organised for access and use. *Integration infrastructure* acts as the glue, the systems and processes that bring together heterogeneous networks, computers, databases and applications.

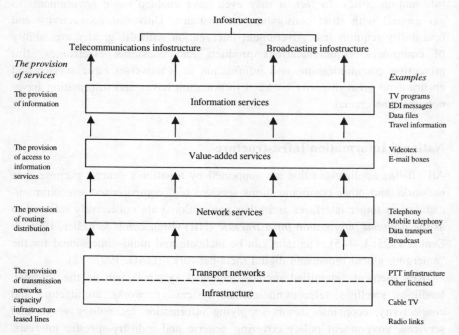

Fig. 9.1. Infostructure connecting telecommunications and broadcasting

The composite vision for a national information infrastructure is to provide a nation-wide assembly of systems, implying a strong role of the government. Five essential components are involved: integrated communications networks, computers and information appliances, information, applications and people. The aim is for people to access information and communicate with each other reliably, securely and cost-effectively in any medium (eg, voice, data, image or video) anytime and anywhere.

With a wide range of technologies, new ways are devised for people to learn, work, entertain and interact with one another. Standard key application areas involve teleworking, distance learning, networking for universities and research centres, telematics services for local enterprises, road traffic management, air traffic control, healthcare networks, electronic tendering, public administration networking, city information highways and others.

To support all these applications and flesh out the national information policy, the national infrastructure will inevitably include the following eight areas: broadband capacity, data compression, network intelligence and flexibility, networked computer servers, interactive capabilities, multimedia services and applications, intelligent information applications and navigational tools (Drake, 1995).

Broadband capacity

Wired, wireless, fibre optics and other innovations facilitate megabit- and gigabit-per-second transmissions as both carrying capacity and speed are enhanced. Broadband capacity is found primarily in long-distance lines used by corporate enterprise networks and specialised local and wide area networks (LANs and WANs). Interactive multimedia such as voice, data, graphics and video will be possible under the same broadband networks.

Data compression

While fibre optic cables have enabled broadband telecommunications to be brought into homes through local extensions of public networks, or the local loop, compression technology obviates the high economic costs. Compression technology effectively squeezes more digital information into a smaller space and allows broadband delivery over hybrid networks scaled up from existing physical capacities.

Network intelligence and flexibility

Computerisation has rendered telecommunications networks into more software-driven and defined information processing systems. Various functions have been unbundled, combined and reconfigured to facilitate different technical operations. With growing intelligence and flexibility of networks and terminals, the abilities of service suppliers and end-users will increase. More customised services and effective management of online information resources will come about.

Networked computer servers

In a network-centric regime, data communications networks such as the Internet maintain files in a variety of workstations and computers. Network users upload or download accordingly and information is effectively and efficiently communicated and exchanged. Technological advancement and convergence will allow more and a greater variety of information to reside on computer servers. A vast array of news, opinion, entertainment and information can be retrieved on demand via personal computers, intelligent televisions, public kiosks, cyber cafes and other terminals.

Interactive capabilities

Interactive communication will be possible with broadband networks. Information will be customised for specific purposes such as education or entertainment. It is a question of what level of interactivity will major network operators build into their systems. Users may be able to originate, as well as retrieve, in video and other forms for direct communication or for storage in publicly accessible servers.

Multimedia services and applications

With the right supporting information infrastructure, a single-medium transmission such as the telephone can have value-added services (eg, call forwarding, conference calling) added on. New modes of wireless delivery can transfer calls to mobile users wherever they roam. Information formats such as sound, video, text and graphics can be mixed in the same transmission to be accessed on the same customer terminal. A number of windows can be viewed simultaneously while participating in a video-telephone conversation, and the possibilities are limited more by human attentiveness and absorption capabilities than by technical constraints.

Intelligent information applications

Advanced networks can be accessed through a variety of intelligent terminals that can be customised for different services and applications. At home or in the office, powerful personal computers, supercomputers, multimedia telephones and intelligent televisions with computerised set-top boxes serve as network interfaces and even high-definition displays. Mobility on the road is enhanced by pocket-sized personal communications systems (PCS), telephones, personal digital assistants (PDAs) and small, flat panel displays.

Navigational tools

Software navigational tools are needed to manage and access information, interface applications and network directories. These act as intelligent personal agents that search the Internet and retrieve files using certain keywords as customer-defined parameters. The task can be performed from anywhere and presented in any format, including customised personal programmes.

Problems and Issues

The promise of the future in a national information infrastructure is enormous, but so are the issues and problems. All previous one-way flows of communication, such as in broadcast and cable television, and two-way flows of communication, such as in the plain old telephone, will be changed, making a new stage of electronic media. Interactive multimedia, multiple information formats, information retrieval and one-to-many or many-to-many transmissions are an explosion of communication, desirable or not.

Gatekeeper

The first issue is that of gatekeeping to the public sphere and arbiters to decide what to keep in or keep out. While the public has a right to free speech, the same free speech over open, public broadcast television has to be reconsidered. Similarly, apart from changing channels and not buying the services, the public may have no control over the content or formation of information received. More opportunities for free expression and control over information may arise with a new information infrastructure.

On the Internet, an unprecedented degree of distributed user empowerment is created. All sorts of virtual communities and groups can be formed between like-minded people to share information, debate and discuss subjects defined by their circle. Users can retrieve an infinite number of files containing information on any subject. They can alter, compose and combine the information as they like, adding customised text and graphics, and share them with others; they are limited only by their technical knowledge, level of interest and ability to pay.

However, as will be amplified in chapter 11, the Internet can be egalitarian and elitist at the same time, depending on whether people possess the means of getting on, including computer literacy, affordability and access. Within national borders, as well as across nations, the gap between the information-poor and information-rich will inevitably escalate.

The role of the government

Elsewhere in chapters 3 and 5 especially, the role of public policy concerning competition and regulation has been raised. A host of issues revolving around architecture and design, technical standards and quality, market entry, tariffs and other forms of regulation, property rights, content rules, consumer protection and many others are germane. These issues are addressed under a wide range of measures from regulations to trade policies (see chapter 11).

Digital paradox

In an era of network-centric systems, computerisation, digitisation and competition makes traditional centralised network control and hegemonic corporate behaviour impossible. With digital processing, the power of the state in allocating spectrum will diminish since spectrum is no longer scarce such as in analogue transmissions.

More precisely, the *digital paradox* in telecommunications is owed to four features (Drake, 1995: 94). First, computers and computational power have fallen dramatically in price in accordance with Moore's Law (see chapter 1) in a relatively short period. Second, computers need to communicate with one another and a stored-programme digital machine cannot work any other way. Third, while processing speed has doubled every two or three years with progress in computational devices, telecommunications speed, which is a measure of traffic capacity, has increased in orders of magnitudes. An order of magnitude is ten times, expressed as a logarithm. This means a dramatic reversal in the traditional equation now that transmission is faster than computation, and telecommunications technology is no longer the bottleneck. Finally, while costs have fallen dramatically for appliances, system components and carriage, they remain high for systems implementation, marketing, software and amortisation of sunken assets and investment capital. With cheap equipment and carriage, customers or users become competitors to carriers for value-added services. With open accessible networks, closed networks are oxymoronic.

Abundance, not scarcity

Spectrum and computer power have become abundant. Together with falling costs and prices, that means greater affordability. These trends have tremendous impact on ways to communicate. Laws and regulation may not keep pace with such massive technological change. Investment plans become difficult to make as windows of opportunity keep emerging and business cannot afford to be blindsided by new technology and devices.

More than a highway system, the national information infrastructure enables value to be added to the content of what is communicated. Digitisation has homogenised all speciality networks, isolated stand-alone networks, closed one-way systems and any incompatible devices.

Policy implications

To summarise, technology is faster and cheaper with connectivity and less network control. The implications include increased competition for value-added services, the *de facto* connection of public and private networks, large and accelerated write-offs of sunk plant and assets and loss of the ability of tariffs to function based on traffic flow or time of use. Policies and regulations inevitably lag behind technology. Human behaviour is vested with financial and political interests.

Nonetheless, results include more flexible and fungible choices among technologies, such as carriers, rates, tariffs and service arbitrage and standards. The role of the state and its regulatory mechanisms has to be re-examined. While there is increased network robustness, there will have to be greater stress placed on network integrity, security, privacy, equity and other socio-political issues (see chapter 10).

US policy

As a key player in global information technology and telecommunications, how the US national information policy and national information infrastructure takes shape is an interesting case study. Two themes are reviewed: first, American dominance in information technology for national security impinging on its global military role and, second, the deadline for a digitised national information infrastructure.

A national strategy of co-operative competition in the US further represents the synergy among economics, the military and technology (Golden, 1994). Even with the demise of the cold war, the US remains a global player in the military and security arena and uses its enormous economic leverage to forge a relationship between its commercial industrial base and its defence industrial base. Information technology is an area where dual-use technologies apply or have spillover effects. Defence research, development and procurement have externalities and possibilities for commercialisation. Co-operation to avoid proliferation and diffusion to adjust to new budget realities is a wise national technology policy and military technology strategy. The two are consistent since they both serve the national economic strategy.

In the US, the debate on the national information infrastructure further involves two separate but interrelated issues (Drake, 1995: 17–20). The first issue involves the positioning of big powerful suppliers as oligopolists while attempting to build a fully commercialised national information infrastructure with no government intervention if possible. The second issue concerns how to build an open and participatory national information infrastructure or distribution sector that is heterogeneous, with many vested interest groups.

As in all industrial economies, rebuilding cable television for two-way interactive digital circuits, overbuilding telephone wire pairs and using spectrum more efficiently are among some policy concerns in the US. The year 2000 has been set as the target date for the switchover from analogue to digital.

All television users will have a microprocessor-based box, giving all homes a supercomputer in practice for the new architecture. How ready and able are consumers for the ubiquitous offering of hundreds of channels and interactivity—from ordering movies to electronic commerce—is an interesting research question.

Chapter 10

Information Technology and the Media in the Global Economy

Introduction

This chapter takes the preceding discussion on a national information infrastructure to a global level. A global information infrastructure (GII) is a logical extension of a national information infrastructure (NII). Information services constitute a growing component of global exchange and international trade, with globalisation rising together with outward and inward flows of direct foreign investment and multinational companies.

A need to balance or level up the disparity in information and communications facilities across developed and developing countries is also recognised. Otherwise, communications will remain lopsided in favour of advanced industrial nations, in turn affecting levels of economic growth and development with commensurate political tensions.

A global information infrastructure needs capital, technology and information to construct and maintain. Advanced industrial nations currently hold the keys to all of them. These nations need to help developing countries access the global information infrastructure for three reasons. First, for their own interests, to complete their technological transitions to sustainable global information economies, there is a need to involve as many countries as possible in new trade practices such as the protection of intellectual property rights and new international rules of the game for information-intensive trade transactions. Second, telecommunications is an international public good that is innovation-intensive. Its cost of service delivery falls with additional customers. Economies of scale and economies and scope need more economies to be opened to competition. Finally, developed countries can contribute to the credibility and sustainability of reforms going on in developing and transition economies. A global information economy is an important part of that contribution.

Global Information Infrastructure

The US sounded the first call for a global information infrastructure in 1994 at an international telecommunications conference in Buenos Aires. The *global information infrastructure* concept of a planetary information network connecting large cities and small villages around the globe is premised on the five principles of private investment, competition, open access, universal service and flexible regulation among all nations.

Starting with national telecommunications and broadcasting infrastructure, and public and private networks, a global information infrastructure will emerge with international cable facilities and satellite networks connecting them all together. The global information infrastructure comprises global information highways, which break the tyranny of time and space, creating intimacy in physical and time dimensions. Local information networks will synergise to form global information networks (Heldman, 1995). Similarly, from information societies at national levels, a global information society will emerge (Martin, 1995).

Similar to a national information infrastructure, the global one will be characterised by maximum interoperability and interconnectivity, universal access, user-friendliness and market-driven applications among others. Both national and global information infrastructures must meet societal needs and enable sustainable growth and development as shown in Fig. 10.1, which is a shorthand expression of Fig. 5.1. The overlapping areas in the three circles

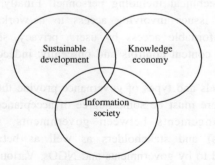

Fig. 10.1. Sustainable development, the knowledge economy and the information society

represent issues that interact with each other and they require co-operation and co-ordination at both national and global levels.

Factors driving the global information infrastructure are technology, the rising demand for information and communications services, multinational suppliers and users and national and transnational competition (Kahin et al., 1997: 533–534). A basic conflict in terms of regulatory regimes and issues between a global information infrastructure and national information infrastructures might be expected as transnational interests are not necessarily the sum total of individual national interests.

A global information infrastructure operates on policy goals including dynamic competition, encouraging private investment and participation, an adaptable regulatory environment and framework, open access networks, universal access to services, equality of opportunity, diversity of content and the participation of as many countries as possible, both developed and developing. But because levels of development and progress are uneven, and resources to level up are not as bountiful, there will be expected differences and possible conflicts between developed and developing countries in shaping a global information infrastructure.

Governance of a global information infrastructure will be tricky in practice, but both core and specific issues arise in three areas. First, there are technical co-operation issues involving spectrum allocation and assignment, the assignment and co-ordination of geostationary orbital slots, interoperability, security and other network standards, an interconnectivity arrangement, revenue sharing, and co-ordination and co-operation in research and development, prototypes and field tests. Second, there are economic issues regarding market entry and licensing, foreign direct investment, competition policies, intellectual property rights, dispute resolution and settlement, and development assistance, both financial and technical including personnel. Finally, there are access, service and content issues involving access to networks by content and service providers, affordable access by users, privacy, security, encryption policies, government content controls and obscenity, indecency, libel, slander and defamation.

While various levels and types of governance provide the principal impetus in all these areas, there must be some degree of acceptance and co-operation for negotiated arrangements between governments, non-governmental organisations (NGOs) and stakeholders as well as between international institutions subscribed to by governments and NGOs. Various *regimes*, defining sets of principles, norms, rules and systems for decision-making in governing international relations must also evolve. Information and communications constitute international public goods with externalities (see chapter 5). It would be useful to start at the regional level if the international level of governance proved too unwieldy and complicated.

In theory, no nation should dominate a global information infrastructure. But, clearly, the US can strongly influence the global information system because it has so many large market players, such as AT&T, in telecommunications. Chapter 9 has noted many strategic alliances in high technology telecommunications industries, especially with US firms (Carlson, 1996). The EU and Japan are laggards even in putting their respective trans-European and national information infrastructures in place. Japan is ambivalent on competition, with rivalry even between its Ministry of Post and Telecommunications (MPT) and Ministry of International Trade and Industry (MITI). Surprisingly, Japan suffers from a low consumer demand for telecommunications and information technology services.

More specifically, the shape of global competition will be affected by the way the US is shifting from an oligopoly revolution to a distributed information revolution. From a telephone monopoly and three national television networks, the distributed information revolution implies the emergence of independent computing networks, competition by telephone, cable and wireless companies for providing local communications services including video services and the rise of network providers of content. A distributed information revolution may set the global strategy as a benchmark for market access.

International Trade in Services

The relationship between trade and infrastructure

The relationship between trade in services, a global information economy and a global information infrastructure has to be established. At the general macro level, information is, increasingly, an important factor of production. But international trade agreements dealing with actual goods, transactions and services rendered do not cover types of information transferred, such as in flows of data, knowledge and information. An elaboration of transborder data flows will make this distinction clearer.

Transborder data flows (TBDF) are defined as the international transfer of digitally encoded units of information for processing, storage or retrieval. To qualify as a transborder data flow, the technical process must involve transmission, storage and processing. The traditional telephone and telegraph do not qualify since they provide transmission but not storage or processing. Data is stored in databases, and processing allows the manipulation of data flows in all forms and orders. Transborder data flows resulting from media products such as news broadcasts, television programming and conventional telecommunications services are excluded from this definition because of the proprietary nature of the transfer of data flows. These technical distinctions are important since they relate to the roots of problems and issues peculiar to the transfer of data flows such as laws, proprietorship and others.

A global information infrastructure delivers services in finance and transport across borders. Without the computer and information technology revolution, much of the consultancy services, computer or financial services would be traded less compared to 24-hour stock exchange transactions and computerised reservations, which intensify the volume and pace.

Communications, information and data play such key roles in production and delivery in both goods and services. Global or multinational corporations are viable because they have networks of communication that give them the benefits of international divisions of labour and international competitiveness. Without telecommunications and computer technology, traditional services such as transport and tourism would be stunted.

A global information infrastructure and its effective governance are thus part and parcel of the international trading system, more so with information-based services and products. The tradability of services and cost of transmitting information across borders depends on telecommunications policies. For instance, the ability of firms to use their networks to establish advanced communications links with suppliers, customers and distributors and between affiliated sister companies would be affected. Trade negotiations have become part of the regulatory process because restrictive practices could effectively limit market access for internationally traded information-based services.

Information-based services that are traded globally can be put into three concentric circles by way of definition (see Fig. 10.2). The innermost circle encompasses services delivered through international communications networks via the crossborder sale of information. These can be direct sales, such as in transborder data flows, or indirectly, such as in computerised network management. The second circle involves the processing and manipulation of information and knowledge. Financial and professional services, for instance, can be delivered either through the movement of people or the local establishment of firms or communications networks. The outmost circle includes all transnational

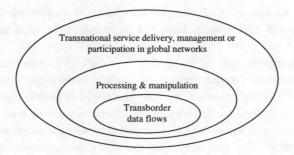

Fig. 10.2. Information-based services in international trade

service delivery, which will be the management of, or participation in, global data networks developed within, between or outside of corporate structures. Examples include marketing or financing activities; even transportation and construction services would be considered as information-based.

The General Agreement on Trade in Services

In 1994, the General Agreement on Trade in Services (GATS) established a new set of principles and rules to govern international trade in services. It is a recognition of the advent of a global information economy with new modes of interaction among nations through an increasingly dense web of public and private communications networks.

As a constitutional framework, GATS covers the whole range of international service sectors, from finance to professions, from telecommunications to transport. The aim is to liberalise trade in such activities amounting to US$1 trillion as estimated by the General Agreement on Tariffs and Trade (GATT) in 1993. Fresh thinking is set on new notions of market access as enabled by new technology and widening sovereign regulatory frameworks to a global framework under the World Trade Organisation, which took over from GATT in 1996.

However, neither the WTO nor GATS could effectively dictate governance of the global information economy, which requires a profound reconceptualisation of the meaning of global integration against the traditions of territorial sovereignty. The broad principles under GATS remain vague and open to interpretation, leaving specific liberalisation commitments and contentious issues regarding the discipline of national monopolies, for instance, to future negotiations. As such, GATS must be viewed as an evolutionary framework; interpretation and enforcement have yet to emerge to give it substance and character.

Trade in services such as under GATS is defined in four parts: from the territory of one nation to the territory of another, in the territory of one nation to a consumer in another nation, by a service supplier of one nation through a commercial presence in the territory of another nation and by a service supplier of one nation through the presence of natural persons of a nation in the territory of another nation. The aim is to cast the widest net possible and yet allow nations to preserve areas they wish to exempt from liberalisation.

Issues in trade in services

One set of issues in trade in services concern networked-based trade. Trade liberalisation involving network-based services revolve around three categories of rights of access that are distinct from, and may conflict with, another type of rights concerning access to local or global generation of information through information networks. To a certain extent, the exclusionary nature of some rights can threaten information generated by local and global information networks.

The first category concerns the rights of access communications service operators or providers, including the right to connect with domestic telecommunications networks, both private and public. This right is for both private networks and equipment such as modems. The right to use one's own protocol or transmission software, the right to establish private networks by linking together leased lines, private intracorporate or local area networks (LANs) and private computer leasing switching lines are all part of this first category of rights of access.

The second category of rights of access is for information service providers who must have the right to use domestic networks on a non-discriminatory basis. This is because local infrastructures for service delivery and the right of access to leased lines available to them will reduce costs.

Finally, the third type of rights of access is for network providers. They must have the right to restrict the use of transnational links to a closed user group such as in examples of the Society for Worldwide Interbank Financial Telecommunications (SWIFT). These are dedicated electronic data interchange networks for specific purposes.

A second set of issues in trade in information-intensive services concerns national regulatory measures. Host and home countries set rules and regulations for service providers operating both within and outside their jurisdiction. Any global regulatory regime must thus take into account the concerns of national regulators to safeguard public interests, protect consumers and ensure against negative externalities. The new service regime has to find effective principles to minimise the trade-restrictive nature of domestic regulations and, at the same time, ensure that the national concerns of regulators continue to be met.

While domestic regulation appears to restrict trade in information-based services, differences among national regulatory systems have to be recognised if the intention to discriminate against foreigners is not blatant. But the means can be subtler than in trade in goods. Regulations regarding licensing, accreditation, registration, supervision and the enforcement of regulations in host countries can act as a costly barrier to entry as well as restrict the provider's preferred mode of delivery.

With the death of distance (Cairncross, 1997), information and communications technology has allowed service providers to implement network strategies based on remote delivery to enjoy economies of scale and economies of scope. Technically, providers can operate entirely from their home bases and sell information services, data processing services or portfolio management services to clients anywhere in the world. National requirements for some degree of local control and local presence would thwart such modes of crossborder delivery of services.

Similar to other areas where non-trade issues such as social clause, human rights and environmental protection inevitably enter as trade concerns, the state's legitimate right to protect the socio-political and cultural content of information should not be mistaken as a trade barrier. Censorship and the banning of certain information and materials remains a sovereign right but should not be a disguised form of trade protection.

Global Trade in Telecommunications

While GATS provided a general framework, individual service sectors and subsectors were left to resolve their national schedules of commitments, including telecommunications and audiovisual services. Both types of services have witnessed clashes between the US, which sought fast pace liberalisation, and the European Union (EU), which was more cautious and preferred to move only incrementally. The Europeans wanted an integrated regional outcome before the radical opening of their markets, mainly because they placed political priority on European integration and probably also because they realised that European services were not yet on par with US telecommunications services. Similar to the Clinton administration's national information infrastructure, a programme for a trans-European network and European information society were launched as part of the Single European Market (SEM). The triad, including Japan, would thus lead the global information economy and society, extending it to all.

Nothing much was done for telecommunications beyond the Uruguay Round and GATS. An annexe to GATS, taking effect only in 1995, and an agreement between parties to negotiate basic telecommunications services at a later date reflected the mood. The EU avoided even drawing strict definitions of basic and enhanced services, falling back instead on concepts such as competitive and reserved services (the latter limited to voice telephony). The difference between initial conditions in the US and Europe have to be noted. Whereas the US has some internal competition among private carriers, public national monopolies persisted in Europe. Propelled by its own deregulation and technology push, the annexe was no mean feat for the US over the EU.

Nonetheless, the WTO has been working hard toward liberalising trade in telecommunications services. Three agreements are particularly relevant as reviewed below.

WTO Basic Telecommunications Agreement

Concluded in 1997, the WTO Basic Telecommunications Agreement to liberalise the basic telecommunications sector comprises 55 schedules, covering 69 WTO members (the 15 EU members counted as one), which account for 90% of global telecommunications revenue. Global telecommunications services account for 2.1% of the global GDP. Of the 69 members who signed the agreement, 30 WTO members already account for 95% of global telecommunications revenue. The quadrilateral countries comprising the EC, the US, Japan and Australia account for a 77% share. Nonetheless, it is worth noting that significant developing countries that are members to the agreement include South Korea, Brazil, Mexico, Argentina, Hong Kong and Singapore.

The effect of the agreement would be lower costs for consumers and greater accessibility and universality, with effect from 1 January 1998. The agreement covers the cross-border supply of telecommunications, abolishing monopolies, easing or abolishing regulations over foreign investments and the opening of services to foreign firms or foreign commercial presence.

Services covered include voice telephone services, data transmission services, telex, telegraph, facsimile services, exclusive line services, private leased-circuits services, fixed and mobile satellite systems and services, cellular telephone services, mobile data services, paging, personal communications systems and all other telecommunications services and networks. Though not part of formal negotiations, value-added services to enhance the form of customer's information, content or storage and retrieval such as online database storage, electronic data exchange (EDI), electronic mail, voice mail and others are also negotiated.

Participating countries submit schedules of their pledges of liberalisation relating to open sectors and reserved sectors in negotiations. The main reserved sectors include a grace period on the liberalisation of regulations and the entry of foreign investment. The three global players made rather immediate offers of liberalisation. Starting in 1998, the EU completely liberalised entry of all basic telecommunications sectors, such as voice telephone services and cellular phones, in all but a few countries such as Portugal. Japan completely liberalised entry of all basic telecommunications sectors, except for limiting foreign ownership of NTT and KDD to 20%. The US liberalised completely, except for maintaining a 20% limit on foreign direct investment in radio stations and recording companies and exclusion of the most-favoured-nation (MFN) obligation for digital satellite broadcasting.

WTO Information Technology Agreement

The WTO Information Technology Agreement (ITA) has reduced tariffs on computers, communications equipment, telecommunications hardware, semiconductors, semiconductor manufacturing devices, computer software and scientific equipment. The agreement covers some 93% of the value of trade in these stated products. Forty-three WTO members agreed to cut tariffs on computer and telecommunications products beginning July 1997 and eliminating all tariffs by the year 2000. They staged, or will stage, four equal rate reductions of 25% each time on 1 July 1997, 1 January 1998, 1 January 1999 and 1 January 2000.

Table 10.1 shows that growth rates in global trade in office and telecommunications equipment have exceeded that of world merchandise trade since 1980. The impact of the Information Technology Agreement will accelerate such trade even further.

Table 10.1. Growth rates in office and telecommunications equipment
and world merchandise trade

	World merchandise	Office & telecoms equipment
1980–85	−1	9
1985–90	12	18
1990–95	7.5	15
1993	−0.5	10
1994	13	24
1995	19	26

(*Source:* WTO)

Table 10.2 shows the ten top exporters and importers of information
technology products in 1995. By the first half of the 1990s, it was electronics
equipment that contributed to the expansion of global trade in manufactured
goods (Jetro, 1997). The electronics equipment industry includes office
equipment, computers, communications equipment, audiovisual equipment and
electronics components including semiconductors.

Table 10.2. Leading exporters and importers of information
technology products, 1995 (US$b)

Leading exporters	
Japan	106.6
United States	98.0
EU15 (extra EU exports)	57.1
Singapore (domestic exports)	41.3
South Korea	33.2
Malaysia	32.8
Taiwan	28.7
China	14.5
Mexico	11.7
Canada	11.6
Total 10	435.4

Table 10.2. (*Continued*)

Leading importers

United States	139.9
EU15 (extra-EU imports)	104.8
Japan	37.7
Singapore (retained imports)	24.7
Malaysia	22.2
Canada	19.8
Taiwan	16.5
South Korea	16.5
China	14.4
Hong Kong (retained imports)	12.1
Total 10	408.7

(*Source:* WTO)

Both North America and Europe imported more than they exported in their trade in electronics equipment (Jetro, 1997). North America exported US$109.5 billion and imported US$150.7 billion of such goods in 1995. For Western Europe, the figures were US$163.1 billion exported and US$201.7 billion imported. Conversely, Asia exported US$304.6 billion and imported US$192.5 billion, enjoying a massive trade surplus. By 1995, Asia accounted for more than half (51.2%) of world's export of electronic equipment.

The trend is more entrenched each year; Asia has become such a large supplier of electronic equipment that the electronics cycle downturn was the reason for Asia's economic slowdown in 1996. The ratio of exports of electronic equipment to total exports is as high as 40–50% in Malaysia and Singapore and 20–30% in South Korea, Taiwan and Hong Kong. While Japan's share is large, some of what it used to make at home and export is increasingly being made in, and exported from, other Asian countries to which Japan's electronic industry has diversified.

Trade-related intellectual property

The Trade-Related Intellectual Property (TRIP) Rights Agreement came into effect on 1 January 1996 when thirty WTO members reviewed their legislation to ensure that their laws and practices complied with the agreement. Developing and transition countries were given five years from 1996, and least developed countries eleven years, to comply with the agreement. Since the objective is to stop the import of counterfeit and pirated products, the TRIP Agreement is highly relevant to trade in information technology products and services. Other multilateral agreements such as the Paris Code and Berne Convention[1] cover other fields of intellectual property rights.

While there are many economic benefits of strong intellectual property protection in stimulating innovation, creating lower cost production and distribution methods for existing products, and developing newer, safer and more effective products, developing countries are clearly disadvantaged by the burden of the agreement at their lower stages of growth. In the long term, technology and product transfers require a conducive environment, especially when so much innovation lies with the private sector. Without adequate protection, creators and innovators will take their products and technology elsewhere, where they are protected.

---

[1] Dating back to 1886, the *Berne Convention* is an international agreement that protects the intellectual property of the creators of literary and artistic works. Some eighty countries have signed the Berne Convention, which is administered by the World Intellectual Property Organisation (WIPO).

Chapter 11

Issues in Media and Information Economics

Introduction

Information technology, digitisation, converging technologies, the knowledge economy, interactive multimedia, a network-centric era, virtual reality, business process reengineering, strategic alliances and a host of exciting developments have been identified and discussed in the foregoing chapters. Mankind is stepping into the virtual world and the promise of things to come in the next millennium has yet to fully unfold.

This chapter is devoted to probing the non-economic, socio-political and legal issues of the information and communications technology revolution and emerging multimedia industry. Some of these issues have been hinted at in previous chapters, including equity, privacy, information overload, the legal and regulatory environment and the status of the nation-state in the new borderless and seamless world.

Equity

Haves and have-nots

Technological convergence coexists, paradoxically, with the new divide between the haves and have-nots. New communications technology accentuates the gap between the information-rich and information-poor. Those with access to the electronic highway—requiring both hardware (ie, equipment) and software (ie, computer literacy)—are the *haves* or *information-rich*. Less developed countries without the requisite infrastructure or means to educate people do not benefit as much from the new communications technology. While unprecedented amounts of information have been generated, the dissemination and transmission of such information cannot be assumed to be free and perfect (Wresch, 1996).

Communication is not merely for personal, social or political reasons: the most important motive must be for production, work and income to be generated. From the discussion in chapter 6 on impact of information technology on work and employment, those unable to access and use new communications technology will definitely lose out as the *have-nots* or *information-poor*.

Based on a 1995 world total of 2,186 million devices, ways to communicate can be divided into 9% by personal computers, 32% by telephone and 59% by television. Access to these three means varies with wealth as shown in Table 11.1 (Cairncross, 1997: 3).

Table 11.1. Access to electronic communication varies with wealth

Communication[+] / Income groups*	Personal computer	Telephone	TV
Low	0.3	2.0	12.9
Middle	1.1	9.1	20.5
Upper	3.3	14.5	26.3
High	20.5	53.1	61.2

[+] Number of TV sets, telephone lines and PCs per 100 inhabitants, 1995
* In GNP per capita, low income = US$725 or less, middle income = US$726–2,895, upper middle income = US$2,896–8,955, high income = US$8,956 or more
(*Source:* International Telecommunications Union, "World Telecommunications Development Report" (1996–97))

The uninformed are effectively like the blind or non-sighted. Since communication is a two-way process, as much as they cannot be informed, the information-poor also cannot provide feedback to articulate their views and preferences effectively. The power influence comes with the power to communicate. The chasm between the information-rich and information-poor may further distort ideals of freedom and democracy. Across countries, the issue may grow into one of electronic colonialism (Martin, 1995) if the developing world becomes aggravated by outside interference.

The development of the niche economy is attributed to new information technology and the "revolt of the rich" where the rich and well-off groups do their best to separate themselves from, and discard, their disadvantaged and lagging countrymen, regions and states (Toffler, 1980). Social eruptions can only be overcome by the transmission of news and information to disaffected areas.

Universal access

At another level, equity can be an issue with a more market-based supply of information technology, telecommunications and media services compared to traditional public broadcasting. With technological convergence and the changing nature of competition, more and more private sector involvement (in response to market demand) based on profit maximisation and efficiency criteria would affect the principle of free universal access when the services were publicly provided.

Three types of structural changes in the institutional infrastructure affect universal access and the universal nature of information technology, telecommunications and media services. They are deregulation of economic activities, privatisation of functions that were once public and commercialisation of activities that were once social and that have expanded with commercial potential. As a corollary, data deprivation may result if the collection of socially vital information is neglected, withheld or eliminated as a consequence of these trends (Schiller, 1996: 55).

Even the Internet is not exempt from commercialisation and for-profit motives as commercial use exceeds non-commercial use (see chapter 7). Pushing the national information infrastructure to the private sector through private ownership and competition may be a useful launch for businesses and homes to come on board and make applications useful. However, can market forces alone ensure that societal goals are met and that the ideals of democracy, such as in universal access and equity, are maintained? Would public interest be adequately served from a social and equitable point? While the market is a powerful institution in making products and services possible and available for distribution, some co-operative private–public sector efforts may be necessary with information as a public good with positive externalities. Leaving everything to market pricing based on profit maximisation is not enough.

For example, advanced digital television means Americans may have to replace 270 million analogue television sets by the year 2006 at prices ranging from US$200 for a digital converter box to US$5,000 or more for a new digital large-screen, standard resolution display (Neuman et al., 1997: 223). The less endowed who cannot afford it would be unable to enjoy digital television so long as it is provided by the market. Both conventional over-the-air and terrestrial (cable) may have to be offered together to ensure universality.

Broadcasters still fight for free spectrum to make possible crystal-clear pictures and CD-quality sound. Allotted broad bandwidth can be used for multichannel conventional television by using advanced electronics to squeeze five channels into space previously occupied by one. The principle of paying for what one gets, such as in pay-television, goes against the grain of public broadcasting with information and communications as public goods with positive externalities.

Falling costs

On the other hand, accessibility may also be favourably affected since long-distance costs are falling and, eventually, there need not be any extra charge for duration and distance for most telephone calls. But as the large profits earned on long-distance and international calls fall, with most of them made by commercial and business users, the practice of subsidising local calls made by private individuals will suffer. In other words, local rates may rise to be more closely aligned with the true costs of such calls.

Table 11.2. Cable and satellite capacity in terms of voice paths

	1990	1995	1996	1997–2000*
TRANSATLANTIC				
Cable	145,000	1,310,800	1,310,800	1,310,800
Satellite	283,000	710,800	710,800	737,500
TRANSPACIFIC				
Cable	37,800	264,000	864,600	234,000
Satellite	39,000	234,000	1,464,600	424,500

* Minimum available
(*Source:* Adapted from Cairncross (1997: 31))

Scarcity is changing to plenty with increases in capacity driving prices down as new fibre optic cables are laid. Much of the capacity will be filled eventually by the Internet, boosted by increasing demand. As the supply of voice paths for transatlantic (North America to Europe) and transpacific (North America to East Asia) cable and satellite capacities rise (see Table 11.2), costs will fall.

For local capacity and local subscribers using copper local-loop technology, the costs per connection for fixed wireless and coaxial cables, fibre-to-curb and fibre-to-home may all range from US$200 to $2,000 upwards.. While not truly comparable, since optical fibres-to-home carry far more information than wireless cables, for instance, these figures give some rough idea of the orders of magnitude.

Developed versus developing world

The gap is likely to widen between developed and developing nations, but opportunities and possibilities of inclusion do exist for the developing world. With the appropriate policy, developing countries can take advantage of the declining cost of access due to technology. They can leapfrog ahead to the latest, most advanced network while developed nations have to be concerned, for instance, with the switchover from analogue to digital. A younger population in developing countries gives them another advantage in terms of mindset changes and the adoption of new technology. Developing countries are also on the threshold of education and other social reforms that impinge on the freedom of speech and liberalisation of markets. Producing citizens with creative talents and proficiency in English, such as exists in India, will help some developing nations to forge ahead. The right policies and institutions are crucial for this leapfrogging process.

In the developed world, the issue is more of excluding the less endowed from the world of networks. But this concern is misplaced because the falling prices of equipment and software, the cost of connecting people with wireless links, communications satellites and multichannels mean more access for the poor than ever before. A revolution of inclusion, rather than exclusion, is predicted; new forms of mobility across electronic highways will even benefit older persons. While the uneducated and the old may be disadvantaged in terms of computer literacy and know-how, they can be retrofitted. But the electronic world will remain dominated by the young who grow up with the new technology.

While developed countries may have started on the Internet earlier, and have a larger number of hosts per 1,000 population, the growth rate of hosts per 1,000 population has been most rapid in developing countries (*The Economist*, 15 February 1997). Between January 1996 and January 1997, Finland had the largest number of hosts per 1,000 population (about 55) and South Africa had the smallest (3). But the growth rate of 160% in Hungary and 106% in South Africa and other developing countries that started from a low base are in contrast to those in developed countries such as Finland at 26%. The growth rate in Hong Kong at 178% was probably due to the then impending handover to China (*The Economist*, 15 February 1997).

The balance of trade in intellectual property, such as royalties and license fees, is also in favour of the US as the leading industrial nation in such products. In 1996, the US enjoyed a surplus of US$20,660 million, followed by US$1,710 million for the UK, while deficits of US$3,350 million and US$2,660 million were incurred by Japan and Germany respectively (Cairncross, 1997: 198). As a corollary, spending on computers and telecommunications (excluding software and services) as a percentage of GDP in 1994 were 10.8% and 10.5% respectively for Switzerland and Austria at the top range of OECD countries, and 4.1% and 4.0% respectively for Italy and Sweden at the low range (*The Economist*, 23 November 1996).

Privacy

The surge in privacy, security and encryption issues is a result of information technology spreading into every facet of life (Cate, 1997: 1). *Privacy* is an expression of one's personality or personhood, rights leading to autonomy and ability to control one's relationship with others. Some secrecy, solitude and anonymity are implied in one's desire for privacy, and one may choose, or not choose, to disclose information if such control is allowed as inherent in privacy. But privacy is not absolute, and a balance has to be made to avoid conflicts of interest with others and with society as a whole.

In information privacy, the most important protection is individual responsibility and action. On the Internet and other networks, the novice computer user or the unacquainted may be unaware of the often invisible actions of softscreens, of finding resources on privacy in print or of some transparent guidance. Some technological or other form of self-help besides passwords, such as an anonymous remailer or encryption software, may help. In giving data, the individual may unwittingly surrender his or her privacy since it is not known how the data collector intends to control the use, dissemination and retention of the information.

Even when new technology is introduced for perfectly benign motives, the cumulative social impact on personal privacy bears some thought. As the new economy goes online, increasing use of credit and debit cards in electronic commerce or electronic communication leaves a *digital trail* captured by computer databases. The resulting potential invasion and abuse of privacy can be immense. Databases are spawned and information overload may occur as the data trails grow. With information and data routinely recorded by many sites that offer free content to users or when purchases are made, the assault on privacy is wide open.

Privacy is also tied to concepts of freedom and democracy. Erosion of one may lead to erosion of the other. While computers and telecommunications have enhanced the ability of governments and organisations to collect, collate, store and disseminate personal information, they may have simultaneously enabled more access to more people than intended (Burnham, 1980).

As much as there is faith that accountable, democratic governments protect freedom and rights, some fair information practices must prevail across society, ranging from employers to doctors with whom a confidentiality pact is implied. Surveys in the US have shown a progressive increase in the public's concern for privacy (Cavoukian & Tapscott, 1996). Control, consent and regulation are emerging issues. Consumers who worry about their personal information being misused can withhold their consent for their information to be used for additional or secondary purposes. In the final analysis, it pays for businesses and private sector organisations to voluntarily employ self-regulating codes that respect the consumer's privacy.

A contractual approach to information privacy may be an explicit agreement between the data subject and data user. If self-regulation by data users is not strong, national laws and collective non-governmental action become critical. *Statutory privacy protection* should include three elements: notice, consent and accountability.

The death of distance due to information and communications technology poses intractable difficulties for national jurisdiction and regulation since national laws cannot extend across borders. The only solution is for governments to co-operate. Effective policing comes with a cost that, perhaps, only rich industrial states can afford and are willing to bear. It is also difficult for governments to identify and comprehend offenders in virtual cyberspace. A trade-off inevitably results, with some risk in exchange for a certain level of personal convenience and freedom by using electronic media. *Self-regulation* has to be exercised, and people and groups will, increasingly, have to protect themselves as governments find it harder and harder to do so.

Perverse privacy

Perversely, the privacy of pornographers, hackers and swindlers can be hidden and their anonymity protected while the privacy of others are violated. Measures to deal with this issue include requiring call records and caller identification that can determine who called whom, when and where.

The same issues confront money laundering, which is related to concealing unlawful sources of money including funds of illicit origin first employed in financial transactions before entering the legal circuit in various forms of investment (Savona, 1997). Money trails are expedited by information technology as legitimate markets, banks and financial intermediaries are involved. Preventative and control policies require strict recording, documentation and reporting, and international co-operation and monitoring.

The Legal and Regulatory Environment

The role of the government

The role of the government includes articulating principles, enacting and enforcing laws, administering data protection systems, registering data collection and use activities and the persons engaged in them, negotiating multinational agreements and adjudicating disputes. Legal cultures range from the European style of giving their governments all or some of these roles to a more limited role of the government in the US (Cate, 1997: 121). Governments are likely to play a greater role with the explosion in digital data and the globalisation of networks, markets and institutions that require national legal protection. Some non-governmental action is also necessary to ensure that self-help and market-based solutions work in a multinational framework.

The law should allow information subjects and users to continue to develop their own privacy protection through mutual agreements, market-based solutions, group action and voluntary codes of conduct. Individual responsibility, not regulation, is the principal and most effective form of privacy protection. But the law should serve as a cap-filler to facilitate individual action in situations where the lack of competition has interfered with private privacy protection. The law should provide limited, basic privacy rights to facilitate—not to interfere with—the development of private mechanisms and individual choice as a means of valuing and protecting privacy.

Cyberlaw

The government should play a circumscribed role, limited primarily to articulating principles for information privacy, enacting laws when necessary to protect rights, adjudicating disputes concerning such rights, facilitating discussion, education and co-operation, and leading multinational negotiations to resolve conflicts between competing national privacy laws. The long-term goal is the promulgation of basic multinational principles to facilitate the activities of information users and the services and products they offer, ensure consistent international privacy protection for personal information and reduce the cost of administering and complying with inconsistent national legal regimes.

Even if *cyberlaw* covering legislation involving all forms of electronic transactions can be drawn up and legislated, the implementation and monitoring of intellectual property rights is not an easy task. The less developed the country, the more strain on its administrative resources to make protection effective and efficient.

Copyright laws confer two main rights—the right to authorise reproduction and the right to authorise distribution. Legal confusion arises when one asks whether an electronic transmission of a copyrighted work is a reproduction, distribution or both (*The Economist*, 27 July 1996). Indeed, the digital age poses difficulties for traditional notions of these two acts.

Copyright law currently makes a distinction between reproduction for public use done with the rightsholder's permission and reproduction for private use. In the latter situation, within limits, it is sometimes allowed to give users reasonable access to some bits of information.

However, when a surfer calls up for information on the Internet, copyright laws may not be infringed upon since accessing the information does not constitute reproduction until the material is copied. The nature of the information distributed or reproduced is also important. A list of addresses or names with no intrinsic property right may have some commercial value to advertisers, for instance. While such personal information is intended to be distributed and reproduced freely and widely, personal privacy is intrinsically at risk.

A distinction would then have to be made to confer *special copyright protection* to more intellectual products such as databases and software. Another issue arises when *distribution rights* control the first sale of a copy but not subsequent sales. Selling something second-hand is legal but it is unclear how a perfect copy of an original should be treated and what kinds of copying should be allowed. A more perplexing issue resulting from borderless economics is that current copyright laws are based on national boundaries. Such territorial restrictions may be used as protectionist measures by developing countries.

Organisations trying to monitor electronic piracy include the Business Software Alliance (BAS), which compares computer sales with software sales, and the International Federation of Phonographic Industry (IFPI). The latter estimates that one in five sales of recorded music is a pirated copy; the estimate jumps to one in three in the case of compact discs (CDs) (*The Economist*, 27 July 1996). Thus, while communication is enhanced thanks to piracy, there are legal and moral issues of ownership and the protection of rights.

New rules are needed to address these new issues. The Geneva-based World Intellectual Property Organisation (WIPO) is trying to update the Berne Convention, which set international standards for copyright laws. The US and the European Union are drawing up amendments to copyrights and related rights in a digitised society. Free information in a pre-digital world may be diminished or not freely allowed. This would impede progress and the world of knowledge if copyright laws overkill distribution and reproduction in a bid to attain their objectives.

The policing of cyberlaws is another major challenge and issue. Most groups would prefer government and international sanctions such as the WTO's trade-related intellectual property rights (TRIPS), the Berne Convention and WIPO. Problems include tracking down the source of illicit materials since uploading and downloading are hard to trace. Anonymity and a hacker mentality in cyberspace are, perversely, almost guaranteed. Even when traced to a particular source, the responsible party is hard to establish, for instance, in the case of operators of a bulletin board or public library.

Policing the electronic world is contradictory to the idea that the electronic world represents information, ideas and technologies of freedom. The only areas where regulation is desirable are for pornography, racist or terrorist materials and the like. In general, censorship works only after three issues are resolved: namely, differentiating between public and private, using technology to screen off offensive materials and establishing who is responsible for doing the screening.

Screening

The technology of screening involves several approaches. In Singapore, since September 1996, it is required that all individual users (not businesses) route requests for access to Internet sites through proxy servers. Large computers check the requests against a blacklist of sites containing objectionable material. It is too costly and burdensome to impose the same on businesses. But not many other Asian countries desire the Singapore system. In fact, Malaysia pronounced no censorship on the Internet in a bid to attract successful multimedia businesses.

A second approach is screening through software that looks for taboo words as a basis to decide whether to block a site. Computers, however, are bad at distinguishing meaning. The law on a violence (V) chip in the US in 1996 is to sanction a circuit that allows parents to automatically block programmes. But the problem is, parents may be less technologically adept and savvy than their children, who can effectively manipulate around the barrier.

A third approach is requiring Internet service providers (ISPs), companies that are responsible for providing Internet access, to screen off objectionable areas of the Internet, such as in Singapore and China. Blocking news groups is relatively straightforward, but not when dealing with Web materials. Sites or bulletin boards that are closed off can reappear hydra-like: if necessary, under a different name. Internet service providers face a Herculean task since they like a postal system that only transports content.

A fourth approach is self-censorship, persuading content owners or third parties to rate sites voluntarily. Electronic tags are placed on sites and families are warned so that owners or Internet service providers can block the sites or allow families to opt in or out. Groups such as parents, specialist companies and others can rate Internet sites according to their own specifications. This effectively averts the problem that what outrages one person may not bother another.

Intellectual property rights and piracy

Copyright conveys a sense of monopoly power. When monopolies have absolute market power, or enjoy entry barriers, consumer welfare suffers higher prices and restricted quantities. If an argument of positive externality can be made for products with intellectual property, they should fall into the realm of other merit products such as education and health.

The rate and effectiveness of communication is strongly conditioned by the protection of intellectual property rights. Intellectual property is unlike ordinary property, making it more difficult to protect. The revolution in digital technology and electronic transmission means that copyrighted materials can be easily downloaded and reproduced. Information ranging from frivolous recreation to commercial applications, such as databases and computer software, can be copied or adapted. Copying is almost effortless, costless, widespread and immediate. It is a business in itself; pirated software, music, articles and films available on the Internet can be had by anyone who is determined, be they amateur or professional.

Two schools of thought emerge on whether pirated materials ultimately enable more widespread communication and transmission of knowledge. On one hand, piracy has been defended as a means of promoting the real product. The argument is that, without the pirated source, many users would never get to know authentic Microsoft software, for instance. "Altruistic" piracy is practised by groups that give away copied software and music for free.

The Robin Hood argument creates a vicious circle. Presently, companies charge more for a small piece of intellectual property precisely because of piracy and their need to recover research and development (R&D) costs.[1] Most users of pirated materials argue that they would never pay the full price for such products. So long as the originators are getting payment from corporate and professional users, they see no harm in benefiting amateurs and less endowed users in the name of knowledge and development for all.

A compromise is to keep payments low and copyrights easy to obtain at minimum compliance costs. The issue is one of base versus rate to generate the same revenue for the originators of copyrighted materials. Payment and costs can be satisfied more equitably. One might suggest that governments and public organisations subscribe to the original materials and allow them to be distributed to the less privileged or developing countries so as not to inhibit education and training.

---

[1] An alternative of subsidising the software creators and innovators with possible flaws is suggested in chapter 4.

However, content providers and companies will continue to exist, though they will inevitably lose profits, causing them to put up a higher price, which in turn drives more activities underground. Certain precautions, such as making frequent updates, may be frustrating to users who paid the legal price. Other sources of income from advertising, sponsorship and other spin-offs from the original products may be suggested.

The line between moral and ethical practices on one hand, and business and legal practices on the other, also implies a political problem. As far as the software and computer industries are concerned, the US (and Silicon Valley) still leads in software (*The Economist*, 25 May 1996, 29 March 1997). Developing countries always have to copy the more advanced developed countries. It is only with technology transfers that development gaps can be bridged. Developing countries may not be able to pay high royalties or licence fees, yet stealing intangible products is no less illegal than stealing tangible ones.

In redesigning copyright regulations, three approaches are possible (Cairncross, 1997: 206). First, content can be sold outright to sponsors or advertisers who can give it away free to attract new customers. A second approach is a combination of a free portion and a chargeable portion, such as in a free razor but not the blades, or a free recording at a concert once the admission fee is paid. Finally, a copyright may be replaced by a serviceright in which charges are made, not for reproduction, but for a continuity of service in the form of updates and maintaining the original material such as in a financial newsletter.

The principle of consent to protect intellectual property in general, and copyright in particular, is necessary for the system to work. The other important principle is for a fair return on an innovation rather than the right to exclude others from replicating it. The latter becomes impossible when the digital replication of materials is so easy.

Piracy rates

Table 11.3 shows the piracy rates of some Asian nations and other selected countries. Piracy is clearly a huge problem to be tackled. As a percentage of the total value of US$15.2 billion lost to piracy, Europe accounts for 39%, Asia for 29%, North America for 21%, Latin America for 9% and Africa and Middle East for 2% (Business Software Alliance reported in *The Economist*, 27 July 1996).

Table 11.3. Software piracy rates in selected countries, 1995

Country	Piracy rates
Vietnam	99
Indonesia	98
China	96
Russia*	94
Pakistan	92
Philippines	91
Thailand	82
India	78
Malaysia	77
Brazil*	77
South Korea	76
Taiwan	70
Hong Kong	62
Japan	55
Italy*	58
Singapore	53
Germany*	50
United Kingdom*	43
United States*	35

* 1994

(*Source:* Business Software Association and Software Publishers Association reported in *The Straits Times* (20 December 1996) and Business Software Alliance reported in *The Economist* (27 July 1996))

Another source estimated lost revenue for business applications (at their retail value) due to software piracy worldwide in 1996 at US$11.3 billion, of which the Asia-Pacific accounted for 33.8%, North America for 24.0%, Western Europe for 22.8%, Latin America for 5.0% and the rest of the world for 14.4% (Cairncross, 1997: 203). Software piracy rates (the number of applications pirated as a percentage of the total number of applications in use) over same period were 68% for Latin America, 55% for the Asia-Pacific, 43% for Western Europe and 28% for North America.

Competition

Be it the telephone or broadcasting, gateways may exert control through the hardware or software of communications on developing certain content that consumers "must" have. While technology has widened hardware gateways, it has not reduced the number of software gateways between customers and the services they want to buy. Instead, technology has created new opportunities for market power such as in encryption systems. A new gateway is in software for encrypting and decoding cable or satellite television.

The communications industry is prone to monopolies for a number of reasons. First, the economics of networking with large networks creates a bias toward monopolies due to economies of scale and scope. Second, the prevalence of several compatible components designed to work together as a system means that one company controlling one part can leverage its way into other parts to extend its market dominance. Finally, the importance of common standards to allow users to communicate with one another also benefits big players. Standards are not public property, but are owned by companies. A company that is first with a standard—even if it is not the best—can retain its monopoly power once the standard is widely used. For instance, though it is an open standard (and not a proprietary one), the QWERTY keyboard is universally used even though the alternative Dvorak keyboard may be faster and more accurate. New media will create new monopolies.

Socio-Political Issues

The clash of civilisations

As command economies collapsed and cultural values appeared to converge, Fukuyama's (1992) thesis of the end of history was quickly followed by Huntington's (1996) clash of civilisations. Again, new communications technology might have been the catalyst in both theses since connectivity and the speed at which cultural reconfiguration and groupings occur must have a role. While Fukuyama is more optimistic, Huntington offers a more pessimistic scenario. Although the cold war has ended, it may well have reinvigorated old antagonisms and affiliations. New communications technology enables interfacing to occur more quickly, intimately and on a much larger scale.

Huntington is hopeful of, not only limiting the clash of civilisations, but also strengthening it in the singular. New communications technology may offer the salvation of individual civilisations. But the future of civilisation has to start with the renewal of the West, which has to arrest its moral decline in anti-social behaviour. This is witnessed in drugs, family decay and the decline in social capital and trust (Fukuyama, 1995), all of which weaken the work ethic and lead to a fall in commitment to learn and grow intellectually. On the other hand, the Asian way, where nepotism and crony capitalism also did their worst in the Asian financial crisis in 1997, is not failproof either.

Information and communications technology provide the means to effect these changes and instil useful role models in both economic and socio-political terms. The commonalities of civilisations lead people to search for and attempt to expand values, institutions and practices in common with peoples of other civilisations. The end of the good life is the same: justifying the means.

Culture industries

The site of social control and power in culture industries include film, television, radio, music, education, theme parks, publishing and computerisation (Schiller, 1996: 2). The information and cultural sector has ascended to a prominent position in the commanding heights of the economy since culture is fused with industrial power. The key is to review and select the cultural products and processes to have—that is, to select what is admitted or rejected for general public consumption. How individuals in cultural industries, such as journalists, broadcasters, editors, administrators, teachers, curators, directors and producers are recruited and employed should also be part of the selection process since they play a pivotal role in the final output of such industries. When information is produced, processed, packaged, stored and sold, its function is redefined in the commodification process and loses its social character if these individuals do not exercise due diligence.

The selection process starts in school as parents try to provide their children with the best in a competitive environment. Schools reflect the social milieu of the community and nation and, together with the family, they are the primary agents and conduits of socialisation and culture.

Infopreneurs are information brokers with the ability to weave through computer databases with great ease for a fee. Even librarians could yield their traditional role as guardians of the public's right to free and unrestricted information, as their social service is acquiesced or discarded with the commercialisation or privatisation of the information function. Librarians and libraries as social sources and repositories of information, which were the bedrock principles and traditional practices, collide with the realities of the marketplace and corporate-driven profit making.

The civil society and democracy

The health and vitality of the civil society is conditioned by the independence of expression. This independence can be both threatened and expedited by an increased corporate presence. Businesses that expedite information, self-destiny and self-determination must be viewed against other businesses that are barriers since they sell information only to those who can afford to pay. Critical issues on the impact of information technology on civil society and democracy were discussed in chapter 5.

The global village and politics

New communications technology spawns a global village in the way information is communicated. In political terms, the wired village leads to more direct rather than representative democracy. Representative democracy is an oxymoron with information technology. Knowledge and information become more accessible, and governments no longer monopolise them. A more self-directed, self-determined destiny by the people redraws rules regarding governance. Global communities emerge in the wired global village and international institutions assume greater influence. All of this ideally takes place in an environment of more participative democracy as communication is improved.

Moreover, governments become demystified under public scrutiny as more information and communication filter through. They no longer enjoy the mystique of being shielded by public relations machinery. No longer are public institutions put on pedestals in an information age. The global village homogenises the impact of information on local, national and social bases.

In periods of punctuated equilibrium, Thurow (1996) warns that new and old technologies and ideologies do not always match up (see chapter 6). Through a complicated process, beliefs filter experiences, condition visions of reality and alter the technologies to be deployed. Only then do new technologies and beliefs offer new choices. Old, well-established social systems have to undergo a visible failure before a new environment is acceptable. Again, new communications could assuage and buffer the process of transition.

An even more ungovernable world with a global information infrastructure results if the entropy argument is taken to its logical conclusion. There is the inevitable problem of the nature of information as an international public good. The global city is a direct outcome of multinational corporations and their producer services such as advertising, design, accounting, financial services, legal services, management, security and personnel services, which can be located and concentrated in a few metropolitan centres (Sassen, 1991).

American pop culture

There is the political role of global media industries such as the Cable News Network (CNN)[2], the British Broadcasting Corporation (BBC) and France's Euronews. Satellites have made borders porous, but the unequal strength lies in Hollywood beaming American culture across the world more fearsomely than any other culture.

While CNN and BBCWST, with 24-hour news and information channels, are rooted in American and European affairs and interests, growing economic interdependence and linkages as well as the impact of international and regional events have resulted in greater awareness of these happenings, as much for commercial as for socio-political reasons. A cultural shock awaits both East and West as the West sees Asian and Middle Eastern events in their living rooms and Asians experience the liberal journalistic styles and methods of the West. Media imperialism will expand as Reuters Television, Worldwide Television News, the Asia Pacific Broadcasting Union, the European Broadcasting Union and others extend their influence over others.

Cultural protection is as feared in Europe as it is in Asia in terms of the threat to European movie and television industries due to the overwhelming influence of Hollywood and the commensurate rise in American imports. Europe accounts for some 80% of box-office receipts of American films and 60% of American film exports since the 1980s (*The Economist*, 24 December 1994). While scriptwriting, movie making and the computer industry can work together at a distance, their concentration in Hollywood remains a practical advantage. Unlike Europe's movie industry, which requires state subsidies as high as 80%, Hollywood is based on competition and audience appeal.

---

[2] See the CNN effect in chapter 5.

Nonetheless, digital equipment is reducing the cost of making television programmes and movies. A second tier industry for television programmes and movies may emerge if lower production costs and digital technology continue.

Star Television is transmitting mostly American-made programmes in English to 38 countries including Kuwait, South Korea, Thailand, Indonesia, Pakistan, the United Arab Emigrates, the Philippines, Saudi Arabia, Hong Kong, Israel, Taiwan, India and China. Major international advertisers are also using Star TV. Media mogul Robert Murdoch[3] is the epitome of power concentrated in the hands of those with money, such as in Time Warner, Viacom, Turner Broadcasting and others.

Entrepreneurial management further produces, patents or franchises products originating from film or television. Movies become selling and marketing programmes in books, recordings, theme parks, clothing, toys, games and all sorts of paraphernalia, even mouse pads. Alliances with fast-food chains and others create more profits (eg, what the Lion King did for Burger King, Kodak and Toys 'R' US). Disney culture is celluloid but distinctly American. The memory of a generation brought up with a certain movie or television programme can be innovatively repackaged for their children such as in the trilogy of Star Trek films.

Commercial messages and images are globalised as Moscow gives way to Beijing as the largest site for McDonald's outlets. A similar invasion is made by other food and beverage products in the rest of Asia, Latin America and elsewhere. The reverse—cultural infiltration from Asia—is still puny by comparison since even Hong Kong movie-making pales in comparison to Hollywood.

Social base

The future of socialising is affected by the mode of communication. The Internet and electronic mail, for instance, has increased communication

---

[3] Beginning from Australia, Murdoch's News Corporation Ltd has expanded to holdings in the US, Great Britain, New Zealand, Hong Kong, Latin America and Germany. The media tycoon and entrepreneur continues, with his growing empire and quest for further opportunities in Asia and Europe, to attain his vision as a global communications company. His media empire includes newspapers, broadcasting, publishing and air transport.

between strangers. On one hand, social life may be enriched as electronic communication becomes easier and less expensive for individuals. The growth of virtual communities of people linked electronically around work, domestic, cultural, ethnic and other interests creates new social, but faceless, bonds.

A new linguistic style is emerging as essentially a written monologue is conducted and whatever conversation occurs may involve an unknown, unseen, heterogeneous mass audience that voluntarily chooses to be on the Internet. On the other hand, the Internet also supports dialogues, video centers and others as well. While the revival of the written form in both cases is heartening, the more or less instantaneous speed and informal environment of the Internet make the language and flow quite unlike ordinary letter writing.

The English language dominates in electronic communication because the US is the world's largest exporter of intellectual property, followed by the UK. However, with digitisation such as in digital television and multichannels, niche programming in minority languages is easy and less expensive. The limitless capacity of cyberspace also means that languages do not have to compete as they do on analogue television and radio.

At a specific technical level within a national setting, the technology of *narrowcasting* gives viewers the choice to watch different versions or editions of the same programme with different angles of filming, languages, audience level (eg, adult versus children versions) and other variations. When so much choice and variety inundates the social base, what becomes the focus or common denominator for people to talk about what they watched on television last night, may be an issue.

Government and the nation-state

With globalisation, the authority of the government may be usurped by extraterritorial and extranational forces. Ohmae (1995) has raised the issue of the end of the nation-state as economic regions rise in the form of the geographic distribution of production, trade and exchange. Expedited by information and communications technology, the predicted demise of the nation-state in economic terms as affecting employment, finance, exchange rates and other macroeconomic policies are already being experienced.

Socio-political effects are further noted above in the context of the culture of the developed world—principally, that of American pop culture, linguistics and socialisation. Political control may be attenuated as more mass appeal of freedom and democracy is transmitted together with American culture and ideology. So long as information and communications technology promise easy and convenient access, national governments have little choice but to tolerate some of the adverse trade-offs.

Part IV

Information Technology in the Asia-Pacific

Chapter 12

Trends and Applications in the Asia-Pacific

Introduction

The economic, technological and socio-political impact of the information and communications technology revolution and transformation to a knowledge economy and society is no less dramatic in the Asia Pacific. Since the late 1980s, high performing Asian economies (HPAEs) or dynamic Asian economies (DAEs), comprising the newly-industrialising economies (NIEs) (ie, Taiwan, South Korea, Hong Kong and Singapore), transition economy China and second-tier NIEs in the Association of Southeast Asian Nations (ASEAN) (ie, Malaysia, Thailand and Indonesia), have been repeating Japan's successful export-led growth. Fuelled by the forces of globalisation, information technology and direct foreign investment, multinational corporations (MNCs) created a network of production and export bases throughout Asia. The synergy and agglomeration of outward and forward-looking policies in the Asia-Pacific, led by development-oriented governments emulating each other, produced what appeared as the East Asian miracle (World Bank, 1993; Leipziger 1997; Rowan, 1997).

Two broad sets of factors brought the miracle to a grinding halt. The first is more innocuous in terms of the limitation of the export-led industrialisation formula. A basic imbalance between demand and supply is not hard to imagine with the production capacity of the HPAEs as a whole offered as exports to traditional markets in North America, Europe and Japan. The economic health of the later has declined due to various oil-induced recessions and an industrial restructuring force paced by technology and globalisation that resulted in massive unemployment made worse by lopsided demographic trends that strained both fiscal and social security systems.

With growing fiscal and trade deficits in the US, the push for a Single European Market (SEM) in the EU, and Japan not taking up the slack, export-led growth by the HPAEs is reaching a constraint due to severe competition between HPAE members and resistance from ailing industrial economies. That China, after the devaluation of its currency in 1994, has accumulated a trade surplus of some US$40 billion—in contrast to the combined trade deficit of US$45 billion from ASEAN plus South Korea—is telling evidence of global supply and demand and competition. With a trade deficit of over US$200 billion, the US cannot afford to absorb more Asian exports, which would incur a million jobs lost if it did.

The second set of factors stems from financial indiscipline that triggered Asia's currency and financial crisis in July 1997. While the HPAEs are resource rich and have huge potential in terms of growth, with rising per capita income and domestic demand, the most unfortunate turn has been the diversion of relatively cheap and plentiful foreign capital from productive investments to speculative short-term activities. Instead of producing goods and services that create wealth, wealth was manipulated as investments in the real estate and stock markets and portfolio investment since economic growth inevitably engendered a bubble economy in virtually every Asian capital. It was faster and easier to get rich through all sorts of financial speculations including currency trading. Even established manufacturing conglomerates realised larger profit shares from real estate and financial transactions than from exports.

Weak, poorly regulated and supervised financial systems were abetted by political patronage and corruption in many state-owned and linked enterprises in all HPAEs except the more sanitised Singapore and Hong Kong. The two city-states with no natural resources have more astute policies because of their vulnerable, knife-edge existences. But the contagion effect of the currency and financial crisis set off in other, poorly managed and myopic HPAEs resulted in an Asian meltdown for one and all.

This brief overview of the economic situation in the Asia-Pacific highlights the region's growing competition and need to have a more internally-pulled growth impetus. If the export-led formula were to continue, more intra-Asian trade has to grow in addition to diversifying more exports to markets other than the triad of the US, Europe and Japan. More logically, domestic markets in the region should be built and stimulated as Asia has over 60% of the world's population.

With such industrial restructuring and export-oriented growth strategies, information technology and knowledge-based industries will undoubtedly play a significant role in the Asia-Pacific region. The global shift of the electronics industry with a high concentration in Asia, as discussed in section 2, is highly relevant given the centrality of the electronics industry to information technology, communications and the media in the countries involved. Because of the strategic role of information technology in the economy and society, other sections in this chapter will look at information technology policies and attempts at building a national information infrastructure in some of the Asian economies. Specifically, case studies from Singapore, Malaysia and Hong Kong will be explored with more general observations for HPAEs and other members of ASEAN.

A *political economy* approach that encompasses political and economic means in achieving its ends has to be invoked in evaluating strategies and policies. Institutions are inevitably political and economic in nature and scope, and they seek to set and redefine rules and norms as the information and communications revolution unfolds. At the same time, the political economy approach has to ensure an acceptable pattern of possible winners and losers that will emerge domestically and internationally.

Geographic Shifts in the Electronics Industry

One of the most distinctive trends in the electronics industry is its geographical shift in production and distribution. This can be due to product cycles and the push and pull in various countries, starting from the industrial countries where the electronics industry was born. The industry has spread from the US, Japan, West Germany, France, Britain and Italy to the NIEs and other HPAEs, India, Brazil and other Latin American countries.

Japanese domination in discrete semiconductor electronics has declined, partly due to its own economic downturn in the early 1990s and partly because US firms clawed back by 1992 (see chapter 3). But Japan continues to control production of memory chips, especially DRAMs. South Korea has been making a presence through Samsung Electronics since 1991. But in more sophisticated, design intensive and more expensive chips, such as microprocessors and programmable logic chips, US firms such as Motorola and Intel dominate.

As labour-intensive producers involved in assembly and test operations, Southeast Asia is very far down in the technology hierarchy. While Singapore and Malaysia are setting up wafer fabrication facilities to get into the higher end of semiconductor electronics, the biggest players in Asia remain Japan, South Korea, Taiwan and Hong Kong.

In consumer electronics, which is very heterogeneous, the shift to Asia is more pronounced. For instance, China is the largest producer of television receivers; it overtook Japan in 1986, while South Korea overtook Japan in 1988. As a whole, Asia contributes the highest share in the world export of both colour and monochrome television receivers, followed by Europe. Exports of Asian colour receivers are mainly from Japan, South Korea and Singapore, though Germany and, to a lesser extent, the UK, Austria and France are strong competitors from Europe. High definition television (HDTV) and big screen televisions are concentrated in a few countries: namely, Japan, the US, Europe and South Korea.

The production of radio receivers has experienced a similar geographical shift as for semiconductors and television receivers. While the industry started in the US, by 1990, Asia emerged as the largest world producer.

Factors for the global shift

The literature is extant in tracing and explaining such global shifts (eg, Dicken, 1992; Grunwald & Flamm, 1985; Henderson, 1989; UNTNC 1986, 1987). A distinction is made between internationalisation and globalisation, both of which have a bearing on the geographical relocation of the electronics industry (Dicken, 1992: 1). *Internationalisation*, or a global shift, denotes the movement in locations of production and refers to the increasing geographical spread of economic activities across national boundaries. *Globalisation* is a more advanced and complex form of internationalisation, implying a degree of functional integration between internationally dispersed economic activities (see chapter 6).

In the case of semiconductors, the most powerful motivation for relocation to Asia is cost minimisation. The distinctive stages of semiconductors, for instance, are illustrative of the shift. These stages range from high level science, technical and engineering activities at the wafer fabrication end, which requires an extremely pure production environment and the availability of suitable utilities (eg, water supplies, waste disposal facilities for noxious chemical wastes), to low-skilled assembly. A plentiful supply of cheap, relatively skilled female labour in Asia attracts low-end activities.

In particular, aggressive Japanese producers, who are able to ride down the learning curve with economies of scale and large production volumes concentrated in a few firms to compete with American firms, have expanded strategically in Asia. In line with product cycles reaching a maturity stage, American firms also relocated to Asia due to tariff incentives. American tariff provisions (specifically, items 807.00 and 806.30 in the US tariff schedule), allow American firms to export domestic materials or components for processing overseas, and then re-import the processed product on payment of duty only on the value-added during the foreign production. Since American and Japanese direct foreign investments are the largest contributors in Asia, their investments in the electronics industry are in commensuration.

Developing countries are keen to redesign and diversify their industrial structures, and industrialisation is a favoured avenue. Their industrial policies, from import-substituting industrialisation to export-oriented strategies, ride on direct foreign investment and MNCs for infusions of capital, technology and expertise as well as markets. Fiscal and other incentives, one-stop investment boards and skills and education programmes geared to the industry are among the various pull factors, apart from other supply factors such as labour and other resources.

Other factors, including privileges of the Generalised System of Preference (GSP) accorded to Asian developing countries, may have embroiled these countries in trade frictions between the US and Japan in semiconductors as the developing nations became export platforms for Japan. The rising Japanese yen, Taiwan dollar and Singapore dollar may have the effect of pushing investment and industries out with higher costs resulting from the currency appreciation. In the final analysis, globalisation to enhance international competitiveness constitutes the most basic argument for the global shift of the electronics industry. The same factors must have motivated Korean and Taiwanese electronics firms to relocate to Southeast Asia as they are caught up in rising labour and other business costs.

Distinctive features of the semiconductor industry in Asia

Three distinctive features of semiconductor industry in Asia have been observed (Ismail, 1995: 96–97; UNTNC, 1986; UNTNC/ESCAP, 1987) as it emerged as the most important global producer. First, almost all semiconductor firms are subsidiaries of American, Japanese or European electronics firms. On the other hand, a few indigenously owned electronic firms have emerged in South Korea and Taiwan because of more active industrial policies by their governments. Also, the size of their economies, including domestic markets, enable them to cut their teeth.

Because of foreign ownership and domination, the second characteristic follows, in that export-orientation is very high. Most Southeast Asian electronic exports are destined for the US as parent companies import components to enhance the firm's competitiveness and to take advantage of the tariff structure. Only South Korea and Hong Kong are relatively less dependent on the US, a the former is more focused on Japan and the latter, on Europe. Japanese firms as a rule are less prone to importing components and finished products back into Japan, which is often accused of being restrictive and not as open as the US in trade.

Finally, almost all semiconductor exports from Southeast Asia are devices assembled from imported dies (prefabricated silicon chips), except for some wafer fabrication in Singapore and Malaysia. Nonetheless, they still involve discrete semiconductors, not integrated circuits, since IC design is very demanding of skills and talents.

In view of such dependencies and limitations in the Southeast Asian electronics industry, South Korea offers a more interesting role model. Samsung, in particular, has pronounced its ambition to be the largest MNC in the world; it is currently the only viable contender, apart from Japanese firms, for dominance in the electronics industry. Elsewhere in Southeast Asia, state-owned enterprises (SOEs) or government-linked companies such as in Singapore probably stand a better chance (being bigger and more resourceful) to make up for the advantages of the Japanese keiretsus or Korean chaebols.

In consumer electronics, production stages are still distinct, though fewer in number. The design stage for television receivers is not as technologically dynamic and advanced as that of semiconductors, though it still requires intensive research and development (R&D). Multimedia and HDTV, which represent the integration of media, television and radio broadcasting, telecommunications and computers to deliver products in education, entertainment, communications and all sorts of business and household applications, are the more dynamic and advanced areas.

Some components, such as picture tubes, are capital intensive while assembly is labour-intensive and low-skilled. As a consequence, consumer electronics is more globally distributed to optimise comparative advantage (ie, a geographical advantage based on resource endowment) and competitive advantage (ie, an acquired or nurtured advantage based on industrial policies or government incentives). Unlike for semiconductors where the components that are relocated to developing countries involve more labour intensive assembly activities, the transfer of both assembly and manufacture activities of some crucial components such as picture tubes, flyback transformers and housing in television can also take place. Matured product lines may be transferred out, leaving basic research and R&D in home countries. A wider array of technologies is thus possible across Southeast Asian countries in consumer electronics.

Increasing competition also affects shifts in consumer electronics, be it competition between American firms (which pushed some out to minimise costs) or between American and Japanese firms. Apart from being export platforms, Japanese consumer firms may also be attracted by the growing consumer market, driven by a growing per capita income and a large population base. Countries such as Malaysia and Singapore that have, respectively, a multimedia supercorridor (MSC) and Singapore ONE (One Network for Everyone), are actively promoting multimedia and information technology. With young, technologically savvy consumers and users adopting electronics products and embracing a high technology lifestyle, the consumption of consumer electronics products is destined to accelerate rapidly in Asia.

However, the export-oriented trend is still stronger as Asian countries realise the value of a more outward-looking development strategy. Growing intra-industry and intra-firm sales are further contributors to higher exports of electronics components. Intra-industry sales and increasing returns to scale arising from economies of scale in the electronics industry have become new explanatory dimensions in international trade theory.

As with semiconductors, import barriers in the US and Europe (both tariff and non-tariff barriers (NTBs) such as voluntary export restraints (VERs)) may have induced some relocation from Asian countries to these countries as tariff-jumping measures. Both the Single European Market and the North American Free Trade Agreement (NAFTA) may have prompted such transfers as part of the protection of market shares and market penetration.

Another development that may prompt more relocation back to developed countries, apart from heuristic demand to stop exporting employment abroad, is increasing automation. This reduces any cost advantage in labour as well as enhances productivity and zero-defect output.

The national electronics industry

The electronics industry appears to be the *de facto* industry representing security and prosperity for a nation. Advanced industrial nations have emphasised their electronics industries and developing countries are just as anxious to use theirs as the avenue for modernisation and technological upgrading.

As the US loses its hegemony in both economic and political spheres in an increasingly pluralistic world, its domination in the electronics industry has similarly slipped. First Japan, then other East Asian economies, notably South Korea and Taiwan, with China in the queue, either have challenged or will challenge the US and Western Europe in high technology industries.

Even if other NIEs such as Singapore are too small and insignificant in the global electronics industry, the heterogeneity and diversity of the electronics spectrum may enable niches to be carved out by those daring to try. Regardless, the revolution in information technology and microelectronics is changing geopolitics and geoeconomics. In light of this, a quick overview of the electronics industry in the major economies is germane. Major non-Asian countries are included in this overview because they have offshore facilities in Asia.

The United States

The US electronics industry became a full-fledged, globally competitive manufacturing industry because of both public and private sector support since its inception. Between 1949 and 1959, the US government funded some 60% of all R&D projects within the US computer industry. Not surprisingly, the Department of Defence was the key governmental agency, with its funds going mainly to the National Cash Register (NCR), IBM and many research universities. NASA's space programme has greatly enhanced its visibility and growth in electronics as well: many of NASA's hardware and software achievements have direct applications in computer and telecommunications industries as well as commercial spin-offs in the electronics industry. Undoubtedly, the government's direct and indirect investment in education, science and technology and infrastructure, and its encouragement of domestic competition created its technological lead in the industry. The government recognised its necessary interest, given the externalities and security sensitivity of the industry.

The US easily dominated other nations as the international centre for technological invention and innovation. It sustained this position of leadership throughout the 1960s and 1970s. However, by the 1980s, the US macroeconomy changed drastically, with unprecedented challenges and competition, particularly from Japanese firms. The US economy is relatively open with free competition in its domestic markets and low intervention in international trade. Under one decade, US companies lost their dominance in semiconductors, whether out of complacency or the sheer aggressiveness of Japanese companies. Semiconductor trade accounted for a large portion of the country's growing trade deficits, which created pressure for the government to intervene in the arena of international trade.

Japan

Japan entered the electronics industry only in the late 1950s and lagged behind the US in technology throughout the 1960s.[1] Japanese firms relied heavily on foreign suppliers, but acquired critical electronic products and manufacturing technologies through joint ventures and licensing agreements with US and European firms. Under an aggressive industrial policy, the government, through its Ministry of Finance and Ministry of International Trade and Industry (MITI), nurtured the electronics industry through active promotion, protection, technology acquisition and massive R&D funding.

Two MITI plans, the first concentrating on R&D in the computer industry and the other assisting Japanese firms to attain competitive performance-cost ratios, were launched in 1971. Japan did no differently than the US in subsidising and funding R&D. Whereas the US market was open and no protection was deemed necessary, especially when there was no contender

---

[1] The Japanese government tried to shift the economy's industrial structure away from traditional heavy industries to knowledge-intensive industries and an information society in which research is the most important input (Morris-Suzuki, 1994). A number of regional cities designated "technopolises" by the Ministry of International Trade and Industry (MITI) were to be the targets of increased infrastructure and special grants to make them attractive sites for advanced industries and research centres. The technopolises were supposed to infuse the energy of high technology industry into the city's culture, traditions and natural abundance. Their role was also to harmonise industry, learning and lifestyle in the 20 regions identified in the 1980s (see Sasaki, 1981). For profiles of nine giants in Japan—namely, Hitachi, Matshushita, Toshiba, NEC, Mitsubishi, Fujitsu, Sony, Sharp and Sanyo—see Dodwell, 1988.

yet, the Japanese saw fit to protect its growing industry by controlling foreign investments and restricting electronic imports through high tariffs, import quotas and foreign exchange allocations. Few foreign firms, such as IBM Japan, have modest success selling in Japan. As Japanese companies became more competitive internationally, explicit trade barriers in tariffs and import quotas were lowered, but implicit barriers such as R&D subsidies and government procurements remained.

High investment and low capital costs were the central factors driving advances in the productivity, quality, product development and cost competitiveness of the Japanese electronic industry. Japanese firms sustained their investment in television and video recorders long after their US counterparts abandoned them. Within the electronic components industry, automation achieved high quality and high volume production at low cost. With ample production capacity in its firms, Japan seized the opportunity to capture world market share in 1978 when US suppliers with limited capacity were overwhelmed by the demand for dynamic 16K RAM.

Japan has unconsciously set itself as a role model for other Asian NIEs, which recognised the importance of building their domestic electronics industries. Government intervention, such as direct funding, investment loans and assistance for companies as well as national research institutes, was seen as necessary. Japan also pursued the acquisition and transfer of technology with appropriate educational and manpower support.

Western Europe

While governments in Western Europe also traditionally backed indigenous European computer and semiconductor firms, their technological capabilities lagged behind that of US and Japanese firms. High tariffs and rules of origin blocked the use of imported semiconductors throughout the European Community. Non-tariff barriers (NTBs) including preferential procurement further protected the European electronics industry, and national champions such as Thomson and Siemens enjoyed state subsidies as well. But unlike Japan, production by foreign producers was encouraged to serve the domestic market in Europe regardless of ownership. Many US electronic firms took advantage of this situation as did the Japanese.

France launched its first national plan to create an independent electronics industry in 1967, comprising integrated circuits, computer manufacturing, software engineering and telecommunications. The greatest efforts to nationalise and restructure French electronics were under Mitterand's government. The programme envisaged accelerating electronic technologies in large-scale integration, computer-aided design and manufacturing, software engineering and basic electronic components and subsystems for minicomputers and supercomputers. France achieved the greatest success in its telecommunications software engineering industries; it was not as successful in its semiconductor and computer industries.

The European Community (EC) initiated co-operation efforts in large-scale projects to ensure the flow of technological information between member states and to establish EC standards in telecommunications and other electronic products. The vision of a European information society would enable Europe to be independent of US and Japanese suppliers of electronic products. Key national firms, research institutes and universities were linked in projects devoted to microelectronics, information processing systems and information technology applications. Among its achievements are a 10K gate array bipolar circuit, a silicon compiler that is a computer-aided design system for designing very large-scale integrated circuits (VLSI), a logical programming language (PROLOG), and a gallium arsenide chip.

South Korea

The South Korean electronics industry started even later than the Japanese since, until the early 1980s, there was little indigenous electronic manufacturing capability except in assembling semiconductors for foreign firms. In 1982, a plan for promoting the semiconductor industry was launched, and Samsung, Lucky-Goldstar and Hyundai were among three of the leading chaebols to be committed to enter the industry. With funding controlled by the government, South Korea used its influence over chaebols in its industrial policy to restructure the economy and promote an export orientation since its first president Park Chung Hee.

By 1985, South Korean firms began full-scale production of 64K DRAMs at the same time when Japanese firms implemented an aggressive pricing strategy to beat off the competition. With accumulated monopoly profits, Japan's 64K DRAMs were priced at less than half of South Korea's production cost. Despite substantial losses, Korean firms stayed on, diversifying tenaciously into areas where Japanese pricing strategy was destroying profitability.

The South Korean government actively promoted joint funding with companies and universities to develop 1M and 4M DRAMs based on acquired

US technology. There was protection of local markets through import licensing and high tariffs. Not stopping at the recruitment of technological and skilled personnel from Silicon Valley, Korean students and personnel were wooed back to jumpstart R&D—a Taiwanese strategy unabashedly copied by all Asian NIEs.

Funding from the South Korean to help recruit a scientific and technological international brainpool totalled US$3.4 billion in 1995 (Pecht et al., 1997: 19). Both South Korea and Taiwan have close affiliations with the US, especially US-trained faculty members and graduates. South Korea also tapped Japan and even Russia for technology. But the nation lags behind competitors in basic materials technology, which has to be imported, essentially top heavy in the high technology area. Except for bonding techniques and testing software, Korean fabrication processes also lag behind its competitors. South Korea's strength lies in its people, with their rigorous implementation of total quality management (TQM), statistical process control and International Standards Organisation (ISO) certification.

Taiwan

Three stages in Taiwan's science and technology development can be identified. The first stage was between 1966 and 1976, following the termination of US economic assistance and the beginning of a new self-reliance that saw the establishment of the National Science Council, the Chung Shan Institute of Science and Technology and the Industrial Technology Research Institute. The second stage was from 1976 to 1986, heralded by the formation of the Hsinchu Science Industrial Park in 1980 (Wang, 1994). The last stage started in 1986 and is likely to take Taiwan into the next millennium as it joins the league of developed countries. Of the four Asian NIEs, Taiwan probably has the best technology, in terms of local small- and medium-sized enterprises (SMEs) as supporting industries in electronics.

Taiwan's semiconductor industry has much greater technological breadth than South Korea's, but it is still unable to achieve an absolute top position in any segment (Lee et al., 1997: 41). Taiwan's production and exports focus on lower- to mid-range technological categories. At the product level, there is a breakthrough in three companies producing 486 SX microprocessors. Two factors at work beyond government support are US investments and demand pull from Taiwan's computer industry.

As early as the 1950s, the Taiwanese government promoted the consumer electronics industry through tax incentives, financial assistance, protection and public procurement. In 1972, the government made plans to acquire semiconductor design and production capabilities by forming a publicly-owned company. By 1976, this state-owned company opened its first model shop in wafer fabrication. Targeted areas included large-scale integrated circuits, automation, lasers and computer hardware and software.

The same strategies to acquire foreign technology, direct funding and training of engineers and programmers, and mission-oriented national research institutes such as in Japan and other NIEs were followed. Taiwan has more market-oriented incentives to promote the export of electronic products and probably invited less trade friction that way than Japan.

Singapore, Malaysia and Thailand

All three ASEAN countries have open domestic markets and are heavily dependent on foreign direct investment and MNCs as conduits for capital, technology, skills and markets. The first US electronic firms making television receivers arrived in Singapore in the late 1970s. It was an opportune time since the Singaporean government was identifying industrial clusters for promotion with the usual package of tax and financial incentives. Singapore has been very efficient in pioneering the one-stop investment centre—the Economic Development Board (EDB)—which took care of investment promotion, industrial financing and developing industrial estates until 1968. It retained investment promotion while the Jurong Town Corporation (JTC) and the Development Bank of Singapore (DBS) took care of industrial estates and financing respectively. With EDB's help, foreign investors are able to start up their turnkey projects quickly and efficiently, and cut across bureaucratic red-tape and any schizophrenia regarding foreign ownership, a legacy left in many former colonies in Southeast Asia.

Singapore has clear-sighted strategies that take into consideration its strengths and weaknesses (Low et al., 1993). Because of its small size, its best strategy is niche industries in industry clusters including business hubs capitalising on Singapore's prime location for regional headquarters and business service provisions, logistics services and a regional communications and media hub. The country has a strong physical infrastructure for communications and telecommunications as well as a strong, soft infrastructure in education and health care.

A policy of regionalisation was initiated in 1993 where local companies were urged to tap regional resources and markets. Helped by the government's fiscal and financial incentives and collaborations in business councils, regionalisation enabled second "S" corporations, or Singapore MNCs, to emerge alongside most well-developed companies that are at the top of the "S" curve. The government spares no effort supporting business initiatives such as in collective national marketing that champions Singapore as a brand name and quality product. Singapore's strategies have explicit intents for the Asia-Pacific region in strategic alliances and international partnerships.

By nurturing strategic clusters including electronics, chemicals, petrochemicals, precision equipment and instruments, aerospace and biotechnology—twinned with services such as telecommunications, transportation and logistics—Singapore provides competitive advantages for time-sensitive, high technology and skill-intensive industries. It has gained a high ranking in terms of world competitiveness judged by all criteria including the strength of its domestic macroeconomy, internationalisation in terms of its participation in international trade and investment, government policies, finance, infrastructure, management science and technology, and the availability and qualifications of its human resources. The quality of Singapore's judicial and political institutions provides a very transparent and conducive business environment, whatever may be said of its political economy (Low, 1998).

Electronics may account for the largest share of Singapore's GDP, output and employment but, from 1973 to 1990, the ratio of value-added to gross output as a measure of the level of technical development fell from 32.2% in 1978 to 27.7% in 1990. Nonetheless, almost every international electronics producer is represented in Singapore, and the country has started to capitalise on their presence as worldclass leaders in terms of technology transfer and technological upgrading.

Singapore's strength in electronics lies in disk drives, semiconductors, surface mount technology and process control instrumentation with worldclass key players in each of these technologies represented with a presence (Beane et al., 1997). Singapore's production capability is comparable to that of South Korea and Taiwan, but it owns a broader base of technologies and caters to a more diverse regional and international market. Its current core capabilities are in digitisation, wireless technology, miniaturisation, automation, human interface technology, product intelligence and product management. Singapore is moving into wafer fabrication to handle memory and ASICs. Its semiconductor sector is primarily involved in integrated circuit design and automated assembly and testing. New areas pioneered in Singapore include metal injection moulding, Personal Computer Memory Card International Association (PCMCIA), connectors and high-density multilayer printed circuit boards (PCBs).

Singapore's electronics industry has become the top export and value-added earning industry and is central to all science and technology and industrial cluster plans. Singapore is presently aiming to develop its wafer fabrication capabilities since more high skilled, high technology pursuits are necessary, both with its resource constraints and competition from more resource abundant regions. Malaysia is doing the same.

But while the city-state suffers from its small size, which limits its domestic market and economies of scale, it has made virtue out of its size in macroeconomic management. With a pro-market and effective government in terms of being both the planner and player, its industrialisation strategy in general and its development of the electronics industry in particular has been well orchestrated and implemented. It has spared no effort in infrastructure growth, including human resource development.

As Singapore's domestic market is small and factors of production are soon exhausted, many MNCs relocated and diversified outward into the region. A hypothesis of MNCs using Singapore as a beachhead to expand into Malaysia and Thailand has found empirical evidence (Tan & Narayan, 1992). The government has encouraged such outward expansion into ASEAN countries through, for example, tax incentives for establishing overseas headquarters (OHQs) and business headquarters (BHQs) to ensure value-adding and linkages back to Singapore. Both direct foreign investment and MNCs have woven a web of integrated production between the three ASEAN countries. While competition at the national level is keen, the global corporate culture of MNCs allowed greater co-operation between subsidiaries, sister companies and other affiliates. Thus, even when MNCs relocated out of Singapore to Penang, many Singaporean subcontractors followed.

In infrastructure and other supporting facilities and policies, both Malaysia and Thailand are laggards, though they have put effort into their electronics industries, more so probably in Malaysia. While all ASEAN economies aspire to develop its indigenous capabilities, high technology industries and a role as a regional headquarters, a strong argument for co-opition (ie, co-operation at the industry and firm levels with competition at the macroeconomic level) exists, especially in the electronics industry.

Following Singapore's successful development of its electronics industry, Malaysia seemed to have replicated its neighbour's strategies to the letter. It produced an introspective array of plans including its Industrial Master Plan and institutions such as the Malaysian Technology Development Corporation (MTDC) and Malaysian Institute of Microelectronics Systems (MIMOS). The take-off in Malaysian electronics occurred around 1986, though it was more a lateral expansion with the value-added per worker reflecting the fact that productivity did not increase significantly (Beane et al., 1997).

Malaysia's free trade zones (FTZs) for electronics are in Batu Berendam (Malacca), Ulu Klang, Technology Park (Kuala Lumpur), Bayan Lepas, Prai (Penang), Kulim Hi-Tech (Kedah), Shah Alam, Sungei Way, Subang Hi-Tech Park (Selangor) and Johor Technology Park (Johor). But it is in Penang that Malaysia's electronic industry is secured.

The first Malaysian semiconductor operation began in 1971, and became the third largest world producer by 1985 (Narayanan et al., 1989). Penang was Hewlett-Packard's first choice for a wafer fabrication plant, which was subsequently set up in Singapore because of Malaysia's tardiness in reaching a decision (one year compared to three months in respective locations) and tax incentives offered by Singapore (Narayanan et al., 1989: 30, 46). In 1972, National Semiconductor established a lower-end wafer plant in Penang.

Of the twelve top semiconductor producers, five are located in Penang, which is emerging as a strong contender to Singapore. The top semiconductor producers in Penang are NEC, Fujitsu, Texas Instruments, Matsushita and SGS-Thomson, together with National Semiconductors and AT&T. Unlike the experiences of Japan, Taiwan and South Korea, Malaysia was even more behind than the Philippines in having no local sub-contractors for the MNCs (UNCTNC, 1986).

What is similar in the initial stage of all electronic industries in ASEAN economies is the acquisition of technology through direct foreign investment, joint ventures, licensing, original equipment manufacturing and subcontracting. South Korea and Taiwan advanced to the later stage of their own-design and manufacture, and Singaporean government-linked companies advanced to overseas acquisitions, equity investments and strategic partnerships for technology. Other informal approaches such as overseas training and assistance from suppliers and buyers are also common. With a heavier dependence on direct foreign investment and an external orientation, Singapore has essentially maximised this reliance, rather than harbour xenophobic or nationalistic sentiments about foreign technology.

Hong Kong and China

More and more Hong Kong manufacturing operations have shifted to China, especially to the Pearl River Delta region, which is also dubbed the Southern China growth triangle. Like Singapore, Hong Kong remains a major international centre of finance and trade. Both city-states function as the brain centres for physical manufacturing plants that are relocated in respective hinterland or nearby regional offshore bases. The Greater China concept involving Taiwan—economically, if not politically and culturally—further gives scope and potential to the electronics industry in Hong Kong and China.

Hong Kong manufacturing remains dominated by textiles and garments, though its diversification into electronics and precision machinery and instruments has taken place. Its electronics industry went through considerable transformation, from the assembly of transistor radios to the production of digital watches, photographic equipment, semiconductors and integrated circuits and personal computers. But while educational facilities and a social infrastructure are provided, the colonial government is less aggressive than its twin city-state of Singapore in promoting science and technology or indigenous electronics companies. There is no parallel of state-owned enterprises or government-linked companies in Hong Kong as it is the epitome of *laissez faire* economics. Thus, its electronics industry developed on its own steam under free trade and free capital and labour movements.

China may be an industrial laggard with its economic and political reforms only beginning in 1978, but its sheer size makes it a class of its own. By the year 2000, according to the Boston-based International Data Corporation, China will have the world's third largest market for personal computers, with the number of PC installations reaching 16.8 million. Many venture funds are attracted there, with as many as 800,000 primary and secondary schools to tap for educational software alone.

China's packaged software market, for instance, is projected by its Ministry of Electronics Industry to explode, with local companies capturing an increasing share. China's nascent software industry can produce everything from word-processing, accounting and publishing programmes to educational software and games. Indigenous software companies do not have to compete directly with giants such as Microsoft since there is almost unbounded territory in simply translating English language software into Chinese for Microsoft Windows operating systems until protection of intellectual property rights catch up with it. While China does have Most Favoured Nation (MFN) status in the US, it is not yet a member of the WTO. Small- to medium-sized entrepreneurs in China have the experience and talent to be very cost competitive. Whereas the lack of physical infrastructure may impede the setting up of production and distribution networks, software engineering and programming require more intellectual capital and entrepreneurial skills.

Latin America

As a comparative and potential source of competition to Asia, the Latin American attempt to develop its electronics industry is best witnessed in Mexico and Brazil since the early 1970s. Since the electronics industry is relatively more intensive in capital, R&D and technology than other sectors, governments in both Mexico and Brazil, representing potential NIEs in Latin America, have created agencies to address this issue.

Brazil's national companies produce domestically designed computers under tight control of foreign investment and imports to protect domestic markets and producers. However, most national electronics firms incurred substantial losses and needed rescuing from the government. Thus, despite government intervention and support, Brazil's electronics industry, unlike that of Singapore or Malaysia, has not taken off to become internationally competitive.

Plunged into being the most indebted nation in the world in the 1970s and 1980s, Mexico's oil dependent economy tried to emphasise economic growth and industrial restructuring in its National Development Plan of 1983–1988. To raise productivity, improve use of its natural resources and encourage an export orientation, the government has attracted direct foreign investment from small- to medium-sized firms in automotives, mining, electronics and other industries. Firms from the US, Japan and South Korea responded to the call for investment and these companies are exporting low-end electronics, especially television sets, from Mexico destined for the US. The NAFTA arrangement has encouraged more such investment to jump tariff walls and tap Mexican comparative advantages.

International economic competition in electronics

Geographical structures and shifts have resulted in a new mode of industrialisation (Henderson, 1989; Line, 1990; Flamm, 1996). As noted, a knowledge economy with the new raw material in electronics has emerged. Electronics information processing to enable communication has a singularly important utility to the entire realm of human activity. The electronics industry has generated a social and technical division of labour and organised a combination of "technically disarticulated" labour processes in "world factories" (Henderson, 1989: 3–6).

The global electronics industry shows that the world's leading nations do indeed engage in an important degree of economic competition. It refutes Krugman's pronouncements that a country's economic fortunes are not determined largely by its success in world markets (Krugman, 1994a) and that low productivity is a problem, not a disaster, and is irrelevant (Krugman, 1994b).

Using company-level data for six clusters of global electronic companies comprising electronic components, computer manufacturing, computer software, telecommunications equipment, industrial instruments and consumer electronics, Japan is found to be the dominant player with its success attributed to its giant electronic companies (Line, 1990: 12). Japan's lead over the US is in microelectronics, semiconductor manufacturing equipment, opto-electronics, precision robots, factory automation, high definition television transmission, reception and video recording and liquid crystal displays and alternative flat screen technologies (see chapter 3).

Comparative analyses indicate that Japan has developed the strongest technology chain in the world. Every clustering industry in the Japanese chain has generated a large amount of national wealth for its economy. Japanese companies have paid greater attention to economic growth and market share, and less attention to cost efficiency and profit margins. Consequently, their labour productivity has generally increased, though it fluctuates with world demand conditions.

On the other hand, economic erosion appears to be occurring in all clustering industries in the US electronic technology chain. Declining market share and profit margins are observed in all clustering groups for US companies, indicating that they have been less successful than Japan's firms in the global electronics market. Only mid-sized American companies in the same clusters exhibited excellent performance. American's giant firms did not, but giant companies are at the gravity centre of the global electronics competition. Their impact on the global marketplace affects the international trade balance, employment, national wealth and standards of living.

The US may have had the world's largest electronics industry in the 1980s but development was distorted by its continued emphasis on defence electronics and sharp appreciation of the dollar between 1980 and 1985 also attracted imports (Line, 1990: 87). American electronics companies have increased market values and provided higher returns on invested capital.

Incongruously, as these companies maximised profits, at the macro level, the US is the world's largest debtor with increasing trade deficits. Rational companies and individuals do not add up to rational behaviour of a nation as a whole; this is an example of the inconsistencies of microeconomic theory at the macro level.

In contrast, Japanese electronics companies have maximised their market shares and long-term economic growth by emphasising investment in labour, capital and technology and by reducing profit margins and sacrificing cost efficiency. American companies are market-driven concentrating on increasing stockholder values while Japanese companies are market-driven concentrating on increasing stakeholder values reflecting stockholder values and stakeholder capitalism respectively (*The Economist*, 10 February 1996).

The behaviour of Japanese companies contradicts conventional economic theory and is thus said to be irrational. But workers and investors accepting smaller returns on their services of labour and capital respectively have contributed to the vitality of Japanese firms. A firm's expansion is seen as beneficial to secure and create more job opportunities and more income for present and future generations. The Japanese standard of living may not be commensurate with its wealth, since its people live in small houses, drive small cars or not at all, save more than spend, and delay or postpone gratification compared to Americans who enjoy instant gratification and consumption and are less willing to work long hours without extra pay. The economic principles of maximising utility and the consumer theory of income elasticity and price elasticity all appear to have failed to explain Japanese consumer behaviour. At the national level, however, irrational Japanese firms and consumers have generated a large amount of wealth for their nation as they are bent on export promotion.

Yet, both American and Japanese firms are capitalist firms with private ownership of property and assets. While US firms follow conventional economic doctrine, American companies found difficulties translating their national goals into corporate goals. By discarding conventional capitalist beliefs, Japanese companies managed to meet both national and corporate goals while competing aggressively and collaboratively in the global marketplace.

The appreciating yen prolonged Japan's economic decline between 1991 and 1994, rendering its exports less price competitive and home-made electronic products more costly, leading to import substitution. US electronics companies meanwhile recovered with massive downsizing and layoffs in the early 1990s to cut costs and improve efficiency (see chapter 6).

Giant Japanese companies have changed their management strategies in three areas. First, they moved offshore to reduce labour and material costs imposed by the strong yen. Second, they expanded imports of components and finished products since foreign goods were cheaper, induced by yen appreciation. Third, strategic restructuring of business operations on a global basis included reducing or eliminating unprofitable products, cutting off excess domestic capacity and personnel, and raising productivity and profit margins by investing in technologies and new products.

These new management strategies reduced risks in the medium- and long-term for Japanese companies highly exposed to yen appreciation. There was no large-scale downsizing as in American firms since Japanese restructuring involved the reallocation of production facilities, the elimination of unprofitable operations, the consolidation of businesses with small market shares, investment in potentially faster growing businesses and the elimination of unnecessary workers of parent companies in Japan. While parent companies did poorly on a consolidated basis for parent and subsidiary companies, their sales, assets, capital spending and employment did better. Globalising operations around the world and diversifying along the entire electronics technology chain and beyond enabled giant Japanese electronics companies to overcome difficulties caused by an unprecedented yen appreciation and a decelerating domestic market. They still sacrifice short-term profits for long-term growth.

American electronics companies have learnt the lesson of moving into areas of emerging revolutionary technologies instead of cutting on capital expenditure as they did during the 1985 recession. During the same time, Japanese electronics companies did the reverse. They aggressively spent money on new facilities and equipment for manufacturing new memory chips; this buffered them against the rising yen in 1986 and onward. Technology is seen as a national resource and a source of national wealth that can generate real productive capacity and ensure the health of competitive international trade.

The European experience with semiconductors is unlike that of the US, where demand is driven by the military (as the largest consumer of leading edge components), a highly competitive commercial computer industry, a high degree of labour mobility and the ready availability of venture capital. The European strategy to protect national markets from the 1960s, select national champions which led to the failure to keep up with competition in a changing marketplace. It protected the domestic chip market but permitted free investment within Europe by foreign producers.

In contrast, Japan built formidable walls around its domestic chip market, blocked both trade and investment, and regulated foreign imported technology without favouring a single national champion (Flamm, 1996: 27). Typically, Japan's semiconductor industry ascended in the truly Japan Inc fashion with intense domestic competition.

Europe's output of electronic components lagged behind Japan and the US; the EU is a net importer of all types of electronics equipment except computers, computer peripherals and office equipment. Its weaknesses lie in the fragmented state of the European electronics industry with a limited number of strong, diversified electronics companies, and limited bilateral and multilateral government support for R&D. The European computer market is dominated by US firms where IBM Europe has larger sales and turnover than IBM USA.

Trade conflicts

The rivalry between American and Japanese electronic firms has a further repercussion in their bilateral trade and balance of payments; this lead to the Semiconductor Trade Arrangement (STA) in 1991, replacing the agreement of 1986.[2] The 1986 Semiconductor Trade Agreement obliged the Japanese government to improve market access for US companies, assist foreign companies in achieving 20% market share within five years and require Japanese producers to terminate dumping activities.

The agreement was violated by mid-1987 by Japanese firms selling semiconductors below foreign market values in the Far East and failing to increase semiconductor purchases from the US. Trade sanctions followed under the Bush administration, with duties as high as 100% on imported Japanese television sets, computers and peripherals and other electronic products. Stronger Japanese efforts to improve market access occurred in late 1987. By the same token, some European, Korean and Taiwanese companies also gained some market shares in Japan.

As a bilateral agreement, one criticism of the STA is its failure to recognise the increasing globalisation of the semiconductor industry, with Asia as the world's fourth largest producer. The web of strategic alliances and complex sourcing arrangements between international companies makes

---

[2] For the history and impact of the Semiconductor Trade Arrangement, see Flamm, 1996: 159–304.

distinctions between national and foreign difficult. The WTO and its stance on competition policy should be a proper mechanism for trade disputes as under the STA.

Two lessons from such mismanaged trade in electronics are drawn. The first is a contradiction between tactical and strategic compromises, such that long-standing principles in US trade policy have come home to roost. The second lesson is the need to continue working to guarantee open, competitive markets for high technology products (Flamm, 1996: 457–458). High R&D costs are characteristic of a high technology industry, which virtually guarantees government intervention. A further rationale comes from the possibility that shifting technology created profits from foreign producers and consumers— that is, technology-based returns can be captured overseas for national producers, which would increase national income and standards of living. The challenge is how to neutralise subsidies to R&D as a tool of profit-shifting trade competition and still preserve the government's ability to engage in socially beneficial, public investment in R&D. Reciprocity in R&D is permitting companies from other countries to join one's subsidised programmes in exchange for one's own companies being permitted to join in a commensurate portion of another country's R&D projects.

Clearly, competition is driven by many forces including, economies of scale, learning economies, enabling technology, high stakes political intervention, and rapid and sustained technological innovation. As a consequence, a broad array of global companies with various degrees of government support are engaged in mortal economic combat on contested terrain. Moreover, in military and defence applications, there are policies by governments and companies designed with strategic objectives. The R&D to sales ratio in electronics exceeds the average for manufacturing, which means that electronic components are near the top of technology intensive industries.

The empirical evidence from global electronics industries and companies may upstage another traditional economic doctrine in showing that free trade is irrelevant within an international system. Nations compete and co-operate in order to enjoy political peace and economic prosperity. Comparative advantage of nations is subject to dynamic changes over time and natural endowments related to simple technologies are not as relevant. Modern economies are built on advanced technologies, knowledge-based investments, highly skilled personnel and abundant financial assets. Competitive advantage can be acquired, created and accumulated by nations pursuing industrialisation the way Japan did as shown in Fig. 8.2.

The technology revolution has completely altered production methods and offers a relatively equal opportunity to all nations in the world. Developing countries willing to invest in electronic infrastructure, starting from virgin greenfield projects, have bested and leapfrogged ahead of more established nations through technology and capabilities transferred through direct foreign investment and MNCs. Changing comparative advantages in the global electronics industry that facilitate government promotion of corporations, industries and national economies have thus upset and violated many economic credos including the logic of government intervention as good rather than bad.

Singapore's National Information Infrastructure

More than in other East Asian and ASEAN states, the urgency to be competitive in a knowledge economy in general, and electronics in particular, is greater in Singapore. A brief overview of its broadcasting and telecommunications sectors and policies is germane as background to its efforts to build a national information infrastructure.

Singapore epitomises what are called latecoming, semi-industrialised countries (LSCs). LSCs are partially industrialised nations engaged in a medium level of development, sharing many strengths and weaknesses of industrialised and developing nations (Storper et al., 1998). Similar to other NIEs, and second generation NIEs, LSCs are latecomers in some common arenas with developed countries, but they face unequal terms. While they have succeeded in generalising education, acquiring basic infrastructure and absorbing the rudiments of technology transfer and innovation, science and technology is still supply pushed since LSCs lack R&D and industrial culture and demand. They also are deficient in soft factors such as intra/interfirm organisation, co-operation, collective goods and civic culture.

LSCs realise that international competitiveness has to be based on learning, where the post-industrial, post-Fordist learning economy is the information or knowledge society. It is a society where the capability to learn is critical to success. Four kinds of knowledge and learning are distinguished: know-what (eg, facts), know-why (eg, scientific principles and laws), know-how (eg, skills and capabilities) and know-who (eg, social skills) (Nielsen et al., 1998: 35–36).

Broadcasting

Radio and Television Singapore (RTS) became the Singapore Broadcasting Corporation (SBC) in 1980. Until October 1994, SBC, like the BBC in the UK, was a statutory board that could run its day-to-day operations somewhat independently of the government in terms of programme content. But SBC's policies fell directly under the Ministry of Information and the Arts, and a bureaucratic structure persisted. The apparent monopoly position of SBC is still faced with competition from neighbouring countries' channels, especially quasi-private and free-to-air services from Malaysia and videotapes. As an international financial centre and business hub, with a widely travelled populace and an information superhighway in place, the enforceability of an overly strict media policy is questionable.

The emergent landscape has thus changed broadcasting policy in terms of an offensive strategy to entrench Singaporean values and culture and develop an immune system as well as to ensure adequate funding and support for cultivating and nurturing Asian programmes and media companies. As such, SBC hived off some of its commercial operations into a wholly-owned subsidiary, SBC Enterprises, in 1986. Business ventures such as locally produced Chinese programmes are being marketed aggressively in the region. Caldecott Productions, set up in 1990 as an independent arm of SBC, produces commercials and video entertainment. In 1994, the Singapore Broadcasting Authority Act initiated a process of privatisation.

First, regulatory powers were separated from broadcasting operations under the Singapore Broadcasting Authority (SBA) and Singapore International Media (SIM) as a holding company, respectively. Under SIM, the Television Corporation of Singapore (TCS) controls the free-to-air channels 5 and 8 for English and Mandarin programmes respectively, with TV12 as a public television service for Malay and Tamil programmes and the Radio Corporation of Singapore (RCS) in radio services. Eventually, TV12 will operate a UHF channel for documentary, arts and other public service programmes of a largely non-commercial nature. A fourth SIM company is SIM Communications for the operation of all transmission facilities and uplink systems to satellites. Privatisation will follow these corporatisation efforts when SIM's operating companies are listed as public offerings or other placements.

Given strict broadcasting and censorship policies, the domain of predominantly government-owned and controlled systems is most likely to prevail with partial privatisation of more commercially viable services. Instead of a separate private broadcaster competing directly with SIM, private programme producers, especially foreign ones to inject creativity and talent, would be encouraged.

Telecommunications

The corporatisation of the Telecommunication Authority of Singapore (TAS) into TAS remaining as the regulatory body, and Singapore Telecommunication (SingTel) absorbing the operations side, occurred even earlier than for SBC. The public flotation of SingTel in 1993 was a flagship of the privatisation programme, and a policy of asset enhancement for Singaporeans encouraged the use of Central Provident Fund (CPF) savings for approved investments (Low, 1996; Hukill, 1994). This is a unique method of deregulation and pricing because of the equally intimate involvement of the state in the economy. Instead of using a rate of return, price caps or other traditional, accountable pricing mechanisms, TAS makes an internal price comparison against a benchmark of the lowest three for similar services offered in other countries. Domestic telephone charges have been time-based since 1991. While there is no transparent tariff policy as such, TAS's immense licensing power is used to affect SingTel's competitiveness.

The original 15-year exclusive licence for all basic services until 2007, which would automatically continue on a non-exclusive basis until 2017, was rescinded with a compensation of S$1.5 billion for ending the fixed-line monopoly in 2000. In mobile communication, the monopoly ended in 1997 with SingTel Mobile and MobileOne (M1) competing in the cellular market. While its public offering in September 1993 benefited from the bull run in the market, SingTel's performance since has been affected. Profits from long-distance services have slowed down because of repeated tariff cuts forced by competition from external carriers including call-back services. Because domestic penetration rates are already high, SingTel has to venture abroad, from China and Vietnam to Norway and Britain, to expand.

A consortium, Starhub, led by Singapore Technologies and Singapore Power (both government-linked companies) together with British Telecom and Nippon Telegraph & Telephone won a licence to compete with SingTel in offering basic or fixed-licence services (*The Straits Times*, 24 April 1998). The Starhub consortium also won one of two mobile telephone licences; the other licence initially went to P2P Communications, made up of Natsteel, Teledata and GTE Corp. However, TAS rescinded the P2P's contract after

GTE Corp denied that it was part of the consortium (*The Straits Times*, 28 April 1998). They were to begin operations in April 2000, two years after Hong Kong opened its telecommunications market to competition. The two city-states would be in neck-to-neck competition as the region's telecommunications hub.

There is a growing trend in Singapore of government-linked companies such as SingTel and SIM to have equity holdings in telecommunications and television in the region, such as in Thailand and Sri Lanka. Aside from Singapore's policy of regionalisation and growing trade in services, the issue of the need to act reciprocally as the nation expands regionally and internationally will arise eventually. For instance, Singapore Telecom International has set up and manages a commercial television channel in Colombo, Sri Lanka. Whether Singapore will be pressured to allow private systems in reciprocity may be moot now since, for instance, the goal to tap foreign talent and resources for Tamil language programmes is an overriding concern, but the possibility of Singapore emerging as a regional broadcasting hub is constrained by its domestic socio-political and censorship policies. It has neither the *lasseiz-faire* climate nor the creative entrepreneurial mass of Hong Kong.

Cable television

Singapore Cable Television (SCV) is a government-linked company under Temasek Holdings, with ownership also by SIM, Singapore Technologies Ventures, Singapore Press Holdings and the US-based Continental Cable Vision. Its first channel, NewsVision, offers 24-hour news services mainly featuring live CNN news. Two other channels offer English Movie-Vision and Chinese Variety-Vision. An ambitious plan has been mooted to build a nation-wide 30-channel cable television network that will eventually provide direct-to-home fibre optic cable links.

While neither SBC successor companies nor Singapore Telecom have equity interests in the cable system, SCV is moving into it. Similar to other global telecommunications companies, Singapore Telecom is using its fibre optic network to join the competition in cable television, video-on-demand and other services. Even Singapore Power, an electric and gas utilities provider, is a contender. While Singapore is a small market of some three million people, its affluent consumer base and position as an international financial and business hub are attractive apart from possibilities of regionalising from Singapore. Local programmes to serve minority groups such as the Malays and Tamils are also viable as these groups are generally in need of supplementary programmes.

While firmly committed to enable access to all homes by the end of 1999, SCV realises it cannot do it alone as a private company without support from TAS, SBA, SingTel, HDB and others. Low, trial offer prices for external cabling of landed properties, which is more complicated than cabling for public and private high-rise properties, have been offered with an installation cost subsidy to such owners (*The Straits Times*, 21 and 23 March 1998).

Satellite broadcasting

Singapore had its first television receive-only (TVRO) satellite dishes installed in 1988 and 1990 respectively, banning private satellite dishes as a commercial and social protectionist measure. Official satellite dishes enable the national broadcasting enterprise to automatically track satellites such as Intelsat, AsiaSat and Palapa over regions around the Indian and Pacific Oceans. This enables news from a broad spectrum of the world's top television agencies to be selected and packaged as part of Singapore's national news fare.

Singapore's first satellite, SingTel 1, is jointly owned by SingTel and the Taiwanese firm, Chunghwa Telecom International. SingTel 1 will provide telecommunications services over East Asia and India over the next twelve years. While potential demand remains high, the currency crisis has stopped satellite projects in Indonesia, Thailand and Laos. Strong competition comes from over two hundred commercial satellites in operation including Intelsat, Palapa, AsiaSat, Panamasat and others in Hong Kong, Malaysia, Thailand and China among others.

The national information infrastructure

To overcome its physical constraints, Singapore was one of the first countries to implement in 1992 a national information infrastructure to explore information technology for the economy (Wong, 1992; Harvard Business School, 1995a, 1995b). The objective was to deploy a broadband national network. But a physical network infrastructure by itself is of limited value since the rapidly declining cost-performance ratio of telecommunications equipment implies that any country can attain some network functionality within a small timeframe at a fraction of the previous cost. More innovative applications have since come about. The clearest vision for Singapore's national information infrastructure was formulated under the IT2000 Report prepared by the National Computer Board (NCB)[3] (Low, 1996). Aimed at creating a new national competitive advantage and enhancing the quality of life in order to take Singapore into the next lap as a developed country (Low & Kuo, 1997), a vision of an intelligent island is clearly spelt out in the report.

Having provided as many citizens as possible with a home under its 100% home ownership policy, the government—through Singapore ONE—is attempting to provide many of these homes with information technology and multimedia capabilities. When this happens, at least the physical dimension of an information society will have been reached. The premise being that when the facilities and capabilities are available, the applications and creativity expected from information societies will follow.

In terms of regulating the social impact of the Internet, SBA promised not to monitor Internet users. It placed the onus of ensuring privacy on Internet providers instead (*The Straits Times*, 27 September 1996). The National Internet Advisory Committee (NIAC) was established to look into issues regarding privacy and promoting the use of Internet services as well as fine-tuning SBA rules (*The Straits Times*, 10 October 1996). Three subcommittees on legal, industrial and public education were formed. One of NIAC's first tasks was to assess the effect of proxy servers, which are devices installed in computer networks to speed up access to often-accessed Web pages. Proxy servers are also responsible for blocking access to sites deemed objectionable by SBA as covered by the Internet Access Service Providers regulation implemented on 15 September 1996.

Singapore ONE is an island-wide network for multimedia applications and services that started at the end of 1997. It was spearheaded by TAS, NCB, and the National Science and Technology Board (NSTB) in June 1996. Leading technology companies are investing more than S$100 million to provide high speed Internet services and online access to government services,

---

[3] In 1997 NCB, formerly under the Ministry of Finance, was placed under the Ministry of Trade and Industry (MTI), which oversees vital economic statutory boards such as NSTB to meet rising competition posed by information technology.

school curricula and educational information for a start.[4] Singapore ONE will also offer companies a nation-wide testbed before expanding into the region.

Telemedicine is a major candidate for information highways since a specialised and wide range of information technologies (eg, computing systems, computer workstations, database designs, software and others) are used with telecommunications to deliver medical services (Cooper et al., 1997: 30–53). Benefits include improved access for unserved and underserved areas, reduced travel costs, the duplication of services, technologies and specialists, reduced professional isolation for peer and specialist contacts and continuing education, improved quality of care through enhanced decision-making of hereto impractical collaborative efforts, and improved overall productivity.

Barriers to technology adoption in telemedicine include technological issues such as integrating existing equipment to work together, the availability of advanced telecommunications networks, regulatory barriers, financial issues, organisational issues and convincing individual adopters. The possibilities include technology commercialisation, growth of a technology-based entrepreneurial community and others. At the grassroots level are individual physicians, nurses, administrators, inventors, entrepreneurs and financiers linked in the network.

One immediate application is the electronic commerce hotbed (ECH) launched in August 1996 to catalyse electronic commerce by identifying new applications with economic potential to demonstrate the technical feasibility of using a national information infrastructure for commercial purposes. A new form of communication in S-mail was established as a prototype virtual mail for the retail industry (*The Straits Times*, 6 May 1997). A public-key cryptosystem to facilitate electronic payments has been experimented with under a Secure Electronic Transaction (Set) mechanism.

The Electronic Transactions Bill, proposed by the Electronic Commerce Policy Committee comprising a wide spectrum of government agencies and

---

[4] The Ministry of Education will spend S$300 million in information technology programmes including buying computers, networks, software and training more teachers and students in information technology (*The Sunday Times*, 1 March 1997). This is part of the S$2 billion information technology plan for education to foster creative thinking and independent, continuous learning in schools (*The Straits Times*, 29 April 1997). The future classroom in Singapore will make learning computer-based and rely less on teachers as the search for information shifts to the Internet and other databases. All schools will be fitted with computers by 2002, wired to the Internet and multimedia workstations.

departments and set up in January 1996, gives similar legal weight to electronic transactions and documents as to their paper counterparts (*The Straits Times*, 14 April 1997). Legal certainty, accountability and predictability, including settlement procedures for crossborder cyber disputes, have to be established before Singapore can aim to be a regional hub for electronic commerce. The growth of agencies authorised to issue digital certificates recognised by other countries, acceptance of electronic filing by government ministries, departments, agencies and statutory boards and the issuing of licences and permits online as well as the need for enforcement and investigation agencies are among matters of electronic commerce considered in the proposed bill.

The Singapore Stock Exchange will start online Internet shares trading by the end of 1998, allowing small investors to buy limited shares that will bypass and save on the costs of remisiers (*The Straits Times*, 25 March 1998). The current charge for brokers is 1% commission on small trades. The system would be similar to authorised trading centres, which allow small investors to trade in Singapore shares without having to open trading accounts with brokerage firms.

Beyond the domestic market, new applications can include value-added services in regional trade as Singapore emerges as the electronics marketplace to broker regional products. Widespread adoption of information technology has led to declining co-ordination or overall business transaction costs within or between different firms. An electronic broker serves as the nexus of contractual relationships between different buyers and sellers, which in turn allows the broker to police the market. It can enforce standards for fair trading, discourage opportunistic behaviour and reduce contractual risks.

Greater market efficiency results and greater use of the market mechanism will occur by firms that already have suppliers in the region. Economies of scale and economies of scope will be enjoyed and a second multiplier effect will be generated as Singapore becomes a central brokering house for the region. Further indirect effects will be created for ancillary services such as finance and transportation as trade volume grows in positive feedback loops. Singapore as an international business hub would be entrenched.

Malaysia's National Information Infrastructure

The Multimedia Supercorridor

Initially, Malaysia appeared hesitant with the new communications technologies until it began to realise its economic potential (Low, 1996). Slightly different from Singapore's explicit national information infrastructure is Malaysia's more piecemeal but ambitious attempt to develop its Multimedia Supercorridor (MSC). The MSC covers Malaysia's the new administrative capital, Putrajaya, an intelligent city called Cyberjaya and the new Kuala Lumpur Airport to be served by a 2.5 to 10 gigabit fully digitised fibre optic network that will link the MSC to other countries in Asia, US and Europe (*The Economist*, 1 March 1997). In the MSC, two telesuburbs, a technology park, a multimedia university and an intellectual property protection park will also be built in the US$40 billion project. Public relations, subsidies and incentives have attracted high technology foreign companies such as Microsoft, IBM, Apple, Sun Microsystems, Oracle and Motorola.

The Multimedia University was mooted with an academic programme and staffing from the Massachusetts Institute of Technology, Stanford University, Simon Fraser University and Nippon Telegraph and Telephone's Multimedia University (*The Straits Times*, 10 January 1997). A package of infrastructure, law, manpower training and talent scouting was to have put in place designated flagships in telemedicine, distance learning, government, smart cards and remote manufacturing. However, skilled manpower will be a major constraint on MSC's development.

Malaysia's new cyberlaw is to govern the convergence of technologies and support the development of the MSC (*The Business Times*, 9 October 1996). In contrast, Indonesia, wants to curb foreign participation in broadcasting and advertising in a new broadcasting bill passed in 1997 (*The Business Times*, 9 October 1996). Protecting the socio-political sensitivity of the industry is the main motivation for the bill.

Telecommunications and broadcasting

Like most telecommunications monopolies, Malaysia privatised its Department of Telecommunications in two stages, beginning with its corporatisation in 1987, which established Syarikat Telekom Malaysia Berhad before it was listed on the Kuala Lumpur Stock Exchange. The regulating body is the

Department of Telecommunications under the Ministry of Energy, Post and Telecommunications.

In 1994, Malaysia's fixed telephone market was further liberalised with the entry of three firms, namely, Selkom, Binarian and Time Engineering, that ended Telecom Malaysia's monopoly. Since 1994, two more companies have obtained fixed telephone licences.

In the mobile telephone market, competition started in 1987 with Selkom, and has progressed to include six such companies in operation currently. There are some 36 licences issued in the pager market, though not all are operational in practice. Nonetheless, the Malaysian telecommunications market appears competitive. With the economic and currency crisis in 1998, the further merger and acquisition of smaller operators struggling with huge deficits may be imminent. The larger and more profitable Telecom Malaysia may seek greater horizontal integration from fixed lines to the mobile telephone and pager business.

The privatisation of broadcasting is less straightforward because racial harmony is a key component in Malaysia's nation-building, based on an extremely nationalistic economic policy that sanctions and protects the special rights and position of Malays. Apart from state-owned public broadcasting concerns, the alternative of TV3 is the most interesting, unabashed example of political influence as its major shareholder, Fleet Holdings, is owned by the dominant ruling political party, the United Malay National Organisation (UMNO).

The newest Malaysian, second national commercial network is NTV7, which started broadcasting in April 1998 (*The Straits Times*, 8 April 1998). It is owned by Nati-Seven TV, a wholly-owned unit of the diversified Encorp Group based in Sarawak with broadcast centres in both West and East Malaysia in all the official languages and in Hindi.

While parabolic antennae remain banned in Singapore and Malaysia, Indonesia is liberal and Thailand is *laissez-faire*, having dropped a licensing system in 1992. Without a background of colonisation, and strong ethnic and communal relations such as in Malaysia, the role of the media in Thailand's nation-building is different. A relatively greater degree of freedom is enjoyed while radio and television remain state monopolies.

Apart from a tight grip on broadcasting policy to reflect sensitive socio-political areas, the mass media (eg, newspapers) in Asia are as generally controlled. Similar to Singapore, there have been a steady series of skirmishes with foreign press in Malaysia in particular since correspondents are charged under their respective Official Secrets Act and face temporary, restricted or total bans on the circulation of foreign newspapers and magazines.

Malaysia is intense in its intent to attain the highest level of communications technology, though there is contestation between different ethnic groups in its formation and media policy (French & Richards, 1996: 157–180). If successful, Malaysia may pose an interesting case of attaining the ultimate cyber age with a modern view of its religious and ethnic relationships. Its determination to succeed is reflected in aggressive policies.

Hong Kong's National Information Infrastructure

There is no pronouncement of a policy on a national information infrastructure in Hong Kong *per se*. But similar to Singapore, Hong Kong has tapped the information and communications technology revolution well ahead of other Asian economies by virtue of its international networking in trade and finance. A brief overview of its telecommunications sector will bear out Hong Kong's trends and developments before looking at its trade-related electronic data interchange called Tradelink (Harvard Business School, 1995c).

Telecommunications and broadcasting

The end of the Hong Kong Telephone Company (HKTC) monopoly on domestic public switched telephone network (PSTN) and basic voice services came with four new fixed telecommunications network service licences issued in July 1995 to HKTC, Wharf Holding's T&T (Hong Kong) Ltd, Hutchinson Communications Ltd and New Telephone Ltd. The monopoly has been whittled away since the mid-1980s by the licensing of competing cellular mobile telephone services, which are partial substitutes to fixed wireless telephones. With a teledensity of 51 in terms of the number of exchange lines in a service per 100 population, in 1995, HKTC's monopoly in existing telephone penetration was high. Other markets such as customer premises equipment and paging are more competitive. The telecommunications authority, as the regulator, can introduce class licensing by issuing generic licences, licences that allow operators who would not be required to hold individual licences to provide any kind of telecommunications service within the prescribed categories of the licence. While appearing competitive, a class licensing system has implications for licensing and regulation so long as radio spectrum still has to be allocated, and public interest and safety standards have to be maintained.

In 1993, Hong Kong Telecom became the first operator in the world to complete the switching of its local telephone network to digital technology (*Far Eastern Economic Review*, June 1998). With greater capacity and higher signal quality, digitisation enabled Hong Kong to launch the world's first commercial interactive television, delivered over Hong Kong Telecom's lines in March 1998. With technology as the first step, the Hong Kong telecommunications industry should witness greater deregulation, more competition and newer products. Ironically, Hong Kong Telecom's pact with the government had been its monopoly on domestic and international calls for controlled profits, which still enabled it to acquire new equipment and new technology.

After 1997, there is no more long-distance telecommunications traffic, only local and international traffic. The distinction is unlikely to survive 2006, when the exclusive licence of Hong Kong Telecom International (HKTI) to provide international network services and international basic voice services expires. However, competition does not necessarily guarantee consumer benefits in lower prices and wider choices of services and tariff schemes. The new fixed telecommunications network service face the uphill task of breaking HKTC's stronghold and issues of universal service obligations and calculations of access deficit charges and revenue-sharing arrangements remain contested.

Aside from the common challenge of new technology and multimedia services, telecommunications and media industries in Hong Kong have a peculiar variant in terms of the socio-political environment after 1997 and the territory's existence as a Special Administrative Region (SAR) under China's formula of "one country, two systems". Hong Kong has greater pressures and passion for democracy than other colonies because of its peculiar format within the larger context of Greater China. Broadcasting policy is thus not easy to formulate since Hong Kong aspires to maintain a pluralistic environment and international profile even under such constraints (Lee, 1997: 201–224).

Through Star Television, Hong Kong is also a prime player in technology-driven, regional direct broadcasting by satellite since 1991. Owned equally in the beginning by Hutchinson Whampoa, Cable & Wireless and China International Trust & Investment Corporation (CITIC), most of Star Television's programmes are carried by Asia Satellite Telecommunications (AsiaSat) satellites AsiaSat 1 and AsiaSat 2. Launched in 1990 and 1995 respectively, AsiaSat 1 and AsiaSat 2 already cover two-thirds of the world's population. Greater magnitude, scope and diversity are created by the multiplier effects of, for example, CNN or the BBC World Service Television (BBCWST) beamed via AsiaSat 1 across Asia. It was more to placate the Chinese government that BBCWST was dropped from AsiaSat 1's northern footprint in April 1994 as Rupert Murdoch's purchase of Star Television in 1994 had unsettled Beijing. China made sweeping restrictions against private ownership of parabolic antennae after Murdoch's pronouncement that satellite technology would mean the end of totalitarian regimes (*Australian Financial Review*, 15 June 1994).

Another Hong Kong-based satellite company is APT Satellite (with majority ownership by several Chinese ministries), which has Apstar-1 in space. These satellites have enhanced the region's telecommunications and broadcasting capacity, which will progress naturally to interactive multimedia as a logical sequence.

With Hong Kong's talents in the production and distribution of Asian programmes, it is natural for its broadcasting services to aim for regionalisation. Culturally, aside from the Western and Asian worlds, Star Television, for instance, can even bridge cultural gaps in India. The power and resources of moguls such as Rupert Murdoch in STAR, and other spin-offs like Phoenix Satellite Television, cannot be underscored. Hong Kong is indubitably one of the titans in Mandarin broadcasting and caters, not just to Asian markets, but to Mandarin-speaking viewers around the world.

Television exchanges between Hong Kong, Taiwan and China may be limited by ideological and political barriers, but strong economic, cultural and technological affinities may prevail over them. This regional and geolinguistic role of Hong Kong may give its information technology and media industry more scope and latitude. Even Singapore is a long way behind in such regionalisation efforts as it lacks the necessary talent and creativity. Broadcasting and media policies tend to be more circumscribed and parochial in the more politically controlled Singapore and other ASEAN states. As such, Hong Kong's current status as a regional player should remain strong provided it harnesses its resources judiciously and wisely.

Hong Kong is technologically weak, especially in technology innovation, and it buys most of what it needs. China is also weak in telecommunications infrastructure and backward in equipment manufacturing, but Hong Kong is the base from which China can access sources of high technology in telecommunications.

In one project initiated by the non-profit Hong Kong Trade Facilitation Council in 1983, electronic data interchange and a centralised database of consignment data was created to improve trade activities. Unlike Singapore's

Tradenet, spearheaded by its Trade Development Board (TDB), a consortium of private companies worked on an international computer network linking freight carriers, banks and trading companies. Cable & Wireless initiated its own electronic data interchange system, called Intertrade, as early as June 1989. As a private company, Tradelink Electronic Document Services is a response to the information technology age to reduce paperwork and enhance productivity and turnaround time. But Tradelink is seen strictly as a business proposition rather than a technological watershed. The issues centred more on the sort of government backing required for an exclusive franchise to computerise processing of trade-related documents. Unlike Tradenet in Singapore, Hong Kong's government was not champion to Tradelink.

Comparative Analysis and Issues in the Rest of Asia

Asia and Southeast Asia are fast catching up to the West in information technology and the media, and an information society is inevitable given exposure to foreign trade, capital, labour, technology and other flows. The end of the nation-state and sovereignty in regulation as state-controlled, authoritarian media policies are marked by an irrevocable transition to an international political economy. Direct broadcasting by satellite (DBS) bypasses all state-owned and controlled terrestrial relay equipment, making traditional broadcasting policies largely irrelevant.

The sizeable and growing Asian consumer market is seductive in all areas of information technology and communications. For instance, the size of Asia's market for personal computers is growing, with the Asia-Pacific region accounting for 7% of the world's personal computer market and projected to expand 20–30% in each of the next several years (*Far Eastern Economic Review*, 15 June 1995). Despite the recession, the Japanese market, which accounts for half of all Asia Pacific sales, grew one third to account for 3.4 million computers sold in 1994. China grew by two-thirds to account for 548,000 computers sold during the same year, putting it in fourth place after Australia and South Korea.

In broadcasting, Western media moguls are attracted to the growing audience in Asia, as witnessed by the penetration of Star Television and others. Television broadcasting in Asia is changing from a skimpy collection of state-controlled programmes to a vast array of channels providing a virtual wonderland of viewing options (*Asian Business*, June 1995). Foreign broadcasting companies such as the National Broadcasting Corporation (NBC), the British Broadcasting Corporation (BBC) and the Cable News Network (CNN) are already carried on Star TV. Regional news is broadcast from Singapore by Asia Business News (ABN), owned by Dow Jones, while Hong Kong's Chinese Television Network has had a 24-hour Mandarin language news channel since November 1994. Western broadcast companies do not just export their products to Asia, but customise them with inputs from Asian cities. Even the pioneer Star TV has moved away from pan-Asia coverage to cater to individual Asian markets. Users have become more sophisticated.

In particular, the Murdoch empire includes newspapers (published in Britain, the US and Australia), television (ie, the Fox Broadcasting Network and eight US station affiliates; the BSkyB satellite delivery system for Britain; and Star TV for Asia, the Middle East and India), film (ie, Twentieth Century-Fox), book publishing (ie, HarperCollins), a magazine (ie, TV Guide) and multimedia (ie, a Delphi Internet Services and MCI joint venture) (*Business Week*, 29 May 1995). His reach has certainly entered Asia via Star TV, acquired from Li Ka-shing's Hutchinson Whampoa in 1993. Star TV can potentially beam programmes to 220 million households, but measuring such footprints is not easy. Plans are afoot to use digitisation to customise programmes for different markets.

However, a jungle, rather than an ordered and structured industry, is found in practice with CATV largely still untested in Asia. Although Japan has the most developed and regulated cable market, only about 5% of an estimated 42 million homes with TVs have cable though cable is available to 25% of Japanese homes. Until 1993, pressured by the US over copyright infringements, cable TV was illegal in Taiwan. India's cable industry is in greater disarray with an estimated 40,000 to 60,000 cable companies and all of them operating outside the law until 1995 when a bill was ratified to legalise and regulate the business. But enforcing the new rules would be difficult with India's lax registration requirements.

Indonesia's Palapa satellite may be the first in Asia, but its ownership and control by the Indonesian government for national purposes first and foremost has rendered it less dynamic compared to AsiaSat 1. Palapa's footprint covers an area from northern Australia to southern China and Bangladesh, and its most important customer is CNN, which began a free-to-air service in 1991, and the Australia Broadcasting Corporation, which began a free-to-air service in 1993 (Atkins, 1995).

Interactive media in the digital age and Asian governments build their own acceptable versions of information highways. Singapore is wiring up every home and office with fibre optic cable for future interactive services, which the government plans to control in the "intelligent island". South Korea also has plans for fibre optic multimedia to transform the nation into a full-fledged information society by 2010. As noted, Malaysia has its MSC, while Thailand, the Philippines and Indonesia also aspire to have broadband infrastructure and access by 2002 and 2010 respectively. Table 12.1 shows Asia's switch to digitisation led by Hong Kong and Singapore.

Table 12.1. Asia's use of digital lines, %

Hong Kong	100.0
Singapore	100.0
Vietnam	100.0
China	99.5
Taiwan	97.8
Indonesia	96.0
Malaysia	96.0
Cambodia	94.0
India	87.0
Thailand	87.0
Japan	84.0
Pakistan	78.0
Philippines	70.0
South Korea	65.1

(*Source:* ITU and Merrill Lynch estimates)

For selected ASEAN countries, Table 12.2 shows the penetration of telephone and cellular lines and Table 12.3 shows the growth of new Internet hosts and users.

Many issues as a result of information and communications technology can be raised as traditional state monopoly and authoritarian policies are challenged. A diversity of responses and sustainability of such policies have emerged in Asia. The outcome is inevitably the same: that state control over the mass media is eroding and the most important issue is how best to live with the international marketplace in information technology and mass media.

Table 12.2. Telephone lines/cellular penetration in ASEAN, 1994–95

	Residential telephone lines* 1995	Cellular lines* 1994
Indonesia	2.2	0.09
Malaysia	60.2	4.70
Philippines	6.7	0.50
Singapore	100.0	9.40
Thailand	18.4	2.0
Vietnam	2.6	0.16

* Per 100 households
(*Source:* World Competitiveness Report (1997))

Table 12.3. Internet growth in ASEAN

	Growth of new hosts, %, 1994–95	No. of users		No. of ISPs* 1996
		1996	1997	
Indonesia	1,228.2	50,000	100,000	20
Malaysia	161.1	200,000	300,000	2
Philippines	430.2	20,000	30,000	80
Singapore	333.5	150,000	150,000	3
Thailand	134.7	100,000	150,000	16
Vietnam	na	4,000	6,000	2

* ISP = Internet Service Provider
(*Source:* World Competitiveness Report (1997))

Democracy

The power of telecommunications has let the genie out of the bottle in Asia. As Western information filters through, there is a concomitant need by Southeast Asian governments to try to balance the unbalanced flow of news. Unfortunately, there are times when this occurred along North-South and East-West lines. Yet, this has to be so because the West dominates in the development of the information society and sets the pace for deregulation of the telecommunications industry and other standards. Cultural imperialism may be subtle and indirect, but it is certainly much alive.

Telecommunications and information technology have together released more democracy, since self-determination and self-interests can be pursued. As the world shifts from the importance of the state to that of the individual, opportunities for individual freedom and enterprise are totally unprecedented. The issue is, with newly acquired independence in many Southeast Asian states, are they ready for such unbridled democracy and self-determination? The socio-political and cultural environment is so different from that in the West.

One impending issue arising from information technology and the information society is should the government hinder the process of changes affecting people's lives, in work, entertainment, learning, shopping and communicating, or should it pursue a simple principle that, wherever possible, changes should reflect the free choice of its citizens? When governments have to be afraid or are nervous of the people's ability to judge what is good for them, it becomes a frightening world. Cheaper communication should be viewed as a way to promote competition and progress rather than a challenge to governance, culture and values. Nonetheless, in many Asian countries, an information gap between the government and its people may exist as do gaps between haves and have-nots in society and between developed and developing countries.

Simultaneously, the information technology revolution has brought about a need for balance between the tribal and universal to a new level. Tribalism is not to be confused with nationalism since it is the belief in fidelity to one's own kind, defined by ethnicity, language, culture, religion or even profession (Kotkin, 1993). Electronic mail makes us more tribal at the same time that it globalises us. The mantra "think globally, act locally" has been turned on its head to become "think locally, act globally" and, as economies globalise, a related paradox is that the more universal we become, the more tribally we act (Naisbitt, 1993: 58).

Censorship

Democracy should not be confused with the sovereign and moral duties of a government to protect society as a whole. The issue of censorship may tread on very thin lines between democracy and the need to protect and preserve core culture and values. Cyberspace censorship needs sterner laws for two reasons (*The Straits Times*, 12 April 1995). The first is that as the debate on pornography reveals, jurisdictional problems arise as cyberspace is seamlessly global. What is legal at one place may be illegal in another. The second reason is that existing legislation is simply anachronistic in the anarchic world of cyberspace. Electronic mail may resemble the postal system in transmitting personal messages, and multimedia web pages where companies display information are similar to advertising in newspapers and magazines. Banning indecent materials transmitted by electronic mail and on the Web is not as feasible.

There is a fundamental dilemma between screening off information deemed offensive and undesirable and allowing a free flow of information in an information society. Framing laws that are sufficiently discriminating between what is desirable and undesirable information is impossible. Some providers such as Penthouse and Playboy can list or warn of contents that are forbidden and, if they were wise and thinking in the long term, they could work with parents to help them protect the children. Defining products that require parental approval (eg, film shows) is not as simple as equally computer literate parents is one prerequisite.

Cyberporn is already causing concern even in industrial countries. In the US, congressmen are asking for new legislation to limit access to images that depict children in sexual acts. The Clinton administration has also declared support for practical measures to curb violence in entertainment. There is a difference between what cannot and should not be censored. Technology-wise, it is not impossible once it is decided what is to be censored. The V-chip (V for violence) is a relatively simple and inexpensive device that enables parents to block television programmes transmitted with a signal identifying them as violent or inappropriate for children. Broadcasters or cable television operators transmit a special rating code along with programme carried in an unused portion of the television signal. A V-chip installed in a TV or cable converter will read the signal and warn parents to activate blocking. This assumes that parents are as computer literate and willing and prepared to act as private censors.

Privacy

The issue of computer privacy may be less relevant when viewed from a long-term perspective and if it is realised that information democracy will improve as information productivity increases. Concerns regarding computer privacy arise in three forms. The first occurs when government controls over ordinary citizens are strengthened and government uses personal data for purposes other than originally intended. The second is when ordinary citizens suffer psychological, social or economic damage when enterprises use managerial personnel data and administrative personal data to their personal advantage. Finally, the right of ordinary citizens to privacy is violated when their personal data is disclosed to a third party. Similarly, health care information highways face problems of confidentiality.

Strictly speaking, the state should not have the right to set up a unified national system of code numbers for all citizens. This may lead to the danger integration of all kinds of databases and records and such information could be used for the wrong purposes. At least, a unified system should not exist without an effective watchdog organ set up by citizens. The human right to know will change into a human right to use information, and the human right to protect secrets will change into a human duty or ethic to share information. But Asian governments are highly authoritarian and often communitarian interests take precedence over individual ones. It will be a while more, even with more education and affluence, for Asians to value privacy the way their Western counterparts do.

Intellectual property rights

Because both legal and policing mechanisms are relatively weak and ineffective in Southeast Asia, the issue of intellectual property rights is significant. There are cogent arguments for such protection without which Asia would not be unable to attract research and development if inventors cannot seek patent rights to be enforced. Yet, for many developing countries, small, medium enterprises (SMEs) survive through copying and imitating proven technologies, which they can neither initiate nor pay for. Without a *carte blanche* to adopt and adapt technologies with a view to make the products more cheaply and efficiently, even Japan would not have become the industrial power it is today. But latecomers such as the rest of the NIEs and Southeast Asian countries do not have such free and easy access now.

Industrial countries and MNCs are naturally concerned about intellectual property rights and laws safeguarding copyright and patents. In a survey on the piracy of software in Asia, Singapore's software piracy rate was the lowest as shown in Table 11.3. But protection of software piracy in Singapore took a more forceful turn with the intention of preserving its record as the top Asian nation to protect intellectual property rights with more anti-piracy raids and new rules on the manufacture and import of equipment to make master copies and duplicate optical discs. Makers of optical discs, including compact discs and video CDs used for computer software and movies, have to obtain licences to import equipment needed to manufacture master copies and duplicate discs for CDs, CD-read only memory (CD-ROM), video CDs, digital video discs (DVD) and DVD-ROM (*The Straits Times*, 18 April 1998). But the will to protect intellectual property rights is not as forthright in other Asian countries.

If piracy is one criterion of advancement, clearly, Asia is a laggard behind America and Europe. This is so not just in terms of Asia's level of technical proficiency and capability. Asia's socio-legal framework, such as in protecting intellectual property rights, is not yet conducive to spawning an information industry. Yet protection of intellectual property rights is a necessary condition before external technology and capital can be attracted.

Asian nations are not the only culprits in counterfeiting; Italy ranks third after South Korea and Taiwan with an annual turnover estimated at between 6,000 to 10,000 lira (S$5.4 to 9 billion) as revealed by Indicam, a grouping of about one hundred prominent Italian and international firms (*The Straits Times*, 14 April 1998). Italy also spends more money on hiring private detectives and lawyers to combat counterfeiting ranging from designer clothes to aircraft parts.

Equity

The information society presupposes that every individual has both resource accessibility and computer literacy to grow and develop around information. In Southeast Asia, this may not be so since income inequality, high rates of illiteracy, lack of infostructure and even basic electrification programmes are all at less than desired levels. As a consequence, the worry that an information society may worsen income and capability gaps between the haves and have-nots—unless the government intervenes—is a social concern.

Large parts of Southeast Asia's economy are based in agricultural activities and the use and application of information technology is not uniformly widespread. Even in the manufacturing and service sector, the abundance of labour does not argue for labour-saving technologies such as using information technology for automation and mechanisation. Thus, there is less urgency for telecomputing work and other information technology applications that may exacerbate an inequitable situation. The rural-urban structure is quite distinct and dualistic with the less developed Southeast Asian states.

Culture

A global culture implies the supposed decline of the nation as a cultural glue and a political and economic force as new levels of supranational organisations take over functions traditionally performed by national governments. This may appear more tangibly in consumerism with internationally traded branded goods, but culture is deeper than material and commercial symbols. The thesis of the clash of civilisation suggests that there will be local resistance to globalisation. Technology and access may simply offer people greater choice and variety in how they want to be identified by shared values and experiences in consumption, ethnicity, religion, gender or other characteristics.

One criticism of the global information infrastructure is that it may not benefit developing countries that do not have the national infrastructure to tap into it. That the US may hog the flow of cultural information traffic is a concern of developed countries worried that US "colonisation" in an era of computers, telephones and television may "drown" other cultures. This is made worse by a number of monopolies such as Microsoft, the defendant in an anti-trust case for abuse of its dominant position. Bill Gates, chief executive officer (CEO) of Microsoft Corporation, has noted that cyberspace can transform global culture and has questioned cultural issues related to information technology and the role of the government in a regulatory framework (*The Straits Times*, 13 February 1995). Thus far, the government is involved when it comes to deregulation, censorship of undesirable materials and ensuring privacy and security. Television and broadcasting services are purveyors of pop culture as well.

With the rise of Asia, the era of Western dominance is giving way to an Eastern pre-eminence in more than just economic terms. Both China and Japan have political and military potential, but that is not an immediate concern. Asia is challenging the cultural hegemony of the West as Asian values seep through with rising Asian self-confidence. Southeast Asian leaders in particular, such as Singapore's Senior Minister Lee Kuan Yew, Indonesia's former president Suharto (who was the chair of the non-aligned movement (NAM) in 1994) and Malaysia's Premier Mahathir have not just defended Asian values, they have attacked what they see as the moral decay of the

West, its overweening media and a Western-style democracy deemed ill-suited to developing countries.

This has led to stricter censorship of Western transmissions as Asia reaffirms its culture, tradition and values. Instead of American cartoons and documentaries that interpret the meaning of events to Asia using American terms of reference, Mr Lee Kuan Yew has predicted that Asia may soon interpret these same events from an Asian perspective (*The Straits Times*, 6 February 1995). He maintained that Singapore is not fighting a losing battle in resisting Western media when they try to impose their will and values on Singaporeans. During the next twenty years, Mr Lee's prognosis is that the influence of Western media will decrease from 60% to 40% as East Asia's economies close the lead that the West now has (*The Straits Times*, 6 February 1995).

Asian influence on such matters will rise as its information society finds the wherewithal and capabilities to form its own destiny. But the diversity of Asia will have to be taken into account even as the trend is unstoppable.

The media imperialism argument is about the concern that, with free trade, an unequal volume of Western culture will be exported, reflecting the West's dominance in global politics and economics. Western media practices and products will create Western-oriented elites in developing countries, reinforcing Western imperialism. There will be a growth of interconnected infrastructure and networks and an increase in ownership and participation by MNCs and the private sector that disseminate particular types of media genre and content. The subsequent influence of American programming may undermine and displace the indigenous cultures of receiving countries.

Criticisms of medial imperialism have put the argument as both too strong and too weak (French et al., 1996: 29). There may be over optimism about American rhetoric and its influence. Also, Japanese investment in Hollywood and other dimensions of American culture is not puny. Moreover, television is still a luxury good and the whole nation is not equally exposed. Advertising revenue still means local channels and programmes are important and regulatory pressure can still influence programming. The media imperialism thesis may be weakened by globalisation. While television tends to repeat Western dominant practices, authentic national cultures cannot be so easily dislodged. Television is but a form of entertainment and the wherewithal to support the suggested kind of lifestyle and value system brings a reality check.

An Asian dilemma: the case of Singapore

Like most Southeast Asian countries, Singapore has been cautious and wary with information as it embraces the information society. Its enigma is highlighted to show how Singapore aspires to be an "intelligent" city-state so as to use information technology to compete effectively and efficiently, give its people a higher standard of living in work, personal communication, education, recreation, and other social activities and maintain its socio-political high ground. For instance, its cultural and censorship ideals are among the toughest in Asia with a strict "Speak Mandarin" campaign (instead of dialects) and a very paternalistic state.

The government has stated unequivocally that it must control information technology since ideas can kill, though excessive control is undesirable (*The Sunday Times*, 6 June 1995). Although the satellite dish remains banned for private households, it was allowed to be sponsored by some big banks following the Gulf War in 1991, from which Singapore was cut off in terms of instantaneous news. The government has considered allowing companies to operate their own private links, which will liberalise the telecommunications sector further (*Business Times*, 5–6 November 1994). The Telecommunication Authority of Singapore (TAS) would license very small aperture terminals (VSATs) for intra-corporate use and closed user networks under the plan.

In accepting the recommendations of the Censorship Review Committee (in 1992) under the Ministry for Information and the Arts (MITA), MITA's former minister, Brigadier-General George Yeo, stressed the need to strike a balance between permitting room for creative expression and maintaining society's moral standards. There is a tenuous link between moral depravity and the decline of civilisations, and no society should be steamrolled into doing what is fashionable or what appears as liberalisation and modernisation. Censorship is defensible especially when pornography and obscene materials are involved; it helps prevent such an immoral industry from proliferating.

The government is mindful that regulatory measures should not degrade performance. Under consideration is legislation and licensing by an inter-ministry group. From April 1998, a one-stop centre for censorship merged three sections in MITA, the Board of Film Censors and the Censorship and Licensing sections under the Film and Publications Department (*The Sunday Times*, 1 March 1998). The centre will cover imports of publications, audio materials, film distributors, video library operators and members of public. Legislation would mean laws such as the Indecent Advertising Act, the Films Act and the Penal Code.

Licensing would require that the content that Internet providers host on their servers (computers) is clean. If a subscriber is caught distributing pornography, Internet service providers should terminate his account. A common code of practice is needed to endure uniform policies among different service providers. Singapore is not alone on the problem of online pornography as the US and New Zealand are currently actively pushing for such legislation.

There is no intention to go through people's files such as what Technet, an Internet service provider, did in 1994 to warn users found with pornography materials. Instead, the government would adopt the same approach it presently has by targeting distributors or gateway operators rather than the general public.

The government does not want to stifle the growth of Internet but, at the same time, it wants to protect children from pornography. Using filters slows down access and downloading, adds to the costs of doing so and acts as a deterrent; it is a blunt across-the-board instrument that adversely affects access to desirable information. MITA's former minister, Brigadier-General George Yeo, has noted the need for Singapore to strike a balance between becoming a global hub and preserving value; like "open windows but swat the flies" in the information technology age (*The Straits Times*, 8 March 1995).

Thus, corporatising the Singapore Broadcasting Corporation (SBC) should mean a certain degree of deregulation. But the government has stressed that there will be adequate legislation to ensure enough control, for instance, to stop "Rupert Murdoch from getting out of control" (*The Straits Times*, 16 April 1994). There is no escaping multimedia, but Brigadier-General George Yeo noted that Singapore will try

> "to determine where are the high grounds, and in an orderly way retreat back into the high grounds, and then learn to swim and set sail, because it is going to be a very watery, a very fluid environment. There is no escaping it". (*The Straits Times*, 16 April 1994)

Censorship on the Internet can be effected through technology, using filters. Trials are conducted by the National Computer Board (NCB), the National Science and Technology Board (NSTB) and the National University of Singapore (NUS). However, parental responsibility, rather than censorship, may be more effective. Brigadier-General George Yeo has also mentioned the possibility of an immune system: an internalised value system to block out undesirable values. The role of parents, school authorities and other community groups become important in this regard.

Although Singapore is in many respects in a class of its own and may not proffer the model information society for the rest of Southeast Asia, the issues it has to wrestle with are not that unique. Where Singapore may be a hard model for others to follow is in the law, regulations and other social measures to implement its goals. However, if it is appreciated that it is precisely its small size, and openness with respect to trade, capital, technology, labour and other factor inflows that makes it vulnerable and subject to strict a regime of social discipline and communitarian ideology, its policies may be redeemed. Caught between the need to survive based on efficiency and effectiveness rather than more idealistic ideologies, Singapore has pursued a very pragmatic path instead.

A compromise is made in a thesis that the PAP exercises power not by suspending ideology and legitimising coercion, but by achieving legitimacy through "ideological efficacy" (Chua, 1995). Ideological efficacy is underpinned by survivalism and pragmatism. The first creates a state of uncertainty and operational room for the second concept, interpreted as doing whatever is necessary to survive, including overt state intervention and even authoritarianism. While having served Singapore well in the last three decades, ideological efficacy is reaching its limits when security, stability and sustained economic growth have become taken for granted. Beyond survivalism and pragmatism, a new ideological threshold of communitarianism is tendered.

Nonetheless, with respect to the attempt to maintain a balance between technology and progress and certain socio-political values in an information society, two guiding principles may be discerned in Singapore, and may prove useful for other Southeast Asian countries as well. First, clear and unambiguous legal instruments and enforcement mechanisms must continue to be kept efficient and effective. This makes control and screening harder, but it is necessary to keep up with the rapid pace of technology. Singapore's already efficient administrative system can be made even more effective by harnessing information technology in various ministries and agencies, at least to keep up with the private sector. Second, when it comes to soft issues like culture, values and governance, the government has to be paternalistic in a benevolent manner since individual freedom, while valuable, can be easily abused. That advanced countries are reconsidering the importance of discipline and protecting the young is a point to be noted. In the US, this is seen in Clinton's support of efforts to beat cyberporn, violence and even cigarette consumption among young Americans. Imaginative and creative administrations eventually lead to higher orders of achievement in the final analysis.

Conclusion and Policy Implications

The fourth wave of technology and the information society has arrived (see Fig. 7.1), unleashing immense benefits as well as dangers if information as an input to production and a higher standard of life is abused and misdirected. But mankind has thus far survived similar risks and costs of progress under previous waves of progress, and we are confident that, after some initial problems and issues, the information society will bring welfare and overall good. But, unlike the materialistic results of previous cycles of progress, the information society allows greater individual freedom and democracy. This is a concern for governments, especially those in developing countries. There has been increasing interest in the link between democracy and growth, but not much consensus on whether democracy is necessary for growth (Barro, 1994; Streeten, 1994). In many of developing countries, including those in Southeast Asia, democracy is a luxury good and many Asian governments assert that discipline is more important (Barro, 1994).

Lessons from developed countries

The development of information societies in advanced industrial nations (ie, the US, Europe and Japan) may offer possible lessons and implications for East and Southeast Asia (Longhorn, 1994: 5). The US national information infrastructure (NII), released in September 1993, focused on building an electronic superhighway policy to permit rapid improvements to be made on its communications infrastructure. But progress toward an information society has not been smooth. For one, some of the biggest business alliances have never been completed, causing delays in interactive video-on-demand trails. US companies are also faced with conflicting signals and uncertainty concerning regulatory issues.

In Europe, the European Commission's white paper (1993) included dramatic improvements in trans-European networks, greater use of technology and co-ordinated implementation of a European information society. A special task force was set up in February 1994 composed of high-level experts (drawn from European industries) who are both users and providers of products and services. At the European Corfu Summit in June 1994, the task force recommended establishment of a European Information Infrastructure to match that of the US. The main goal was to use market mechanisms to foster an entrepreneurial mentality and a common regulatory approach.

They identified ten priority applications including teleworking; distance learning; university research centre networks; telematic services for small, medium enterprises (SMEs); road traffic management; air traffic control; health care networks; electronic tendering; public administration networks and city information highways. But different national policies rendered telecommunications deregulation uneven throughout the European Union. The European approach to an information society places less stress on technology per se and more on the wise, innovative use of existing technology or near-future developments. But because Europe is so diverse, there is a diverse state of readiness for an information society.

Progress is even slower in Japan since the impetus for an information society comes from various sources, primarily the Ministry of International Trade and Industry (MITI), the Ministry of Posts and Telecommunications (MPT) and Nippon Telephone and Telegraph (NTT). Other players include numerous cable television (CATV) companies (many of which operate at a loss due to government restrictions on ownership and distribution), telecommunications equipment suppliers and media owners. But NTT remains a near monopoly, which increases the cost of everything from microwave transmission to database hook-ups. A new vision of an information society in Japan was launched in September 1994 for an Advanced Information and Telecommunications Society Promotion Headquarters. Its objective is to prepare comprehensive measures for social awareness, deregulation and better definition of the role of private-public sectors in an information society.

The Japanese vision of an information society has social functions, and the teletopia services provided may well be the same for other Southeast Asian countries (Connors, 1993: 138). Social functions comprise improved living conditions, improved health and welfare, improved response to education needs, improved disaster warning and accident prevention, promotion of regional industries, development of data communications businesses, modernisation of agriculture, promotion of energy and resources conservation, reinforcement of local communities, alleviation of isolation, enhancement of local health authorities and promotion of regional internationalisation. Many of these social functions are related to teletopia services.

The Ministry of Posts and Telecommunications's offer of teletopia services include community/town types of services (eg, interactive cable television, CATV and videotex), health/welfare services (eg, regional health information and home examination/diagnosis services), academic services (eg, technical and reference systems), services for traditional/regional industries (eg, information system for small businesses), services for advanced industries and agriculture, services for urban problems (eg, disaster, police and environmental management systems), commerce and distribution services, tourism and recreation services, international services (eg, international teleconferencing and automatic interpreting systems) and services serving outlying islands.

The problems and prospects of an information society in Japan arise as the Japanese public in general does not seem very interested or involved (Sakaiya, 1990: 231–233; *The Economist*, 12 August 1995). Government agencies have to increase the public's awareness of the benefits and applications of information technology in a more concerted and directed educational programme.

Essentially, Japan's telecommunications industry is shackled by government policies such as legal barriers put up by the MPT and stifling the market by keeping costs high and the number of customers limited. Companies are prevented from entering hybrid alliances such as those in the US. By restricting domestic operations in what amounts to a negative industrial policy, Japan is an enigma despite its leadership in optical discs, memory chips and other technologies in the telecommunications industry. This domestic problem also imposes on Japan's competitiveness at the global level, despite its technological lead in Asia and among developed countries.

On differences and implications to be drawn between the three industrial countries, Japan is similar to the US in offering vendors and developers a single national market without Europe's multicultural and multilingual characteristics and partially deregulated telecommunications industry. Japan is similar to Europe in lagging behind the US in the availability of inexpensive high-speed networks and CATV penetration. In both Japan and the US, telecommunications liberalisation and trade issues can be effectively addressed through a single legislative framework within a single government. Thus, emphasis, methodologies, goals and priorities differ according to political, cultural and business environments, but common issues include creating awareness of the possibilities offered by an information society, education at all levels of society on how to use the information infrastructure and an co-ordinated effort on global issues such as standardisation, intellectual property rights, privacy and competition rules.

In all three industrial countries, deregulation has removed or reduced some monopolistic power. More complex issues on applications, social aspects, intellectual property rights, cross ownership of media, censorship, security of electronic information and universal access have arisen over the traditional issues of national telecommunications infrastructure and access to international lines.

Policy implications

As latecomers, and with so much of the content and value of programmes originating from the West, there is a double concern that Asian values and culture may be diluted at best or corrupted at worst. There is an incipient trend toward a universal mass culture that affects traditional life in developing countries as they absorb capital inflows and technology transfers. Products such as Sony electronic goods, CNN programmes and Nintendo games are household words in many parts of the world. It is not possible to prevent such a cultural invasion nor is it strictly necessary.

As an information society generates greater goal-directed activity and self-interest for individuals, governments are understandably concerned. It may be more difficult to assume that the individual in pursuing activities that spawn self-interest and self-determination would also promote the common weal. At least, this may take a bit more time in the context of Southeast Asia.

All developing countries, including those in Southeast Asia, are grappling with how best to harness an information society without drowning in it. The goal is to devise an operational information policy to promote economic and market efficiency, government effectiveness and the ability of principals to evaluate agents (Norman, 1993: 229). At the same time, operational information policies should not crowd out scientific information policies, which aim to promote a rapid rate of invention and innovation (Norman, 1993: 238). There should thus be no conflict between the two. But whereas there is no conflict between scientific curiosity and invention, there is a trade-off between scientific curiosity and innovation as privacy and trade secrets are involved.

Among Southeast Asian countries, most have taken a very protective attitude, at least in the initial stage, in terms of absorbing the softer sides of the information technology revolution. Governments such as Malaysia and Singapore have resorted to banning the satellite dish (just as the Middle East completely bans satellite broadcasting) or adopting strict censorship policies or both to the extent possible. But a long-term perspective may render such harsh rules neither desirable nor practical as both technology and the will of the people dictate otherwise.

The Singapore model of dealing with an information society may be considered, although it is in a class of its own among Southeast Asian countries. It is, however, Singapore's approach in implementation, rather than its goals, that are different and difficult for others to follow. In other words, issues of democracy, privacy, censorship and protection of intellectual property rights are similar. Two guiding principles have been noted in Singapore's case to deal with these issues in an information society. They involve having efficient and effective laws and enforcement mechanisms and the state being as highly advanced in matters of information technology as the private sector and exercising paternalism as the gatekeeper on ideological and cultural matters.

Following the trends and principles in Southeast Asia, a number of policy implications may be drawn. First, as latecomers to the information society, it is important to learn from the experiences of industrial countries such as the US, Europe and Japan. Being Asian societies, some Asian models, such as Japan, Singapore and the other Asian NIEs, should be more relevant than others.

Second, since information technology is an advanced and globally diffused commodity with many externalities involved, it pays Southeast Asian countries to build co-operation and consultation both within and outside Asia. It is also time that Asia as a whole assert a higher profile in the international arena in terms of influencing trends and events, even if not leading them. An Asian blend of information societies is not beyond Southeast Asia since highly wired and information technology "intelligent" societies such as Singapore and Hong Kong have the infostructure and software capabilities to take some lead. Both city-states have the advantage of proficiency in English as well as being centres of Chinese, Malay and other ethnic cultures. Singapore, in particular, could play a bigger role with the 1997 issue in Hong Kong forming a foregone conclusion to some extent. However, Singapore has to be sensitive to the bigger regional societies around it, while using scientific and technological bases for rationalising its information technology policies.

In particular, human resource development and training in information technology to enhance and build an Asian-oriented information society would fit in with Singapore's current policies. As an international service hub, it could easily design the right policies to promote its quaternary industries in a similar fashion.

Since infostructure is all about communications, and it takes two or more—and the more the better—to build an information society, another implication is for Southeast Asian countries to devote more resources to building their national information infrastructures. More ASEAN-based and other regionally based efforts could be encouraged while preserving the spirit of sovereignty among newly independent states in Southeast Asia.

What telematics is doing for the European Union can be considered in ASEAN countries, trans-ASEAN telecommunications networks, integrated services digital networks (ISDNs), telematics networks and others (Turner, 1997). The interconnection between different networks and their interoperability (eg, the compatibility of ISDN or national standards), alongside common standards and universality is delivering a set of public services over advanced communications networks in a market-led revolution.

While the EU may see an open skies policy as part of its broad policy of harmonisation and integration, the same is not viewed in ASEAN countries, where it is too premature with nation building in many states yet to stabilise. Because the media is such an important agent of nation building, ASEAN states have to control it and make it a partner of national policies.

In the final analysis, it appears that the information society will put more pressure on governments in Southeast Asia for a variety of reasons. The need to build a national information infrastructure or infostructure is one reason. Protection against cyberpornography and other undesirable influences is another, from a cultural standpoint. Another socio-political concern is whether relatively newly independent nation-states in Southeast Asia are ready for the democracy and personal freedom promised by the information technology revolution. To remain competitive, governments must also ensure that intellectual property rights are upheld such that research and development can be encouraged. Ensuring equity and improving accessibility to the information society for all the people is another challenge for authorities and non-governmental organisations (NGOs).

With so many matters for governments to exercise their authority and influence over, there may be a tendency for many to err on the side of conservatism, attracting Western condemnation for repressive, authoritarian governance. There is a dilemma here that can only be resolved if Southeast Asian governments stand firm and resolute by their priorities and goals, and not be swayed by how others live in their information societies. In other words, the socio-cultural and political environment in which an information society thrives must be taken into strong consideration by Southeast Asian and non-Asian parties. Eventually, Asia as a whole may evolve its own blend suitable to Asian constituents.

It would be too complicated to try to compare the impact of the information and communications technology revolution or evaluate national and global information infrastructures across nations. Empirical evidence and materials at both the national and global levels may be neither comprehensive nor truly comparable, and comparisons would be fraught with the difficulties of country-specific parameters according to different socio-political, ideological and economic considerations. As noted from the cases above, Asian nations cannot be easily compared with Western industrial countries in areas of information and communications policies. Few developing countries have a clear sight or documentation of their national information policy or infrastructure, unlike the US (GOA, 1994, 1995) or the EU and OECD in general.

Glossary of Terms in Information Technology and the Media

affective information information that is based on sensitivity and production of emotion. It embraces all the information that conveys sensory feelings, such as 'comfort', 'pain' and the emotional feelings of 'happy' and 'sad'.

analogue information represented as a continuously changing physical quantity, such as a radio signal.

Artificial Intelligence (AI) techniques to enable computer-based systems to respond in similar ways to intelligent human beings.

arts industries the industries that process, retrieve and service affective information or produce and sell related equipment. *See* **information industries**.

Asynchronous Transfer Mode (ATM) network communication technique capable of handling high-bandwidth multimedia information applications, including video.

ATM automatic teller machine as device for delivering cash and carrying out other transactions for authorised customers using, say, a bank or credit card.

bandwidth indication of amount of information a telecommunication channel can carry (usually measured in bits per second).

bit (Bi)nary digi(t) used in a mathematical system that recognises only two states, typically represented as '0' and '1'.

bps bits per second

broadband is telecommunication medium, like optical fibre, which can cope with the large volumes of data required for multimedia applications.

BT British Telecommunications

Bulletin Board System (BBS) a computer system allowing users of an electronic network to leave messages that can be read by many other users.

Business Process Re-engineering (BPR) approach to restructuring organisations by optimising the processes needed to meet specific goals, which often requires changing existing departmental boundaries.

CAD computer-aided design

CAM computer-aided manufacture

CCITT international standards-making body representing telecommunications operators, suppliers, and other interested parties.

CD compact disc

cellular radio a mobile-telephone service which divides the areas covered into small cells to assist in managing the network efficiently.

circuit switching way of linking systems and devices on a network by directly connecting transmission circuits, as with traditional telephone exchanges.

CNC computer numerically controlled machine

coaxial cable transmission medium used for cable networks, with a bandwidth narrower than optical fibre but broader than copper wires.

cognitive information information that is a projection of the future; it is logical and action-selective. The projection means that the cognitive information is used for detecting and forecasting.

common carrier telecommunications network supplier which carries communications from others.

Computer Aided Instruction (CAI) computer-oriented self-learning system.

computer conferencing group discussion based on the exchange of electronic messages on a computer network.

Computer Integrated Manufacture (CIM) use of computers and networks to support all aspects of the manufacturing process.

computer numerical control machine software-controlled machine tools.

Computer-Aided Software Engineering (CASE) set of methods, techniques, and tools which seek to apply engineering rigour to software development.

Computopia computer utopia, an ideal global society in which multi-centred, multi-layered voluntary communities of citizens participating voluntarily in shared goals and ideas flourish simultaneously throughout the world. *See* **voluntary community**.

convergence coming together of all information and communication forms into common underlying approaches based on digital techniques.

cross-ownership where one company owns many different major media operations, such as television, films, and print publishing.

cross-subsidy use of revenues from a profitable activity for less profitable ones, for instance to support telecommunications services to remote areas.

CSCW computer-supported co-operative working

CTA constructive technology assessment

cultural imperialism strong influence by one country over other nations through a domination of electronic media and computer software production and distribution.

cyberspace term indicating the virtual universe created by networked information flows.

DAE dynamic Asian economy

DBS direct broadcasting by satellite

dial-up access connecting to a network by dialling a number, rather than being connected to it permanently.

digital compression techniques which enable large volumes of information to be sent using fewer bits.

digital represented by strings of 1's and 0's, such as the bits (0/1 or on/off) used by digital information and communication technologies.

direct satellite broadcasting transmission of television or radio programmes directly from a satellite to an antenna connected to viewers' TV sets.

distance learning use of electronic networks to deliver educational services.

download to send an electronic document, software, or other computer file across a network.

EDI electronic data interchange

EFTPoS electronic fund transfer at point of sale

electronic data interchange ability to exchange documents and other information, such as orders and invoices, between organisations electronically.

electronic democracy applications of electronic networks to support democratic processes.

electronic funds transfer using electronic networks for money-based transactions.

electronic mail network service allowing typed messages to be sent between people using personal electronic mailboxes to store messages until they are read.

electronic service delivery using electronic networks to provide customers and clients directly with a variety of public and commercial services.

ESPRIT European Strategic Programme for R&D in Information Technology

ethics industries the industries that process, retrieve and service ethical information.

ethnography social science method for analysing group behaviour through observation, for example to observe a work environment when new technology is introduced into it.

ethnomethodology form of ethnography employing a range of systematic techniques for recording and studying group behaviour.

EU European Union

expert system artificial intelligence technique for developing software incorporating human expertise on particular subjects.

FCC Federal Communications Commission (USA)

File Transfer Protocol (FTP) standard for exchanging computer files across the Internet.

Flexible manufacturing systems (FMS) application of information and communication technologies to tailor production relatively easily to different customer requirements.

Fordism rigid, routinized assembly-line work processes, based on Taylorism, which Henry Ford introduced in the early twentieth century to build cars.

futurization future actualisation; this implies actualising the future, bringing it into reality. Expressed metaphorically, it means to paint a design on the invisible canvas of the future, and then to actualise the design.

GATS General Agreement on Trade and Services

GATT General Agreement on Tariffs and Trade

GDP gross domestic product

GIU global information utility, a global information infrastructure using a combination of computers, communication networks and satellites. *See* **information utility**.

GNP gross national product

Graphical User Interface (GUI) use of icons and pointer devices to simplify users' interaction with a computer, as in Microsoft Windows and Apple Macintosh systems.

hacking accessing a computer-based system unlawfully.

HCI human-computer interaction (or Interface)

High-definition television (HDTV) television pictures with a high resolution involving the presentation of more information on a screen to give sharper ages than traditional lower-resolution images. This requires higher bandwidth networks.

ICT information and communication technology

IIO International Information Organization

ILO International Labour Organization

information and communication technologies (ICT) all the kinds of electronic systems used for broadcasting, telecommunications, and computer-mediated communications.

information cycle informative cycle of subject-object-signal-action. The subject receives a signal from the object, identifies the signal and evaluates it according to an acquired standard of judgement, selects a course of action, and finally achieves some use-value by implementing the action.

information economy an economy in which the processing and transmission of information is a prime activity.

information gap the relative absence of information processing and transmission technology between industrialised and developing countries, to which must be added the human factors of levels of intellectual development and behavioural patterns in such countries.

information industries the industries that process, retrieve and service cognitive information, or produce and sell related equipment. *See* **knowledge industries**.

information infrastructure provision of underlying network capabilities to support a variety of services based on computing and telecommunications capabilities.

information service provider organisation, group, or individual who creates and packages information content carried by electronic networks.

information society refers to the increasing centrality of ICTs to all forms of social and economic activity.

information society a society that grows and develops around information, and brings about a general flourishing state of human intellectual creativity, instead of affluent material consumption.

information superhighway term coined by US Clinton Administration for an advanced information infrastructure accessible to all individuals, groups and firms.

information technology computer-based techniques for storing, processing, managing, and transmitting information.

information utility an information infrastructure consisting of public information processing and service facilities that combine computer and communication networks. From these facilities anyone anywhere at any time will be able easily, quickly and inexpensively to get any information which one wants to get.

information relationships an informed situational relation between a subject and an object that makes possible the action selection by which the subject itself can achieve some sort of use-value.

informational voluntary communities a completely new type of voluntary community. It is the technological base of computer-communications networks that will make this possible. *See* **voluntary community**.

Integrated Services Digital Network (ISDN) service using digital techniques throughout the network.

interactive television networked service allowing TV sets to be used for two-way communication with various services, such as for teleshopping.

Internet international 'network of networks' offering electronic mail and database services to millions of people.

IPR intellectual property rights

IT information technology

Just In Time (JIT) use of information and computer technologies to co-ordinate deliveries from suppliers to ensure a minimum of locally stored inventory is needed to support production processes.

knowledge cognitive information that has been generalised and abstracted from an understanding of the cause-and-effect relations of a particular phenomenon occurring in the external environment. See **cognitive information, information, technology**.

knowledge industries the industries that produce, sell service knowledge and knowledge related equipment. *See* **information industries**.

leased line link from a telecommunications operator dedicated to a particular customer for the payment of a regular fee.

liberalisation opening up of public telecommunications supply to competition.

Local Area Network (LAN) computer-based network which serves a particular room, building or campus.

magnetic stripe method of storing digital information, as on most bank and credit cards.

modem MOdulator/DEModulator which converts between analogue and digital techniques to allow computers to be connected via non-digital networks.

Mosaic simple graphical user interface, developed for World Wide Web, which has influenced interface designs of many other tools for exploring information networks.

multimedia integration of text, video and audio capabilities in computer and telecommunication systems.

narrowband telecommunication channel which can handle only relatively small volumes of data, such as copper wires used for voice-only telephony.

narrowcasting targeting communication media at specific segments of the audience.

NC numerically controlled machine

NIE newly industrialising economy

NII national information infrastructure

OECD Organization of Economic Co-operation and Development

ONA Open network architecture

online activity involving direct interaction with a computer-based system via a telecommunications link.

open system the aim of enabling any computer system to interconnect and be compatible with any other.

Open Systems Interconnection (OSI) model for open-system compatibility developed by the International Standards Organisation and CCITT.

operating system software, such as Microsoft DOS and Windows, Unix and IBM MVS, which manages the computer's basic functions so they can be exploited effectively by users.

optical fibres broadband telecommunication links using light to transmit information.

packet switching method for coding and transmitting digital information as small packets of information rather than a single continuous stream and then reassembling them at their destination.

participatory democracy a form of government in which policy decisions both for the state and for local self-government bodies will be made through the participation of ordinary citizens.

PC personal computer

PICT programme on information and communication technologies

Plain old telephone service (POTS) basic voice-only telephony services.

political economy the overlap and interaction between economic and political power in the context of prevailing control structures.

PoS point of sale

Post, telegraph, and telephone (PTT) usually a public monopoly telecommunication operator, generally owned by a national government.

post-Fordism new forms of work organisation which move away from the automated mass-production line of Fordism.

preferred reading the interpretation which a producer of media content or software would like the audience or user to follow.

Private Automatic Branch exchange (PABX) system located on a user's premises which links phones inside the organisation and connects them to the public network.

privatisation opening up of the public telecommunications supply industry to private ownership.

problem solving a method or means of eliminating risks that may stand in the way of accomplishing an aim.

process the development in time of a situation created artificially by the interaction between the purposeful action on the field of the subject of action and the reaction of the field to it.

protocol detailed definition of the procedures and rules required to transmit information across a telecommunications link.

PTO Public telecommunication operator

Public switched telephone network (PSTN) telecommunication network available to the public.

public telecommunication operator supplier offering telecommunication infrastructure capabilities to individuals and companies.

QA quality assurance

quarternary industries a new classification of industries; it is reasonable to distinguish information-related industries from service industries, and classify them as quarternary industries to provide a clear concept of the industrial structure of an information society.

R&D research and development

semiotics study of the underlying meanings of symbols and metaphors.

share of voice measurement of cross-media ownership based on the proportion of total media consumption rather than technologically defined markets, such as newspaper circulation or television audience shares on their own.

SISP strategic information systems planning

smartcard credit-card-sized device including a microprocessor for storing and processing information.

synergy a combined functional action by a group to achieve a common goal.

systems industries the structure of the systems industries will consist of a complex of industries formed by linking up existing industries with the information industries.

tariff rebalancing shifting the basis of telecommunication charges to reflect the direct costs of each service, without allowing for cross-subsidies.

Taylorism way of organising work which emphasises routinization as a means of optimising productivity, originally developed by engineer F. W. Taylor in the late nineteenth century but also often employed in modern computer-based automation.

technology cognitive information that is useful in effectively carrying out production-oriented labour requiring a certain degree of prescribed expertise.

Telco telecommunication company

telebanking interactive networked service allowing transactions with banks to be undertaken from home.

telecommuting using telecommunications to perform work at home or a work centre that would otherwise involve commuting physically to a more distant place of work.

teleconferencing meeting involving people in different locations communicating simultaneously through electronic media.

telematics information and communication networks and their applications.

teleport site-specific telecommunication infrastructure, such as a land-station link to a satellite, associated with related land and building development.

teleshopping ability to order goods and services from home directly through an interactive network.

teletext service transmitted by television signal which allows users to call up a wide variety of information on a TV screen.

telework use of an electronic network to enable individuals to work from home or a decentralised work centre.

time-sharing system the system by which several users have access to a computer simultaneously.

time-value the value which man creates in the purposeful use of future time. Put in more picturesque terms, man designs a goal on the invisible canvas of the future, and goes on to attain it.

TQM Total quality management

Transmission Control Protocol/Internet Protocol interconnection standard used for the Internet.

universal service provision of a minimum set of telecommunication services to all households.

Usenet international collection of electronic discussion groups on a multiplicity of topics, accessible through the Internet.

Value added network (VAN) an enhanced service built on the basic telecommunications network, such as electronic mail and telebanking.

videoconferencing teleconferencing involving video communication.

video-on-demand interactive network service which allows customers to view a video whenever they wish.

videotex computer-based network service which delivers textual and graphical information, typically as pages of information stored on remote computers.

Violence-chip (V-chip) an electronic device that can be installed in a TV set to block out objectionable' material, which is detected by a rating that must be encoded in the television signal.

virtual organisation operation involving many individuals, groups, and firms in different locations using electronic networks to act as if they were a single organisation at one site.

Virtual reality (VR) computer-based visualisation of a total environment that gives the user a perception of being within the environment rather than viewing it on a screen.

virtual reality computer-based visualisation of a total environment that gives the user a perception of being within the environment rather than viewing it on a screen.

VLSI very large scale integration

voice mail the ability to store spoken messages on a network for subsequent retrieval by the recipient.

voluntary community a community in which a group of people carry on life together voluntarily with a common social solidarity. The fundamental bond to bring and bind people together will be their common philosophy and goals in day to day life. *See* **informational voluntary communities**.

Wide area network (WAN) telecommunications network that extends beyond individual buildings or campuses.

World Wide Web (WWW) system which allows information sites around the world to be accessed via the Internet through the Mosaic interface.

WTO World Trade Organization

Bibliography

Ahamed, Syed, V and Lawrence, Victor, B, (1997), *Intelligent Broadband Multimedia Networks: Generic Aspects and Architectures*. Boston: Kluwer Academic Publishers.

Alexande, Donald, L, ed, (1997), *Telecommunications Policy: Have Regulators Dialed the Wrong Number?* Westport: Praeger.

Amin, A, ed, 1994, *Post-Fordism: A Reader*. Oxford: Blackwell.

Antonelli, Cristiano, ed, (1992), *The Economics of Information Networks*. Amsterdam: North-Holland.

Archibugi, D and J Michie, (1995), "The Globalisation of Technology: New Taxanomy", *Cambridge Journal of Economics*, Vol. 18, pp. 121040.

Arrow, Kenneth, (1962a), "Economic Welfare and the Allocation of Resources for Invention", Nelson, Richard, R, ed, *The Rate and Direction of Inventive Activity: Economic and Social Factors*. National Bureau of Economic Research, Princeton: Princetown University Press, pp. 609–24.

Arrow, Kenneth, (1962b), "The Economic Implications of Learning-by-Doing", *Review of Economic Studies*, Vol. 29, pp. 155–73.

Arrow, Kenneth, (1979), "The Economics of Information", in Dertouzos and Moses, J, eds, *The Computer Age: A Twenty-Year Review*. Cambridge: MIT Press, pp. 302–17.

Atkins, William, (1995), "Satellite Television and State Power in Southeast Asia: New Issues in Discourse and Control", Occasional Paper, Centre for Asian Communication, Edith Cowan University.

Audretsch, David, B, (1995), *Innovation and Industry Evolution*. Cambridge, Massachusetts: The MIT Press.

Barro, Robert, J, (1994), "Democracy and Growth", paper presented at Third Asian Development Bank Conference on Development Economics, Manila, 23–25 November.

Bartholomew, Martin, F, (1997), *Successful Business Strategies Using Telecommunications Services*. Boston: Artech House.

Beane, Donald, Shukkla, Anand and Pecht, Micheal, (1997), *The Singapore and Malaysia Electronics Industry*. New York: CRC Press, The Electronics Industry Series.

Beatty, Jack, (1998), *The World According to Peter Drucker*. New York: Free Press.

Blankenburg, WB, (1982), "Newspaper Ownership and Control of Circulation to Increase Profits", *Journalism Quarterly*, Vol. 59, Winter, pp. 390–398.

Bollier, David, (1996), "The Future of Electronic Commerce", Report of the Fourth Annual Aspen Institute Roundtable on Information Technology, 17–20 April 1995, Aspen, Washington DC: Aspen Institute .

Branscomb, Lewis, M and Keller, James, H, (1996), Converging Infrastructures: *Intelligent Transportation and the National Information Infrastructure*. Harvard: The President and Fellows of Harvard College.

Breheny, Michael, J and McQuaid, Ronald, (1987), *The Development of High Technology Industries: An International Survey*. New York: Croom Helm.

Briley, Sheena, ed, (1996), *Women in the Workforce: Human Resource Development Strategies into the Next Cenrury*. Edinburgh: HMSO.

Brooke, Geoffrey, M, (1992), "The Economics of Information Technology: Explaining the Productivity Paradox", Center for Information Systems Research, Working Paper No. 238, Sloan School of Management, Massachusetts Institute of Technology, April.

Brown, Richard, K, ed, (1997), *The Changing Shape of Work*. Houndsmills: Macmillan Press.

Browne, Ray and Fishwick, Marshall, eds, (1995), *Preview 2001+ Poopular Culture Studies in the Future*. Bowling Green: Bowling Green State University Popular Press.

Buckland, MK, (1991), "Information as Things", *Journal of the American Society for Information Science*, Vol. 42, pp. 351–60.

Burnham, David, (1980), *The Rise of the Computer State: The Threat to Our Freedoms, Our Ethics and Our Democratic Process*. New York: Random House.

Byron, Reeves and Nass, Clifford, (1996), *The Media Equation: How People Treat Computers, Television, and New Media Like Real People and Places*. New York: Centre for the Study of Language and Information.

Cadot, Olivier, Gabel, H Landis, Story, Jonathan and Webber, Douglas, eds, (1996), *European Casebook on Industrial Policy*. London: Prentice-Hall.

Cairncross, Frances, (1997), *The Death of Distance: How the Communications Revolution Will Change Our Lives*. London: Orion Publishing.

Candussi, D and Winter, JP, (1988), "Monopoly and Content in Winnipeg", in Picard, Winter, JP, McCombs, M and Lacy, S, eds, *Press Concentration and Monopoly: New Perspectives on Newspaper Ownership and Operation*. Norwood: Ablex, pp. 139-145.

Carnoy, Martin, Castells, Manuel, Cohen, Stephen, S and Cardoso, Fernando Henrique, (1993), *The New Global Economy in the Information Age: Reflections on Our Changing World*. Pennsylvannia: The Pennsylvannia State University.

Castells, M and Hall, P, (1994), *Technopoles of the World: The Making of Twenty-First-Century Industrial Complexes*. London: Routledge.

Castells, Manuel, (1996), *The Rise of the Networked Society*. Cambridge, Massachusetts, Blackwell.

Cate, Fred, H, (1997), *Privacy in the Information Age*. Washington DC: Brookings Institution Press.

Cavoukian, Ann, and Tapscott, Don, (1996), *Who Knows: Safeguarding Your Privacy in a Networked World*. New York: McGraw-Hill.

Celente, Gerald, (1997), *Trends 2000: How to Prepare for and Profit from the Changes of the 21st Century*. New York: Warner Books.

Champy, James, (1995), *Reengineering Management: The Mandate for New Leadership*. New York: HarperBusiness.

Chawla, Sarita and Renesch, John eds, (1995), *Learning Orangisations: Developing Cultures for Tomorrow's Workplace*. Portland, Oregon: Productivity Press.

Chomsky, Naom, (1989), *Necessary Illusions*. Boston: South End Press.

Chua Beng Huat, (1995), *Communitarian Ideology and Democracy in Singapore*. London: Routledge.

Comor, Edward, ed, (1994), *The Global Political Economy of Communication*. London: Macmillan.

Connors, Michael, (1997), *The Race to the Intelligent State: Towards the Global Information Economy of 2005*. Oxford: Blackwell.

Cooper, WW, Thore, S, Gibson, D and Phillips, F, esd, (1997), *Impact*. Westport: Quorum Books.

Couch, Carl, J, (1996), *Information Technologies and Social Orders*. New York: Aldine de Gruyter.

Crandall, Robert, W and Furcgtgott, Harold, (1996), *Cable TV: Regulation or Competition?* Washington DC: Brookings Institution.

Crawford, Richard, (1991), *In the Era of Human Capital: The Emergence of Talent, Intelligence, and Knowledge as the Worldwide Economic Force and What it Means to Managers and Investors*. US: HarperCollins.

Crew, Michael, A, ed, (1996), *Pricing and Regulatory Innovations Under Increasing Competition*. Boston: Kluwer Academic Publishers.

Crozier, Michel, Huntington, Samuel and Watanuki, Joji, (1975), *The Crisis of Democracy*. New York: New York University Press.

Czech-Beckerman, Shimer, Elizabeth, (1991), *Managing Electronic Media*. Boston: Focal Press.

Daly, CP, (1997), *The Magazine Publishing Industry*. Boston: Allyn and Bacon.

Dance, Stephen, G, (1994), *Intrepreneurs*. London: Macmillan.

Daniel Bell, (1973), *The Coming of Post-Industrial Society: A Venture in Social Forecasting*. New York: Basic Books.

Davidson, James, Dale and Rees-Mogg, William, (1997), *The Sovereign Individual: The Coming Economic Revolution, How to Survive and Prosper In It*. London: Macmillan.

Davies, Andrew, (1994), *Telecommunications and Politics: The Decentralised Alternative*. London and New York: Pinter Publishers.

Davis, Stan and Davidson, Bill, (1991), *2020 Vision*. New York: Simon Schuster.

DeFleur, Melvin, L and Ball-Rokeach, Sandram J, (1989), *Theories of Mass Communication*. 5th ed, New York and London: Longman.

DeFleur, Melvin, L and Larsen, Otto, N, (1987), *The Flow of Information: An Experiment in Mass Communication*. New Brunswick: Transaction Books.

Delsen, Lei, and Reday-Mulvey, Geneviere, eds, (1996), *Gradual Retirement in the OECD Countries: Macro and Micro Issues and Policies*. Aldershot: Dartmouth.

Dicken, P, (1992), *Global Shift: The Internationalisation of Economic Activity*. London: Paul Chapman Publishing.

Dizard, Wilson, P, (1989), *The Coming Information Age: An Overview of Technology, Economics, and Politics*. New York and London: Longman.

Dodd, Daniel, (1990), *The World Electronics Industry*. London and New York: Routledge.

Dodwell Marketing Consultants, (1988), *The Structure of the Japanese Electronics Industry*. Tokyo: Dodwell Marketing Consultants, 2nd ed.

Dominick, Joseph, R, (1994), *The Dynamics of Mass Communication*. New York: McGraw-Hill.

Don Tapscott, (1995), *The Digital Economy*. New York: McGraw-hill.

Dordick, Herbert, S, and Wang, Georgette, (1993), *The Information Society: A Retrospective View*. Newbury Park: Sage Publications.

Dorn, James, A, ed, (1997), *The Future of Money in the Information Age*. Massachusetts, Cato Institute.

Drew, Stephen, AW, (1994), *Business Re-engineering in Financial Services: Strategies for Redesigning Processes and Developing New Products*. London: Pitman Publishing.

Drew, Stephen, AW, (1994), *Business Re-engineering in Financial Services: Strategies for Redesigning Processes and Developing New Products*. London: Pitman Publishing.

Driffield, Nigel, L, (1996), *Global Competition and the Labour Market*. Amsterdam: Harwood Academic Publishers.

Drucker, F Peter, (1980), *Managing in Turbulent Times*. New York: Harper & Row.

Drucker, F Peter, (1992a), *Managing for the Future: The 1990s and Beyond*. New York: Truman Tally Books.

Drucker, F Peter, (1992b), *The Age of Discontinuity: Guidelines to Our Changing Society*. New Brunswick: Transaction Publishers.

Drucker, Peter, F, (1993), *Post-Capitalist Society*. Oxford: Butterworth-Heinemann.

Drucker, Peter, F, (1997), *Drucker on Asia: A Dialogue Between Peter Drucker and Isao Nakauchi*. Oxford: Butterworth-Heinemann.

Duch, Raymond, M, (1991), *Privatizing the Economy: Telecommunications Policy in Comparative Perspective*. Ann Arbor: Michigan University Press.

Dutton, William, H, ed, (1996), *Information and Communication Technologies: Visions and Realities*. New York: Oxford University Press.

Duysters, Geert, (1996), *Dynamics of Technical Innovation: The Evolution and Development of Information Technology*. Cheltenham: Edward Elgar.

Ebers, Mark, ed, (1997), *The Formation of Inter-Organizational Networks*. Oxford: Oxford University Press.

Elsevier Advanced Technology, *Yearbook of World Electronics Data Series*, various years, Oxford.

Ernst, Dieter and O'Connor, David, (1992), *Competing in the Electronics Industry: The Experience of Newly Industrialising Economies*. Paris: Organisation for Economic and Co-operation Development, Development Centre.

Evenson, Robert, E and Ranis, Gustav, eds, (1980), *Science and Technology: Lessons for Development Policy*. Boulder: Westview.

Ferguson, JM, (1983), "Daily Newspaper Advertising Rates, Local Media Cross-ownership, Newspaper Chains, and Media Competition", *Journal of law and Economics*, Vol. 28, pp. 635–654.

Flamm, K, (1988), *Creating the Computer: Government, Industry and High Technology*. Washington DC: The Brookings Institution.

Flamm, K, (1989), "Technological Advance and Costs: Computers Versus Communications", in Crandall, RW and Flamm, K, eds, *Changing the Rules: Technological Change, International Competition and Regulation in Communications*. Washington DC: The Brookings Institution.

Flamm, Kenneth, (1996), *Mismanaged Trade? Strategic Policy and the Semiconductor Industry*. Washington DC: Brookings Institution Press.

Frank, Robert and Cook, Philip, (1996), *The Winner-Take-All Society: Why the Few at the Top Get So Much More Than the Rest of Us*. New York: Penguin Books.

French, David and Richards, Michael, eds, (1996), *Contemporary Television: Eastern Perspectives*. London: Sage Publications.

Fukuyama, Francis, (1992), *The End of History and the Last Man*. New York: Free Press.

Fukuyama, Francis, (1995), *Trust: The Social Virtues and the Creation of Prosperity*. New York: Free Press.

Gates, Bill, (1995), *The Road Ahead*. New York: Penguin.

Gattiker, Urs, E, ed, (1994), *Women and Technology*. Berlin and New York: Walter de Gruyter.

Gibson, Rowan ed, (1996 and 1997), *Rethinking the Future*. London: Nicholas Brealey Publishing.

Gibson, Rowan, (1996, 1997), *Rethinking the Future*. London: Nicholas Brealey.

Giodano, Lorraine, (1992), *Beyond Taylorism*. London: Macmillan Press.

Greco, AN, (1997), *The Book Publishing Industry*. Boston: Allyn and Bacon.

Goh Keng Swee, (1995), "The 'Technology Ladder' in Development: The Singapore Case", *Asian Pacific Economic Literature*, May 1995, 10:1, pp. 1–13.

Golden, James, Reed, (1994), *Economics and National Strategy in the Information Age: Global Networks, Technology Policy, and Cooperative Competition*. Westport, Connecticut and London: Praeger.

Goonasekera, Anura and Holoday, Duncan, eds, (1994), *Asian Communication Handbook*. Singapore: Asian Mass Communication Research and Information Center.

Grotta, G, (1971), "Consolidation of Newspapers: What Happens to the Consumer", *Journalism Quarterly*, Vol. 48, Summer, pp. 245–250.

Grunwald, J and Flamm, K, (1985), *The Global Factory — Foreign Assembly in International Trade*. Washington DC: Brookings Institute.

Grycz, Chet, (1998), *The Electronic Publishing Industry*. Boston: Allyn and Bacon.

Hamel, Gary and Pralahad, CK, (1994), *Competing for the Future*. Boston: Harvard School Press.

Hammer, Michael and Champy, James, (1993), *Reengineering the Corporation: A Manifesto for Business Revolution*. New York: HarperBusiness.

Hammer, Michael and Stanton, Steven, A, (1995), *The Reengineering Revolution: A Handbook*. New York: HarperBusiness.

Hammer, Michael, (1996), *Beyond Reengineering: How the Process-centered Organization is Changing Our Work and Our Lives*. New York: HarperBusiness.

Handy, Charles, (1994), *The Empty Raincoat: Making Sense of the Future*. London: Hutchinson.

Handy, Charles, (1984), *The Future of Work: A Guide to a Changing Society*. Oxford: Basil Blackwell.

Harvard Business School, (1995), "Hong Kong TRADELINK: News from the Second City", Case 9-191-026, 8 November.

Harvard Business School, (1995), "Singapore Tradenet: A Tale of One City", Case 9-191-009, 30 September.

Harvard Business School, (1995), "Singapore Tradenet: Beyond Tradenet to the Intelligent Island", Case 9-191-105, 10 October.

Heilbroner, Robert (1995), *Visions of the Future: The Distant Past, Yesterday, Today, Tomorrow*. New York: Oxford University Press.

Heldman, Robert, K, (1995), *The Telecommunications Information Millennium: A Vision and Plan for the Flobal Information Society*. New York: McGraw-Hill, Appendix A, pp. 141–200.

Henderson, Jeffrey, (1989), *The Globalisation of High Technology Production*. London: Routledge.

Herman, Edward, S and Chomsky, Naom, (1987), *Manufacturing Consent*. New York: Pantheon.

Herman, Edward, S, (1995), *Triumph of the Market: Essays on Economics, Politics, and the Media*. Boston: South End Press.

Hobday, Michael, (1995), *Innovation in East Asia: The Challenge to Japan*. Aldershot: Edward Elgar.

Hollings, Robert, L, (1996), *Reinventing Government: An Analysis and Annotated Bibliography*. New York: Nova Science Publishers.

Horton, Thomas, R and Reid, Peter, C, (1991), *Beyond the Trust Gap: Forging a New Partnership Between Management and Their Employers*. Homewood, Illinois: Richard D Irwin.

Hoskisson, Robert, E and Hitt, Michael, A, (1994), *Downscoping: How to tame the Diversified Firm*. New York: Oxford University Press.

Hukill, Mark, A, (1994), "The Privatization and Regulation of Singapore Telecom", in *Journal of Asia Pacific Telecommunity*, Vol. 6, No. 3, pp. 26-30.

Hull, Geofrey, P, (1998), *The Recording Industry*. Boston: Allyn and Bacon.

Huntington, Samuel, (1996), *Clash of Civilisations and Remaking of World Order*. New York: Simon & Schuster.

Huntington, Samuel, P, (1993), "The Clash of Civilizations?" *Foreign Affairs*, Summer, Vol. 72, No. 3, pp. 22–49.

Inmon, William, H, (1986), *Technomics: The Economics of Technology and Computer Industry*. Homewood, Illinois: Dow Jones-Irwin.

Ismail, Mohd Nazari, (1995), *Transnational Corporations and Economic Development: A Study of the Malaysian Electronics Industry*. Kuala Lumpur: University of Malaya Press.

Jackson, Paul, J and Wielen, van der Jos, M, eds, (1998), *Teleworking: International Perspectives: From Telecommuting to the Virtual Organisation*. London and New York: Routledge.

Jessop, B, (1993), "Towards a Schumpeterian W9rkfare State? Preliminary Remarks on Post-Fordist Political Economy", Studies in Political Economy, Vol. 40, pp. 7–39.

Jessop, B, (1994), "Post-Fordism and the State", in Amin, A, ed, *Post-Fordism: A Reader*. Oxford: Blackwell, pp. 251–279.

Jones, Bryn, (1997), *Forcing the Factory of the Future: Cybernation and Societal Institutions*. Cambridge: Cambridge University Press.

Kahin, Brian and Wilson III, Ernest, J, eds, (1997), *National Information Infrastructure Initiatives: Vision and Policy Design*. Cambridge: MIT Press.

Kanter, Rosabeth, Moss, (1990) *When Giants Learn to Dance: Mastering the Challenges of Strategy, Management and Careers in the 1990s*. London and New York: Routledge.

Kellner, Douglas, (1990), *Television and the Crisis of Democracy*. Boulder: Westview.

Kennedy, Paul, (1993), *Preparing for the Twenty-first Century*. Hammersmith: Fontana Press.

Kiesler, Sara, ed, (1997), *Culture of the Internet*. Mahwah, New Jersey: Lawrence Eribaum Associates.

Knoke, William, (1996), *New Bold World: The Essential Road Map to the Twenty-First Century*. New York: Kodansha International.

Korte, WB, Robinson, S and Steinle, WJ eds, (1988), *Telework, Present Situation and Future Development of a New Form of Work Organization*. Amsterdam: Elsevier.

Kotkin, Joel, (1993), *Tribes: How Race, Religion and Identity Determine the Success in the New Global Economy*. New York: Random House.

Kozmetsky, George and Yue, Piyu, (1997), *Global Economic Competition: Today's Warfare in Global Electronics Industries and Companies*. Boston: Kluwer Academic Publishers.

Krugman, P, (1994a), "Competitiveness: A Dangerous Obsession", *Foreign Affairs*, March/April.

Krugman, P, (1994b), *Peddling Prosperity, Economic Sense and Nonsense in the Age of Diminished Expectations*. New York: WW Norton & Co.

Lamberton, Donald, M, ed, (1996), *The Economics of Communication and Information*. Cheltenham: Edward Elgar.

Lasserre, Phillippe and Schutte, Hellmut (1995), *Strategies for Asia Pacific*. London: Macmillan.

Lee Chung-Shing and Pecht, Michael, (1997), *The Taiwan Electronics Industry*. New York: CRC Press, The Electronics Industry Series.

Lee, Paul, SN, (1997), *Telecommunications and Development in China*. Cresskill, New Jersey: Hampton Press.

Levin, HJ, (1971), *The Invisible Resource: Use and Regulation of Radio Spectrum*. Baltimore: Johns Hopkins Press.

Lim, Linda, CY and Pang Eng Fong, (1991), *Foreign Direct Investment and Industrialisation in Malaysia, Singapore, Taiwan and Thailand*. Paris: OECD Development Centre.

Lim, Winston, (1994), *Singapore — A Gateway to Asia's Electronics Industry*. Singapore: Saloman Brothers, December.

Line, Richard, (1990), *The International Electronic Industry*. London: The Economist Intelligience Unit, Special Report No. 2050, December.

Lipnack, Jessica and Stamps, Jeffrey, (1994), *The Age of the Network: Organizing Principles for the 21st Century*. Vermont: Oliver Wight Publications.

Lipseg-Mumme, C, (1983), "The Renaissance of Homeworking in Developed Economies", *Relations Industrielles*, Vol. 38, pp. 545–567.

Litman, Barry, R, (1998), *The Motion Picture Mega Industry*. Boston: Allyn and Bacon.

Lodge, George, C, (1995), *Managing Globalization in the Age of Interdependence*. San Diego: Pfeiffer & Co.

Longhorn, Roger, (1994–5), "The Information Society: Comparisons in the Trio of Europe, North America and Japan", *I&T Magazine*, No. 16, pp. 5–9.

Low, Linda, (1994), "The Privatization of Singapore Telecom", in *Journal of Asia Pacific Telecommunity*, Vol. 6, No. 3, pp. 31–32.

Low, Linda, (1996), "Social and Economic Issues in an Information Society: A Southeast Asian Perspective", *Asian Journal of Communications*, Vol. 6, No. 1, pp. 1–17.

Low, Linda, (1996), "Social and Economic Perspectives from a Southeast Asia Information Society", *Asian Communication Journal*, Vol. 6, No. 1, 1996, pp. 1–16.

Low, Linda, et al, (1990), "The Information Sector: Measuring Its Size and Economic Effects", in Kuo, Eddie, et al, eds, *Information Technology and Singapore Society: Trends, Policies and Application*. Singapore: Singapore University Press, pp. 45–58.

Low, Linda, et al, (1994), *Input-Output Tables 1988: Models and Applications*. Department of Statistics, January, pp. 32–36.

Low, Linda, Toh Mun Heng, Soon Teck Wong and Tan Kong Yam with special contribution from Helen Hughes, (1993), *Challenge and Response: Thirty Years of the Economic Development Board*. Singapore: Times Academic Press.

Low, Linda, (1998), *The Political Economy of a City-State: Government-made Singapore*. Singapore: Oxford University Press.

Makridas, G, Spyros, (1990), *Forecasting, Planning, and Strategy for the 21st Century*. New York: The Free Press.

Mansell, R, (1993), *The New Telecommunications: A Political Economy of Network Evolution*. London" Sage Publications.

Martin, Stan, (1998), *The Radio Industry. Boston*: Allyn and Bacon.

Martin, Wainright, E, DeHayes, Daniel, W, Hoffer, Jeffrey, A, and Perkins, William, C, (1994), *Managing Information Technology: What MAnagers Need to Know*. Upper Saddle River, New Jersey: Prentice Hall.

Martin, William, J, (1996), *The Global Information Society*. Aldershot: Gower.

Masuda, Yoneji, (1990), *Managing in the Information Society: Releasing Synergy Japanese Style*. Oxford: Basil Blackwell.

McCormick, G, ed, (1981), *Bonsai Australia Banzai: Multifunctionpolis and the Making of a Special Relationship with Japan*. Sydney: Pluto Press.

McHugh, Patrick, Merli, Gergio and Wheeler III, William A, (1995), *Beyond Business Process Reengineering: Towards the Holonic Enterprise.* Chichester: John Wiley & Sons.

McRae, Hamish, (1994), *The World in 2020: Power, Culture and Prosperity.* Boston: Harvard Business School Press.

Micklethwait, John and Wooldridge, Adrian, (1996), *The Witch Doctors.* London: Heinemann.

Miller, Steven, E, (1996), *Civilizing Cyberspace: Policy, Power, and the Information Superhighway.* Reading, Massachussets: Addison-Wesley. Chapter 2, "The Policy Starting Point: Markets, Government, and the Public Interest", pp. 19–34.

Moore, Thomas, S, (1996), *The Disposable Workforce: Worker Displacement and Employment Instability in America.* New York: Aldine De Gruyter.

Morris-Suzuki, Tessa, (1994), *The Technological Transfromation of Japan.* Cambridge; Cambridge University Press.

Moschella, David, C, (1997), *Waves of Power: Dynamics of Global Technology Leadership 1964–2010.* New York: Amacom.

Mowlana, Hamid, (1977), *Global Information and World Communication: New Frontiers in International Relations.* London: Sage Publications.

Murlis, Helen, ed, (1996), *Pay at the Crossroads.* London: Institute of Personnel and Development.

Naisbitt, John, (1994), *Global Paradox: The Bigger the World Economy, the More Powerful Its Smallest Players.* New York: William Morrow & Co.

Naisbitt, John, (1995), *Megatrends Asia.* London: Nicholas Brealy Publishing.

Narayanan, Suresh, Rasiah, Rajah, Young Mei Ling and Yeong Beng Jong, (1989), *Changing Dimensions of the Electronics Industry in Malaysia: The 1980s and Beyond.* Penang and Kuala Lumpur: Malaysian Economic Association and Malaysian Institute of Economic Research.

Nielsen, Klaus and Johnson, Bjorn, eds, (1998), *Institutions and Change: New Perspectices on Markets, Firms and Technolohy.* Cheltenham, UK: Edward Elgar.

Norman, Alfred, Lorn, (1993), *Informational Society: An Economic Theory of Discovery, Invention and Innovation.* Boston: Kluwer Academic Publications.

Norris, Pippa, ed, (1997), *Politics and the Press: The News Media and Their Influences.* Boulder and London: Lynne Rienner Publishers.

Ohmae, Kenichi, (1990), *The Borderlesss World: Power and Strategy in the Interlinked Economy.* New York: Harper Business.

Ohmae, Kenichi, (1995), *The End of the Nation State: The Rise of Regional Economies*. New York: Free Press.

Olson, MH, (1988), "Organizational barriers to Telework", in Korte, WB, Robinson, S and Steinle, WJ eds, *Telework, Present Situation and Future Development of a New Form of Work Organization*. Amsterdam: Elsevier, pp. 77–100.

Olson, MH, (1989), "Telework: Effects of Changing Work Patterns in Space and Time", in Ernste, H and Jaeger, C, eds, *Information Society and Spatial Structure*. London: Belhaven, pp. 129–137.

Organisation for Economic Cooperation and Development, (1993), *Competition Policy and A Changing Broadcast Industry*. Paris: OECD, Chapter 5, "Economic Analysis of Broadcast Markets", pp. 77–98 and Chapter 8, "Concentration of Media Ownership", pp. 153–158.

Organisation for Economic Cooperation and Development, (1996), *Employment and Growth in the Knowledge-based Economy*. Paris: OECD.

Osborne, David and Gaebler, (1992), *Reinventing Government: How the Entrepreneurial Spirit is Transforming the Public Sector*. Reading, Massachussetts: Addison-Wesley.

Parker, Marilyn, M and Benson, Robert, J, (1988), *Information Economics: Linking Business Performance to Information Technology*. Englewood Cliffs, New Jersey: Prentice Hall.

Parsons, Patrick, R and Frieden, Robert, M, (1998), *The Cable and Satellite Television Industry*. Boston: Allyn and Bacon.

Pavlick, John, V, (1997), *New Media Technology*. Boston: Allyn and Bacon, 2nd ed.

Pecht, Michael, Bernstein, JB, Searls, D and Peckerer, M, (1997), *The Korean Electronics Industry*. New York: CRC Press, The Electronics Industry Series.

Peck, Jamie, (1996), *Work-Place: The Social Regulation of Labor Markets*. New York and London: The Guilford Press.

Perelman, Michael, (1991), *Information, Social Relations and the Economics of High Technology*. London: Macmillan.

Picard, RG, (1986), "Pricing in Competing and Monopoly Newspapers, 1972–1982", *LSU School of Journalism Research Bulletin*.

Picard, RG, (1989), *Media Economics: Concepts and Issues*. London: Sage Publications.

Picard, RG and Brody, JH, (1997), *The Newspaper Publishing Industry*. Boston: Allyn and Bacon.

Porat, Marc, U, (1977), "Definition and Measurement", Vol. 1 of *The Information Economy*. Washington DC: Government Printing Office, pp. 22–29.

Porter, Michael E, (1990), *The Competitive Advantage of Nations*. London and Basingstoke: Macmillan Press.

Pringle, Peter, King and Starr, Michael, F and McCavitt, William, E, (1995), *Electronic Media Management*. Boston: Focal Point, 3rd ed.

Reich, Robert, (1992), *The Work of Nations: Preparing Ourselves for the 21st Century Capitalism*. New York: Vintage Books.

Rifkin, Jeremy, (1996), *The End of Work: The Decline of the Global Labor Force and the Dawn of the post-Market Era*. New York: GP Putnam's Sons.

Rifkin, Jeremy, (1996), *The End of Work: The Decline of the Global Labor Force and the Dawn of the post-Market Era*. New York: GP Putnam's Sons.

Rosston, Gregory, L and Waterman, David, eds, (1997), *Interconnection and the Internet*. Mahwah, New Jersey: Lawrence Erlbaum Associates.

Rubin, Michael, Rogers, (1983), *Information Economics and Policy in the United States*. Littleton, Colorado: Libraries Unlimited.

Ryan, Daniel, J, ed, (1997), *Privatization and Competition in Telecommunications: International Developments*. Westport: Praeger.

Sakaiya, Taichi, (1991), *The Knowledge-Value Revolution or a History of the Future*. Translated by George Fields and William Marsh, Tokyo: Kodansha International.

Sasaki, M, (1981), "Japan, Australia and the Multifunctionpolis", in McCormick, G, ed, *Bonsai Australia Banzai: Multifunctionpolis and the Making of a Special Relationship with Japan*. Sydney: Pluto Press.

Sassen, Sakia, (1991), *The Global City*. Princeton: Princeton University Press).

Sauer, Christopher, Yeron, Philip, W and Associates, (1997), *Steps to the Future: Fresh Thinking on the Management of IT-based Organizational Transformation*. San Francisco: Jossey-Bass Publishers.

Savona, Ernesto, U, (1997), *Responding to Money Laundering: International Perspectives*. Amsterdam: Harwood Academic Press.

Schiller, Herbert, (1996), *Information Inequality: The Deepening Social Crisis in America*. New York and London: Routledge.

Schwab, Klaus, ed, (1995), *Overcoming Indifference: Ten Key Challenges in Today's Changing World*. London and New York: New York University Press.

Scitovsky, Tibor, (1945), "Some Consequences of the Habit of Judging Quality by Price", *Review of Economic Studies*, Vol. 12, No. 2, pp. 100–5.

Senge, M, Peter, (1990), *The Fifth Discipline: The Art and Practice of the Learning Organization*. London: Century Business.

Senge, M, Peter, Roberts, Charlotte, Ross, Richard, B, Smith, Bryan, J and Kleiner, Art, (1994), *The Fifth Discipline Fieldbook: Strategies and Tools for Building a Learning Organization*. London: Nicholas Brealey.

Shaw, James, (1998), *Telecommunications Deregulation*. Boston and London: Artech House.

Simai, Mihaly, ed, (1995), *Global Employment: An International Inquiry into Future of Work*. Volumes 1 and 2. Tokyo: United Nations University Press.

Simon, Denis, Fred, ed, *The Emerging Technological Trajectory of the Pacific Rim*. New York: ME Sharpe, 1995.

Snooks, Donald, Graeme, (1996), *The Dynamic Society: Exploring the Sources of Global Change*. London and New York: Routledge.

Solow, Robert, (1994), "Is All That European Unemployment Necessary?" Massuchusetts Institute of Technology Working Paper No. 94–06.

Sorlin, Pierre, (1994), *Mass Media*. London and New York: Routledge.

Splichal Slavko, Calabrese, Andrew, Sparks, Colins, eds, (1994), *Information Society and Civil Society: Contemporary Perspectives on the Changing World Order*. West Lafayette: Purdue University Press.

Storper, Michael, Thomadakis, Stavros, B and Tsipouri, Lena, J, eds, (1998), *Latecomers in the Global Economy*. London and New York: Routledge.

Streeten, Paul, (1994), "Governance", paper presented at Third Asian Development Bank Conference on Development Economics, Manila, 23–25 November.

Tan Yew Soon and Soh Yew Peng, (1994), *The Development of Singapore's Modern Media Industry*. Singapore: Times Academic Press.

Tan, LH and Chia, SY, eds, (1989), *Trade, Protectionism and Industrial Asjustment in Consumer Electronics*. Singapore: Institute of Southeast Asian Studies.

Tapscott, Don and Caston, Art, (1993), *Paradigm Shift: The New Promise of Information Technology*. New York: McGraw-Hill.

Tapscott, Don, (1995), *The Digital Economy: Promise and Peril in the Age of Networked Intelligence*. New York: McGraw-Hill.

Thurow, Lester, (1996), *The Future of Capitalism: How Today's Economic Forces Shape Tomorrow's World*. New York: Victor Morrow.

Tilly, Chris, (1996), *Half a Job: Bad and Good Part-Time Jobs in a Changing Labor Market*. Philadelphia: Temple University Press.

Toffler, Alvin, (1980), *The Third Wave*. London: Collins and New York: William Morrow.

Toffler, Alvin, (1990), *Powershift: Knowledge, Wealth, and Violence at the Edge of the 21st Century*. New York: Bantam Books.

Turner, Colin, (1997), *Trans-European Telecommunication Networks*. London and New York: Routledge.

Turow, Joseph, (1992), *Media Systems in Society: Understandimng Industries, Strategies, and Power*. London: Longman.

United Nations Conference on Trade and Development, (1994), *Technological Dimension in Industrial Districts: An Alternative Approach to Industrialization in Developing Countries*. New York and Geneva: UN.

United Nations Industrial Development Organisation, (1996), *Industrial Development Global Report 1996*. New York: Oxford University Press for UNIDO.

United Nations, (1995), *Development of the Export-oriented Electronics Goods Sector in Asia and the Pacific*. New York: United Nations Economic and Social Commission for Asia and the Pacific.

United States Government, (1994), *Global Information Infrastructure: Agenda for Action*. Washington DC.

United States Government, (1995), *Global Information Infrastructure: Agenda for Cooperation*. February, Washington DC.

UNTNC, (1986), *Transnational Corporations in the International Semiconductor Industry*. New York: United Nations.

UNTNC, (1987), *Transnational Corporations and Technology Transfer: Effects and Policy Issues*. New York: United Nations.

UNTNC/ESCAP, (1987), *Transnational Corporations and the Electronics Industry of ASEAN Countries*. New York: United Nations.

Vincent, David, R, (1990), *The Information-based Corporation: Stakeholder Economics nd the Technology Investment*. Homewood, Illinois: Dow Jones-Irwin.

Walker, James and Ferguson, Douglas, (1998), *The Broadcast Television Industry*. Boston: Allyn and Bacon.

Wallace, James, (1997), *Overdrive: Bill Gates and the Race to Control Cyberspace*. New York: John Wiley.

Wang, Ku, ed, (1994), *Science and Technology Parks: Selected Successful Experience in Asia Pacific Region*, Chinese Taipei: Pacific Economic Cooperation Committee, June.

Weitzen, H, Skip and Parkhill, Rick, (1996), *Intreprenurs: Online and Global*. New York: John Wiley.

Welfens, Paul, JJ and Yarrow, George, eds, (1997), *Telecommunications and Energy in Systemic Transformation: International Dynamics, Deregulation and Adjustment in Network Industries*. Berlin: Springer-Verlag.

Wheatley, Margaret, J, (1992), *Leadership and the New Science*. San Francisco: Berrett-Koehler.

White, Barton, C, (1993), *The New Ad Media Reality: Electronic Over Print*. Westport: Quorum Books.

Williams, Frederick, ed, (1988), *Measuring the Information Society*. Newbury Park: Sage Publications.

Wilson, William, Julius, (1996), *When Work Disappears*. New York: Knopf.

Winslow, Charles, D and Bramer, William, L, (1994), *Future Work: Putting Knowledge to Work in the Knowledge Economy*. New York: The Free Press for Andersen Consulting.

Wirth, MO and Wollert, JA, (1984), "The Effects of Market Structure on Television News Pricing", *Journal of Broadcasting*, Vol. 28, Spring, pp. 215–225.

Wolpert, Samuel, A and Wolpert, Joyce, Friedman, (1986), *Economics of Information*. New York: Van Nostrand Reinhold Co.

Wong Hon Seng, (1992), Exploiting Information Technology: A Case Study of Singapore", *World Development*, Vol. 20, No. 2, pp. 1817–1828.

Woodrow, Brian, R and Brown, Chris, eds, (1991), "The Uruguay Round and Beyond: What Future for Services Trade Liberalization?", Second Geneva International Forum on Global Services Trade Liberalization, Applied Services Economics Centre, Geneva, pp. 121–161.

Wresch, William, (1996), *Disconnected: Haves and Have-nots in the Information Age*. New Brunswick: Rutgers University Press.

Yoshino, MY and Rangan, US, (1995), *Strategic Alliances — An Entrepreneurial Approach to Globalization*. Boston: Harvard Business School Press.

Index